LANDMARK COLLECTOR'S LIBRARY

# TICKNALL POTS & POTTERS
## from the Late Fifteenth Century to 1888

Janet Spavold and Sue Brown

LANDMARK COLLECTOR'S LIBRARY

# TICKNALL POTS & POTTERS
## from the Late Fifteenth Century to 1888

Janet Spavold and Sue Brown

Landmark Publishing

Published by

Ashbourne Hall, Cokayne Ave
Ashbourne, Derbyshire DE6 1EJ England
Tel: (01335) 347349 Fax: (01335) 347303
e-mail: landmark@clara.net
web site: www.landmarkpublishing.co.uk

1st edition

ISBN: 1-84306-172-4

British Library Cataloguing in Publication Data: a catalogue record for this book is available from the British Library.

Printed by Cromwell Press, Trowbridge, Wiltshire

Design & reproduction by James Allsopp

**Front cover**: Animal decoration from site 6

**Back cover T**: Lace-based patterns from site 6

**Back cover B & Page 3**: Yellow ware bowl

# Contents

# List of Illustrations

# Reference tables for old values

Reference tables have been included for readers no longer familiar with old values. Original values have been retained in the text.

Money Values
12 pence (12d) = 1 shilling (1s)
One shilling = 5p
20 shillings = one pound (£1 or 1L)
approximately $2^1/_2$d = 1p
Pence and shillings together were written as '1s 6d' or '1/6d'.

Square Measure (area)
40 perches = 1 rood
4 roods = 1 acre
1 acre = 0.4047 hectare
4840 square yards = 1 acre
1 square yard = 0.8361 square metre
Acres, roods and perches were abbreviated to their initials, for example 10a 2r 37p

Linear Measure
12 inches (in) = 1 foot (ft)
3 feet = 1 yard (yd)

Weight
14 pounds (lb) = 1 stone (st)
2 stones = 1 quarter (qtr)
4 quarters = 1 hundredweight (cwt)
20 hundredweights = 1 ton
2.22lb = 1 kilogram

1 score = 20 items

# Abbreviations

| | |
|---|---|
| BL | British Library |
| CRO | Chester Record Office |
| DAJ | Derbyshire Archaeological Journal |
| DLSL | Derby Local Studies Library |
| DRO | Derbyshire Record Office |
| GL | Guildhall Library, London |
| HMC | Historical Manuscripts Commission |
| LA | Lincolnshire Archives |
| LJRO | Lichfield Joint Record Office |
| MH | Lothian Archive, Melbourne Hall, Derbyshire |
| NA | Nottinghamshire Archives |
| NPG | National Portrait Gallery |
| NRO | Northamptonshire Record Office |
| pers. comm. | personal communication |
| ROLLR | Record Office for Leicestershire, Leicester and Rutland |
| SBT | Shakespeare Birthplace Trust |
| SHC | Staffordshire Historical Collection |
| TNA: PRO | The National Archives: Public Record Office |
| WMM | Wedgwood Museum Manuscript |
| WRO | Warwickshire Record Office |
| WIL | Wellcome Institute Library |
| WoRO | Worcestershire Record Office |

# Acknowledgements

We are grateful to all those who have given permission for the essential fieldwalking and who helped us with this research. Major thanks are due to Norman Clarke, the then estate manager for the National Trust, and David Barker, then at the Potteries Museum, Stoke-on-Trent, for their patience with our many queries. We have had invaluable support and assistance throughout from Trevor Spavold and Joan Baker, and this has been greatly appreciated. Jennifer Illsley and Stuart Woodward have kindly lent us their pots and given permission to illustrate them.

Our thanks are due to the staff of the following: Ashby Image and Print; the British Library; Calke Abbey (National Trust), especially the then house manager Kerry Usher and the estate manger Bill Cove; Derby Local Studies Library; Derby Museum, especially Richard Langley and Anneka Bambery; Derby University Visual Media Department, especially Ann Aderogba and Mary Davies; Derbyshire Record Office; the Fitzwilliam Museum Cambridge, especially Dr Poole; the Guildhall Library; the Harpur-Crewe Estates, especially Mr Garnett and Olive Wardle; Keele University Manuscripts Department; Lincolnshire Archives; Lord Ralph Kerr of Melbourne Hall; Lichfield Joint Record Office; the National Archives: Public Record Office; the National Monuments Record; the National Portrait Gallery; the Potteries Museum, Stoke-on-Trent, especially Debbie Ford; Northampton Record Office; Nottinghamshire Archives; Record Office of Leicestershire, Leicester and Rutland; Repton School; Repton Preparatory School (Foremark Hall); the Shakespeare Birthplace Trust; the Victoria and Albert Museum, especially Robin Hildyard; the Wellcome Institute for the History of Medicine; and Wiltshire Record Office (Trowbridge). We have quoted from the Wedgwood manuscripts by courtesy of the Trustees of the Wedgwood Museum, Barlaston, Stoke-on-Trent, Staffordshire, and we are grateful to Gaye Blake Roberts and Helen Burton for their help.

We would also like to thank the following: Rosemary Bailey; Sarah Bailey; Denis Baker; David Bell; Mr Bayliss; Ivan Bird; Sidney Bricknell; Dr Irene Brightmer; Dr David Brown; Russell Brown; Peter and Jean Burden; Sybil Carter; Mike Clarke; John Collier; John Dainty; Tony de Blaquiere; G. N. Draper; Michael Dumelow; Richard and Dorothy Forman; Barbara Foster; Miranda Goodby; Diana Grant; Joe Hallifield; Roy Hallifield; Mark Heath and Julie Tibbert; Mavis Heath; Philip Heath; Adrian Henstock; Prof. David Hey; Dr Jeffrey Hoffman; John Hyde; Ann Irving; Howard Joynes; Roy and Pam Kerby; Richard Kilburn; Diane Kucyj; Ann Lardeur; Deidre O'Sullivan of Leicester University and her students, David Long, Mick Malpass, Alan MacCormick, Peter Marriott, Nigel Melton; Lynn Moralée and her fellow Local History students at Derby; David and Rosemary Mumford; David Musson; Andrew Newton; Maureen Newton; Susan Page; Beverley Parker; Richard Parker; Robert Parker; Claire Pattinson; Roy Paulson; Roger Pegg; Ray Reeves; Brian Rich; John and Alyson Rodgers; Yvonne Sant; Colleen and Dave Shepherd; Patrick Skinner; Lesley Smith at Tutbury Castle; Fred and Dorothy Soar; Harold and Annette Soar; Michael Stanton; Mr and Mrs J. Symonds; Fiona Tebb; Alison and Michael Thornhill; Howard Usher; John Webster; Oswald Webster; Dr Christopher Welch; Rita Whitehorn; Peter Whyte; Roy Wileman; Robin and Val Wilkinson; Muff Wiltshire; Sue Woore; and the many people who have kindly sent us references. This study would have been more difficult without their help.

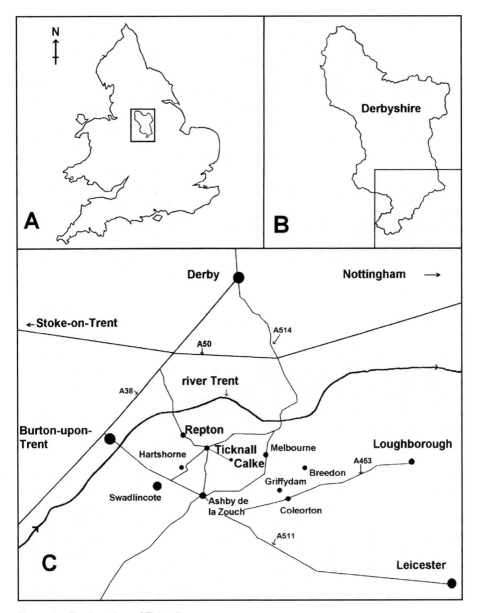

Figure 1 – The Location of Ticknall

Pottery was made at Ticknall for about four hundred years, with varying numbers of sites in production at any one time. Most reference books on pottery note its existence but say nothing about the extent of the trade. When we started our research about seventeen years ago, we faced a number of problems. While there are a number of local booklets about Ticknall giving a good general introduction to the area and its industries, the potteries had not been studied in depth. There was a marked lack of documentary evidence for the potteries as businesses, and almost nothing left of the pottery works themselves. Once production had finished, the land reverted to agriculture. There was little to show of the pottery, especially by comparison with other areas, and we found that there was a good deal of uncertainty even in museums as to what constituted Ticknall pottery. In some places we were told that pottery which had been thought to have been made in Ticknall had more recently been reassigned to Stoke-on-Trent. There was no real agreement over stylistic recognition for slipware designs in the way that there is recognition for the jewelled wares from Stoke-on-Trent, mainly because there is not a large enough body of decorated work from Ticknall to establish its style. Most of the potters' names were unknown, and as far as we have seen from fieldwalking, nobody put even initials on their pots. The date of closure of the last pottery was well known, but not when the potteries had started. We did not know how extensively the potteries were scattered over Ticknall, Calke and Heath End (Figure 5, p.39). Much of the physical evidence has come from systematic fieldwalking during the period of the research, frequently guided by farmers' experience and knowledge of their land. When we began to collect sherds we rapidly recognised that we needed help from expert archaeologists to interpret it.

Our aims are to provide as full a history of the Ticknall potters and potteries as possible, to identify the products of the area, and to reassess Ticknall's importance in the history of the pottery trade. We hope to provide a clear picture of where the potteries were sited, and how and from where they obtained their clay. We hope to provide an insight into the potters' way of life and standards of living at different periods, their patterns of work, and marriage and inter-relationships between potting families. This should lead to a greater understanding of the economics of the pottery industry here, and the reasons for its rise and decline. We hope that the fieldwalking collection will provide a study resource for archaeologists as well as historians. While collecting evidence for Ticknall pottery, we also collected evidence of any other named pottery types for comparison. In time, this enabled us to work out marketing patterns.

We were aware from other research that Ticknall pottery was mentioned in probate inventories. We searched probate records for evidence of where the pottery was sold, in the absence of any other means of tracing the markets, and we have read more than 100,000 probate inventories to this end. Key statistically valid groups, where the entire series has been read, include Leicestershire (1514–1825) and the Lichfield diocese for the 1630s and 1680–4. The diocese covers Derbyshire, Staffordshire, and half each of Warwickshire and Shropshire. The peculiars, including Burton-upon-Trent, have not yet been searched. All the Cheshire inventories for 1631 were read. For Leicestershire, Ticknall references were collected from the start of the inventory series; other pottery types were collected from 1570. The earliest non-Ticknall references outside Leicestershire start in 1447.

We knew of the existence of the large collection of records which belonged to Calke Abbey which we guessed would have information on the potters as tenants of the Harpur family (later Crewe, then Harpur Crewes) and their predecessors. When the records were transferred to Derbyshire County Record Office at Matlock we were able to search them in detail. Meanwhile account books and rentals from other local estates such as Staunton Harold and Foremark proved helpful. To this was added the reconstruction of local families, from the wills and parish records of Ticknall, Calke and the adjacent parishes of Breedon, Ashby de la Zouch and Hartshorne. The quality of these records varies. For instance, Ticknall registers survive from 1626, but there is a gap from 1645 to 1660 and there is evidence of significant under registration for the period before 1700. Calke registers only survive from 1699. Ticknall is fortunate in the amount and variety of parish material that survives but it lacks any manorial records apart from Suit Rolls for 1721–1807. National sources such as taxation returns and musters have also been checked. We have standardised family names throughout the text except where they occur in quotations. All this has enabled us to build up evidence about the potters and the extent of the industry, and we are grateful to those who have allowed us to see information or pots held locally or who have passed on useful pointers.

The use of pottery was very limited during the Middle Ages and the range of pottery goods was restricted to cooking pots, jugs and bowls. Pottery was almost entirely confined to the kitchen. Virtually nothing is known about methods of distribution for medieval pottery, other than that it had a very limited market range, and it was probably distributed by the potters themselves. Households at the lower end of the social scale ate off thick slices of coarse bread, or treen (wooden) plates. They drank from wooden cans made of shaped staves bound top and bottom with split willow, or turned wood cups. At the top end of the scale people used pewter, silver or even gold. Equipment for food preparation was also mainly treen ware such as turned bowls or troughs for kneading dough. During the late fifteenth century a new item began to appear, the pottery cup or mug, and during the early sixteenth century it so rapidly became the preferred choice that a new industry sprang up, producing these items. Cistercian wares such as those found on the early Ticknall sites rapidly gained popularity and were high-status items. Tudor greenwares, another popular type, were not made here but in the south, in Surrey.

The expanding trade with the Continent, especially the Low Countries, brought new ideas and fashions for household items. In some better-off households in the sixteenth century fine stoneware mugs, imported from Westerwald in Germany, were in use. New introductions in pottery types were copied by local potters, including those at Ticknall. They included chamber pots, chafing dishes and firepots (a pot full of hot ashes placed in a wooden box and used to warm the feet of women with sedentary jobs such as spinning), pipkins and skillets (cooking pots with three feet), and bowls with handles. In the early seventeenth century decorated slipwares came in from the Low Countries and Germany, and started the fashion for them among English households; the blue and white tin-glazed Delftwares proved especially popular and started an enduring fashion.

By the seventeenth century English potters had expanded their range to yellow and black wares and there were specialist stoneware potteries in London. With experience, forms were improved and techniques developed to produce better-quality goods in a greater range of forms, and the potters added decoration in the form of applied pads of clay, impressed or slip-trailed designs. These developed into recognisable local styles. Economic growth in England meant that people could afford these new items even though they cost more than treen wares. The decorated wares were clearly bought for show as much as for use, and some appear to have been made to order for special occasions. They indicate that some householders had money to spare for luxury items and were no longer living in a subsistence economy.

Platters and plates in general were only just beginning to appear on English tables in the seventeenth century. For most people, tableware was still treenware: bowls, dishes and trenchers made of wood. Many of the inventories include trenchers and treenware, often in the same entry as the Ticknall ware. For the better off, pewter was favoured and silver was still in use by the very wealthy. Pottery was predominantly used in kitchens, butteries and dairies for preparation, cooking and storage.

# 1. The Social and Industrial Perspective

The earliest reference to landowners in Ticknall occurs in the will of Wulfric Spot in 1004, when he left 'that little land' he owned there to Burton Abbey.[1] The abbey retained it until the Dissolution of the Monasteries, and Sir William Paget bought the abbey's lands in 1546. When the Domesday Survey was taken in 1086, Ticknall was owned by the King, the abbey and Nigel de Stafford, each having a manor. Henry I granted his manor of Ticknall to Richard, 2nd Earl of Chester, who came of age in 1115. Successive earls and other individuals gave large parts of the land to Repton Priory after it had been refounded at Repton by Maud, Countess of Chester.

It is not known when the Francis family first lived in Ticknall, but they held part of the king's manor under the Earls of Chester.[2] Ralph de Tykenhal was an abbey sub-tenant some time between 1229 and 1260;[3] he was also a tenant of the Earl of Chester and lord of the manor.[4] His daughter and co-heiress Agnes married William Francis of Osmaston some time before 1293; thus all this property also passed into Francis hands.[5] Richard Francis of Ticknall, his son Henry and Edward Francis of Petworth, Sussex, sold the manor and its properties to George Biddulphe, alias Biddle, in 1614.[6] Part of the manorial wastes was called Le Holynherst (Hollyhurst), a name associated with deer parks where deer and cattle browsed on holly trees. In 1647 Thomas, son of George Biddulph (Biddle) gentleman, owned Prince Wood or Prince Fee, and it was the property of Thomas Pearston, a descendant, by the end of the century. In about 1711 Sir John Harpur bought the Francis lands and manor in Ticknall from Thomas Pearston.[7]

The Abells appeared in 1291–2 when Thomas, Abbot of Burton, sued Robert Abell and Elyas de Stanton over the abbey's lands in Ticknall.[8] The previous sub-tenant had been Ralph de Tykenhal. This part of the abbey property must descend from Agnes de Tykenhal's sister and co-heiress. By 1362 John Abell was a tenant of the Black Prince whose ownership is remembered in the names Prince Fee and Prince Wood; he also owned Hollyhurst.[9] Abell was also a tenant under a second manorial lord in 1363, this property derived from the de Stafford manor.[10] Edward Abell was lord of these manors when he died in 1597.[11] His son Ralph inherited, and he sold it in about 1625 to the Harpurs.[12]

'Tickenhall Grange', which had been a grange for Repton Priory, was retained as part of the Crown manor after the Dissolution and was let to various tenants. The Crown retained a direct interest in the village, and as late as 1846 Ticknall still paid a chief rent of 27s to Queen Victoria for the remaining Crown lands, as well as one of £13 10s to the Marquess of Anglesey for the Burton Abbey lands.[13]

The first mention of the Harpurs in relation to Ticknall came in 1544 when there was a court case over properties in several villages, including some rents in Ticknall; they lived at Swarkestone.[14] After the Dissolution, Calke passed through several hands until Henry (later Sir Henry) Harpur bought it in 1622; thus the Harpurs became lords of Calke manor. Until the 1620s they owned little land in Ticknall, but they bought the Abell and then the Francis manors, then as much as they could, particularly from 1780 to 1820. It was only after these purchases that they owned most of the parish and by the late eighteenth century they were recognised as sole lords of the manor in Ticknall.[15]

In the early period, the greatest influence in Ticknall must have been the church: Burton Abbey owned part of the manor and Calke was a daughter house of Repton Priory. The Grange in Ticknall supplied food to Calke and Repton. The parish church, originally a chapelry of Repton, held an important place in the village. As Repton Priory was gradually given lands in Ticknall, it would have exercised considerable influence in the village, on both social and religious life. Economic life would not have escaped the priory's scope, and the presence of the grange may have affected common-field agricultural decisions. It is possible that the pottery industry here had started under the auspices of the priory.

One of the puzzles in studying the Ticknall potteries has been to decide when and how the trade began. There are no written records to match the earliest archaeological evidence from the excavation of the Austin Friars in Leicester, which indicates that the potteries were established by about the last quarter of the fifteenth century. It may be that the skills of working in clay derived from the proximity of Repton Priory and its cell at Calke. The priory owned property in Ticknall such as The Grange. Priory staff lived in Ticknall at different times and the Prior himself may have done so too. Evidence that the priory made encaustic tiles was uncovered in 1866 at Repton School when work was being done to level a piece of ground within what had been the priory grounds. The boys discovered deposits of tiles with a twin-chambered, charcoal-fired tile kiln. The tiles were dated to the fourteenth century, and a number of patterns were recovered which showed considerable artistic and technical skill. An account of the discovery was published by the headmaster, Dr Pears, along with a description of the patterns by Llewellyn Jewitt, who noted that several other sets of remains of medieval tile kilns had been discovered in association with religious houses, where tiles were made for sale. He matched some of the Repton patterns to tiles found in churches, for example, at Bakewell, Wirksworth, Duffield and Dale Abbey (all Derbyshire); Exeter Cathedral; Kegworth (Leicestershire); Thurgarton Priory (Nottinghamshire); and Tutbury and Burton-upon-Trent (Staffordshire). In a footnote he recorded that a tile with a Repton pattern was found, among others, 'at Tickenhall, and is now in the possession of Sir John Harpur Crewe ... It probably belonged to the Abbey of Calke and shows that that house ... was supplied with tiles from the Repton kiln'.[16] These tiles were being made during the century before the first evidence for pottery in Ticknall appears, and it poses an intriguing question: did the skills for the pottery derive from the experience of the priory's clay workers? There is a possible link in the use of white clays to produce patterns on a red ground. Both the encaustic tiles and the early Cistercian wares use this technique. The clay for the tiles may have been brought from the priory's lands in Ticknall. Dr Pears commented that the clay for the tiles was 'a stiff red clay, quite unlike the ordinary soil of the place'. Further evidence of early familiarity with clay working is to be found in Prior Overton's Tower, now part of the Repton School buildings, which was built in brick in 1436–8, probably by Dutch craftsmen.

There is also a tantalising mention of an oven or kiln ('furnum') in the late thirteenth century but it is not clear what kind of kiln it might be. It is too early for a malt kiln, but it could be a kiln for bark, pottery or lime. It could even be a communal oven for baking bread. There are two references to it, both in property deeds. 'William ad Furnum' was party to a deed concerning half an acre in a Ticknall field on 'the Faldeworyinges' where the neighbours were John Champion and Alan son of Symon. He was also mentioned as a neighbour of two roods of arable land held by Richard Overton and another William, the rest of whose name is illegible. 'Ricardus fil Henricius Furnum de Tykenall' was similarly identified in another document around the end of the 1200s.[17]

The Dissolution in 1539 must have imposed unimaginable changes on village life. When the monastic properties passed into private hands they became the economic and social focus for large estates, and took on the role and function of the manorial lords. The eventual long-term owners here, the Harpur family, became typical English benevolent landlords, if rather eccentric. For example, they made land available to their tenants for allotment gardens, and provided education and almshouses. In the eighteenth century they played a significant part in fashionable Derbyshire society, supplying a High Sheriff and MP, and responding to changes in taste by remodelling Calke Abbey. As the village's population expanded and the old church became too small, they financed the new church in the 1840s. When they withdrew from public life later in the nineteenth century their reclusiveness did not affect their close control of the estate nor their personal relationships with their tenants. By then, they owned the majority of the village houses.

During the sixteenth century Ticknall was only a small village. The earliest useful listing of occupational structures is from an undated taxation list, probably drawn up between 1538 and 1547. It lists 47 taxpayers for Ticknall with their occupations; seven were potters.[18] With their families, this would give a total population of about 212. By 1700 that figure had grown to around 350, but it had not shown uninterrupted growth. The village had suffered a severe attack of plague in 1645, when one-sixth of the population died. The greatest number of burials took place in August and September, and the plague struck both children and adults in almost equal numbers, often affecting several members of a family. Sixty people died, fifteen in each category of men, women, girls and boys. The previous peak in death rates had been twenty-eight in 1637.[19] For such a small village, the impact of plague must have been disastrous. Although the population recovered, there was another dip in numbers in the 1720s, when more people were buried than baptised. After this the population grew steadily until the mid-nineteenth century but it dropped sharply after that. The earliest census in 1801 recorded 1,125 inhabitants; by 1831 there were 1,278. The population declined slowly until 1851 and more rapidly after that to 731 in 1901. In 1991 there were about 425 inhabitants.[20]

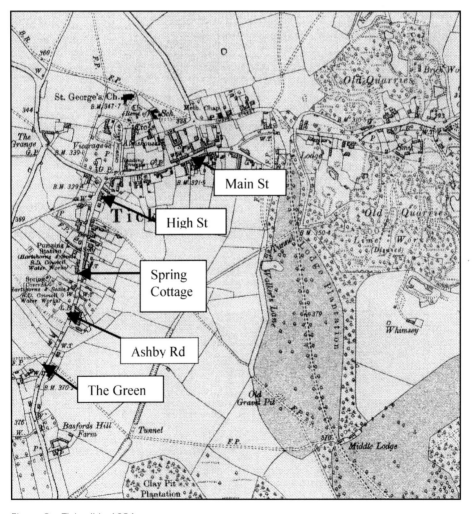

Figure 2 – Ticknall in 1924

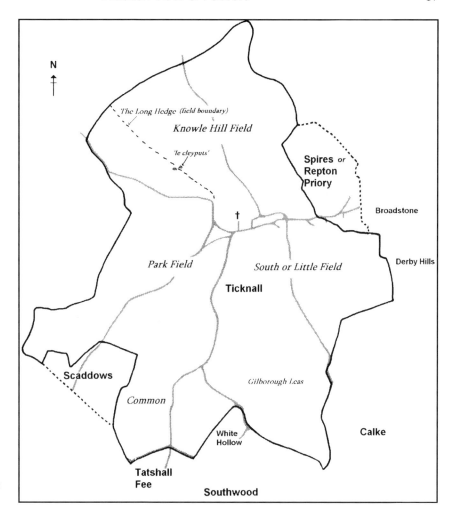

N

The Long Hedge (field boundary)

Knowle Hill Field

'le cleyputs'

Spires or
Repton
Priory

Broadstone

Park Field

South or Little Field

Derby Hills

Ticknall

Scaddows

Gilborough Leas

Common

White
Hollow

Calke

Figure 3 – Ticknall
before enclosure in
1756

Tatshall
Fee

Southwood

The older houses in Ticknall are mostly strung out along High Street and Main Street (see Figure 2). They generally back on to what were then open fields or commons in the typical plot layout of the Middle Ages and early modern period, though there may now be other modern houses behind them, built in their crofts (see Figure 3). The manorial halls and the farms tended to be the larger properties and some of these have significant histories. Spring Cottage, High Street, marked the edge of the medieval village and documentary evidence shows that there was a dwelling (not the present house) on this site in the period 1307–27. Outside the village core, on the present Ashby Road, is an irregular group of cottages at The Green, which were originally intake cottages (illegal settlements nibbled out of the edge of the common), one of which was a pottery. The existing cottages in the village often contain the core of the original houses on the site, and several have been studied in detail to establish the pattern of building and development in the village, using cheap local materials. This gives some insight into the living standards of Ticknall inhabitants at different dates.

Up to the late sixteenth century, the cottages were built on a stone house platform, often with large corner stones, and the gable walls might also be of stone. The stone came from the lime yards and it is mostly roughly coursed and rarely dressed wasters. The other walls were timber framed and the cottages had thatched roofs; the position and depth of the thatch can be seen in the shape of the gable walls now built into the extended cottages. Some were single-storey dwellings, others had steep, ladder-like stairs to a chamber in the roof space, and would have had a small dormer window at floor level. There would have been a wood burning inglenook fireplace against a gable wall, and the stairs were usually beside it. Mostly they were only one room deep, though some seem to have been more than one room wide. One of the cottages studied showed evidence that it was built before the late fourteenth century. There would have been outbuildings such as cowsheds, stables or workshops in the croft behind.

Many of the cottages were rebuilt in the very late sixteenth century or during the seventeenth, to a common pattern of a main room or 'house' (the description almost always used in the inventories for this room) and a narrow service room behind it, if possible on the cold side of the building. Some retained the core of the medieval house, others were extensively rebuilt. The service room was a single-storey outshut built on to the back which was used as a cold store for food and for setting milk. These houses also had a large inglenook fireplace against the gable wall, often fitted with a crane, a fireback and a spit for roasting. There is evidence that by the early seventeenth century it was difficult to obtain suitable wood for these large hearths, and the chimneys were narrowed using large stone blocks to create a hood which was built into the inglenook. The staircases remained beside the fireplace, but were boxed in with a door at the foot to cut down the draughts. The stairs were steep with a tight turn at the top and bottom. The houses were rebuilt in brick or stone, generally incorporating the older stone gables; several were rebuilt deeper from front to back. Bricks were easily obtained as they were made locally. Roofs were still thatched, but the walls were raised a little so that the chambers had better headroom; they still had a dormer window to the front. The 'house' had a window and a door at the front, plus doors through to the service room and out to the back. The service room would only have had a tiny window.

In the late eighteenth or early nineteenth century many of the cottages had their roofs raised to make better bedrooms; the new brick work can still be seen on the upper walls. Roofs were tiled, and larger bedroom windows were installed, often as Yorkshire (sideways sliding) sashes. The local brick makers made the tiles; the potters made the ridge tiles and chimney pots. In some cases the service room was extended for use as a wash-house and coal store, or the staircase was moved from beside the fireplace and installed as a straight flight in the old service room. During the nineteenth century some of the cottages had two-storey extensions added on to a gable end to give another room on each floor. There was some entirely new building in the village in this period, and neat, elegant houses with Regency or early Victorian detailing can be seen. These were better-quality buildings than the older cottages which make up most of Ticknall's housing.

It is likely that the potters lived in houses of the 'house', service room and chamber pattern, with the workshop and kilns in the croft behind the house. The dump for broken or failed pots would have been close by the kiln and explains the position of the waste material found when fieldwalking, even though the property boundaries have changed.

Visitors were often good observers and have left us with descriptions to help elucidate the history. William Wolley's descriptions of the county were published in about 1712; he said Ticknall was 'mostly a Sandy Clay Soile proper for making Course Earthenware for which it is famouse'.[21]

The parish registers show that there was a rapid increase in population from the 1740s onwards, so that by 1789 Pilkington wrote:

*Ticknall is a large village. The whole parish contains one hundred and seventy-five dwellings. These stand chiefly in the village, and form a street of considerable length. During the summer season many persons are employed at the kilns for burning limestone. Formerly a very large quantity of earthen ware was manufactured at this place; but lately the business has very much declined. It is said that since the land in the neighbourhood has been enclosed, it has been difficult to meet with proper clay.*[22]

In 1828 Ticknall was thriving, with 'large lime works, wrought to great advantage; the lime being conveyed by a rail road to the Ashby canal, and from thence forwarded to every part of the country. Ticknall parish contains about 1,300 inhabitants',[23] and the growth was due to the lime yards not the potteries.

The decline of both the potteries and the lime yards was reflected in the directory descriptions such as that for 1895:

*The parish was formerly more prosperous, and since 1851 the population has decreased from 1,241 to 844 in 1891 ... There were formerly extensive lime quarries, brick and tile works, and a pottery worked in Ticknall; of those industries there now remains only the brick kilns, which are worked for estate purposes; the lime quarries are closed, and the pottery has disappeared.*[24]

Wolley wrote that Calke in 1712 was

*a small Hamlet at the East end of that large range of Commons ... Joyning to the Liberty of Hartshorn ... [The park is] well stored with Deere & there is a good large Coney warren on the Common. Here also is made Potts as at Tickenhall to which it joyns North as it doth to Staunton Harrold East.*[25]

In 1789 Calke had thirteen houses, and 'the lime kilns, and a colliery, afford employment to several of the inhabitants'.[26]

Farming as a part-time activity with potting is discussed with the potters' families, but there was of course full-time farming in the parish. Ticknall had the usual range of village trades: carpenters, tailors, shoe makers, blacksmiths, bakers, butchers, tallow chandlers, publicans and a seventeenth-century clay pipe maker. When Farey recorded its occupations, Ticknall had lace running and knitting frames; later there was the repair of fine netting. The village then had malting, brewing, some market gardening and made tallow candles.[27] For a small village, it had a surprisingly wide range of occupations. Residents lived in a healthy place — in 1907, Ticknall was described as 'both externally and internally, the cleanest place within miles of Ashby'.[28]

Ticknall's industrial history was based on its geology. The village lies at the northern tip of the Leicestershire and South Derbyshire Coalfield, where the coalfield dips into a basin centred on Heath End. The Thringstone Fault runs from Hartshorne in the west across the parish to Staunton Harold in the east and provides a geological boundary. South of it are the coal measures clays and north of it the geology is mainly carboniferous limestone, sandstone and gritstone. The limestone inlier is part of a group including Calke, Breedon and Cloud Hill, and Dimminsdale; all these areas exploited their limestone. The geological formation therefore provided the stimulus for Ticknall's main industrial occupations: pottery and brick making, lime burning and coal mining, with the latter supplying the fuel to fire the kilns for the former.

Burning limestone for quicklime to make mortar or to spread on the land was a significant local industry which was documented well before there was any evidence for the potteries. Rough stone from the lime yards was also used widely for local houses. The earliest mention of a lime works in 1462 concerned a 'lymekylne' and houses rented for six years by Symon Ragg from Ellen Assewall at 45s per year.[29] The commercial value of the lime was recognised again when the Prior of Repton kept the right to burn lime on the Calke estate when he leased it to John Prest in 1537.[30] There are references in various seventeenth-century terriers to Limekiln Flat. 'The Lime Kilns in Derby Way' were mentioned when Sir John Harpur bought lands in Knowle Hill Field from Mr Pearston in 1690.[31]

Although the local trade in lime products was well established by the mid-seventeenth

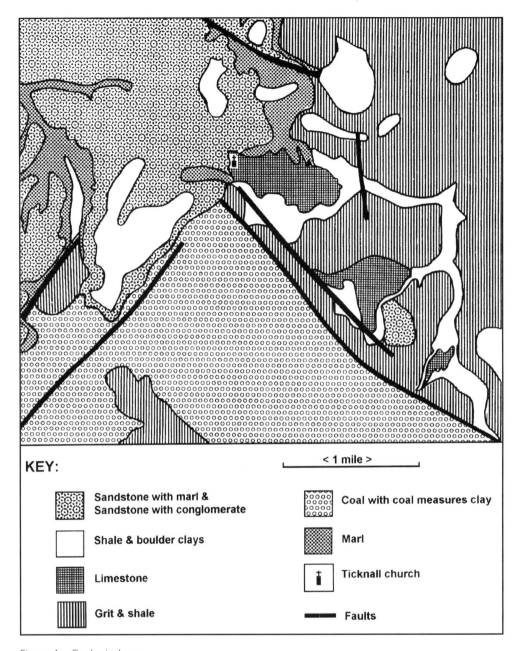

KEY:                                          < 1 mile >

- Sandstone with marl & Sandstone with conglomerate
- Shale & boulder clays
- Limestone
- Grit & shale
- Coal with coal measures clay
- Marl
- ☩ Ticknall church
- Faults

Figure 4 – Geological map

century, it was really from the mid-eighteenth century that it expanded significantly. There were two reasons for this: 'the gradual removal of industrial activity to the margins of the Calke estate, and ... the enclosure of Ticknall's open-field system in 1765'.[32] As well as commercial sales there was a steady demand from the estate itself for building materials. The lime yards south of Main Street were parcelled out as five lots by agreement between the owners, of whom Sir Henry Harpur was the largest. Another was Gilbert Hutchinson, whose great-grandfather William was involved in the lime works before 1670, when his inventory included '9 crows' and hammers, and debts for limestone. His widow Sarah who died in 1680 also had tools and 'limestone already gotten' so she had carried on the business.[33] His grandfather Gilbert was mentioned in the accounts in 1692.[34] Richard Sale and William Gilbert were the other owners. North of Main Street, Sir Henry Harpur and Sir Francis Burdett had the new yards. Gradually the Harpur Crewes acquired all the lime yards and rented them out. They provided seasonal employment in the summer on a large enough scale to draw population in during the nineteenth century.[35] The Ticknall tramway provided good access to the Ashby Canal from 1802 for the lime yards.

Rees recognised the value of Ticknall limestone in his *Cyclopaedia*, where he noted that there were two types of limestone with different properties there, the alluvial and the calcareous; it was the latter that was burnt for sale.[36] After the railways reached the quarries in north Derbyshire, small enterprises like Ticknall's could not compete commercially and the lime yards went into decline other than for local markets; the tramway closed in 1913 and production for the estate itself finally finished in 1940.[37] Because they were simply abandoned, the lime yards preserved their archaeology and nature took over.

Some of the local clays are suitable for making bricks, and the evidence from Prior Overton's Tower at Repton shows that they were made at a very early period. Evidence can still be seen in the village cottages that some bricks were being made in the sixteenth and seventeenth centuries — while the timber framing in walls was generally replaced with wasters from the limestone quarries, the chimneys were built from brick.

Two local streams were called Sedgebrook and Alderbrook; the land lying between them was Great Gilborough or Gilborough Leas (see Figure 3, p.17) and it featured in an undated seventeenth-century law case, probably brought by Robert Bainbridge. The evidence in the case states that 'the Lords & lessies [lessees] of Calke have Alweyes from tyme to tyme used & digged the Soyle within the brookes'. Among the responses to the evidence, the defendants note: 'Summe that have used to make brickes in A Closse of Mr Edward Abells Knowen by the name of Patchers closse ...'[38] (SK358218). The earliest reference we have for a brick kiln is to one that was already working by 1692 and it is probably that in Brick Kiln Plantation (SK370219). After the new lime yards north of Main Street were developed following enclosure in 1765, the estate built a new brick kiln north of the lime quarries. It is marked on the 1882 OS map as 'Brick Yard' (SK358242). The site is derelict and has almost disappeared now but there are traces of gin-driven crushing rollers and a group of buildings. Bricks from this kiln, marked 'IHC' (for John Harpur Crewe), or 'Ticknall', can still be found in the area. It was replaced by another brick yard with a coal-fired Scotch kiln, a moulding shed, an open drying shed and a horse gin which drove crushing rollers arranged above a cart bay so that the crushed clay dropped straight into the cart (SK359243). The moulding shed was demolished soon after the kiln was abandoned in 1939 but the rest was left to decay until the National Trust took over the estate. The kilns produced bricks for estate use as well as for sale, and they made land drains and similar items.

The best coal in the area is centred on the Heath End basin; the coal peters out to very thin seams south and west of it, which rapidly become unworkable. There was a good bed of cannel coal, approximately 12 feet thick and part of the Kilburn seam. It was worked until the mid-nineteenth century from the collieries at Heath End and across the boundary in Staunton Harold park. The shallow accessible seams of coal at the foot of Pistern Hill extending into the present site of Southwood were intensively commercially worked in the sixteenth and seventeenth centuries, and post-war geological surveys showed that the coal was effectively worked out. These shallow seams were worked by means of bell pits. Aerial photographs show regular rows of them to the south of Ticknall village which can still be seen when the land is ploughed, showing up as dark circles. In some places such as Southwood the depressions of the pits are readily found. Coal would have been easily available to the potters, who may have purchased their own fuel from the common as they did their clay.

In 1789 John Byng, Viscount Torrington, left Castle Donington one evening intending to stay at Swarkestone, but found the accommodation 'a most wretched ale house' and the inn at Stanton-by-Bridge too small. He reluctantly rode to Ashby de la Zouch. It was dark before he reached Ticknall, which he described as 'a long, straggling place', and the road was 'stoney, and unpleasant'. Passing through, he 'arrived at a common of a thousand tracks, and covered by coal pits; after crossing this common I came to a cottage, and enquired my road',[39] reaching Ashby at 11pm. The common and coal pits he described would probably be at Southwood. Ogilby's map of the Oxford to Derby road (1720) shows areas of coal working on each side of the road below Pistern Hill. The bell pits must have been working at the time Byng rode by, with lanterns or fires to light them as it was already dark. The cottage was probably at Wicket Nook, just inside Ashby parish.

Fieldwalking evidence shows that a bigger coal mine was developed on land at Heath Farm, probably in the late eighteenth century (SK354207). It was operated by an overhead horse gin to wind the coal, and the site of the mine shaft and the gin circle can still be seen. It was served by a well-constructed driftway through Pisternhill Plantation. In 1811 Farey's list of coal pits had Brians-coppy, Heath End, Pistern, Southwood and White Hollows, all then out of use, and Staunton Harold which was working. In 1829 Glover's Directory listed coal pits at Brian's Coppy, Dimminsdale (Staunton Harold), Pistern, the south-west end of Ticknall and White Hollows, again out of use.[40] By the mid-nineteenth century Heath End was operating again as it is marked on a Staunton Harold estate map in 1859.[41] Pisternhill colliery, near Pisternhill Farm, was one of largest in the area and belonged to the Calke estate. It had a chequered history, and was finally abandoned in 1839.[42] It is the only mine with any surviving buildings.

Lead occurs in the limestone inliers; Calke lies on the most northerly, Dimminsdale on the next one south-east. It is not a major by-product of quarrying in this part of the county as the deposits are generally too small to be economic. In the seventeenth century there were lead mines in Ticknall and Dimminsdale which may have supplied the local trade, and they are discussed further in Chapter 2. The use of lead for glazing has given an insight into another aspect of the potters' lives.

Manufacturing processes are often dangerous, and pottery production had its special hazards. Potters' use of powdered lead to glaze their pots gave rise to an occupational disease, lead poisoning. Lead dust was created when the potters pounded the ore to a powder, usually done dry, and easily breathed in. The lead had to be scattered over the damp pot, and this was done by hand. If the potters were not careful to wash their hands afterwards, and prepared or ate food with contaminated hands, the lead was ingested and the results could be debilitating or even fatal. Lead poisoning was well recognised at the time, and was described by Mr James Wilson, a surgeon from Durisdeer in Scotland, in 1771. He called it mill-reek, the name used by the lead smelters in his area; it was called the bellon in Derbyshire. He described the first stage of the disease thus:

*... an uneasiness and weight is found about the stomach ... and sometimes it appears like a cholic in the intestines. The spittle of the sick is sweet, and something of a blueish colour, resembling what one observes when he chews lead. The pulse is a little low; the skin is all over cold; and a clammy sweat frequently breaks out. The legs become feeble with a prickling numbness; and there is a debility and laziness in all the body. The appetite goes away, and they do not digest what food they take. Sometimes a diarrhoea makes a cure; but, if it continues too long, it is very hurtful. In this stadium [state] the sick are yet able to go about and to work.[43]*

Thomas Kirkland MD (1722–98) came from a long-established Ashby de la Zouch family, and was a well-known and respected doctor in the area. He was also a medical researcher and wrote a number of books on medical practice and theory. In about 1774 he published a 'Commentary on the Apoplectic'. Apoplexy was the condition where there was a sudden paralysis, accompanied by loss of feeling or consciousness, because of a broken blood vessel in the brain. During his discussion of case studies he described the condition of the Ticknall potters that he treated for lead poisoning.

> We have in this neighbourhood pot kilns, in which much lead is used. The workmen, who powder the scoria [ore] of this mineral, are subject to the bellon, and to a paralysis of the limbs, from swallowing the dust which arises in this operation. It is almost impossible to conceive the quantity of lymph, which is secreted into, and becomes ropy in the stomach, &c., and being coloured by the lead, is called by these artificers sludge. I have several times seen both the cholic and paralysis cured by repeated vomiting, and smart purges; for stronger purges are required in this instance than in any I know of. Nor is any good to be expected, till the primae viae [digestive tract] are well cleared. Afterwards I have given a saponaceous emulsion, composed of salt of tartar, oil, and water, by which, and the balsam of pern … the patient has frequently recovered.[44]

Lead poisoning could be contained if the deposits of lead were removed from the body, which was the purpose of Kirkland's purges. Wilson noted that sufferers could recover from this first stage but if treatment was delayed the consequences were severe, particularly if the sufferer drank spirits.

> But, if these symptoms continue long, and spirituous liquors are drunk with an empty stomach, or after working lead, the disease comes to its second stage: In which, to the former complaints, are added a fixed pain in the stomach and guts, especially in the lower part of the abdomen … The patients become very costive [constipated], with the sense of somewhat gnawing their intestines; and the pulse turns quick with heat on the skin. Giddiness, with vehement pain, seizes the head; which is succeeded by an insensibility and delirium, like madness of the worst kind; in so much that they tear their own flesh, and bite their hands; the extremities tremble, and are convulsed: At last, they fall low, the pulse intermits at every third or fourth stroke, and they die in a coma or apoplexy. [If left until giddiness sets in] the success is doubtful; and, when the cure is delayed to be attempted a little longer, the disease almost constantly proves mortal.[45]

He gave advice on controlling or preventing the disease, suggesting the potters should not go to work on an empty stomach, and should eat oily or fatty foods. They should take some medicine twice a year, and, whenever they felt the effects of the disease, avoid hard liquor, or at least not work immediately after drinking. They should not go out into the cold when they were hot from work in the kilns, and the first meal after work should be mainly liquid, like broth. Where possible they should eat meat and avoid a poor diet — not so easy for a poor man. At work, their food should be free from lead contamination, and they should avoid long journeys. He agreed with Kirkland that any cure depended on clearing out the digestive tract and he treated his patients by first blooding them then making them sick and purging them with a dose of emetic which was double that prescribed for anyone else. If it did not work, a stronger dose was prescribed. If the patient was only sick, a large dose of 'jalap and mercury' was ordered. During this treatment, the patient was ordered to drink large helpings of warm broth, and the treatment was to be repeated until all the patient's 'uneasiness' had gone. He could then be given a little opiate at night to induce sleep. If there was a prickling pain in the legs, they were to be rubbed with a coarse cloth or a brush. However, if the madness had begun, 'little else can be done, than to endeavour to keep the patient quiet during the little time he has to live'. Even if a cure was effected, the patient was not restored to full health and strength, and needed to convalesce.

*Some are so wasted before the cure is compleated, that they remain afterwards emaciated, weak, and as if they were hectic, with a giddiness in their head: And sometimes they chat to no purpose, or seem hypochondriac. In this condition, the patient should go to the country, to ride on horse-back some miles every day; and, at the same time, should take bitters with bark [quinine] and steel.[46]*

Presumably the steel was intended to cure anaemia. Another doctor, Thomas Percival, investigated lead poisoning among the Derbyshire lead miners, and described the symptoms in the same way. He recommended taking alum as a prophylactic and as a remedy in the early stages of the disease. The Ticknall potters could have obtained relief locally because of the lime works, though we have no evidence of this being done deliberately. Percival observed that when the lead miners noticed early symptoms, they knew a remedy.

*They usually leave their occupation for a while, and work at the lime kilns, experience having taught them that the fixed air or mephitis arising from the calcinations of limestone, is an effectual and speedy remedy in this disorder. No other change of employment offers them so much relief. The same vapour, in moderate degree, seems to be salutary to the human constitution; for I have been informed by a gentleman of judgement and veracity, who has the direction of a considerable number of lime kilns, that the men employed in burning lime are remarkable for their health and longevity.[47]*

The pattern of mixed or seasonal employment in Ticknall, combining potting, lime burning and farming, may have helped the potters to keep lead poisoning under control for most of the time. As late as 1811 the Revd Davies, writing about Derbyshire, noted that the 'lime kilns find employment for many of the inhabitants during the summer season; while the pursuits of agriculture employ several more'[48] in his description of Ticknall.

Percival's experiments on fine pottery glazed with lead such as Wedgwood's Queen's ware 'shews that vessels of it are improper for the preserving of acid fruits and pickles' because they dissolved the lead from the glaze. This would also have been the case with earlier pottery using older methods of lead glazing and suggests that frequent use this way could produce lead poisoning in users of pottery.

Modern writers on industrial diseases confirm the accuracy of the eighteenth-century observations and the need to clear the lead from the body, noting that it is repeated exposure rather than sudden poisoning that is most dangerous. The potters worked with daily exposure. Symptoms listed are abdominal and muscular pains, anaemia, hypertension, granular kidneys, a blue line on the gums, increased bone density because lead accumulates in the bones, and encephalopathy. In children, the latter can give rise to severe brain damage and mental subnormality. The potters suffered from 'potter's drop', or lead neuropathy, where the motor nerves especially in the upper body are affected, causing the wrist to drop so that it was impossible to control the clay on the wheel. By the time medical examinations were introduced in the industry in about 1870 they could only have helped the potters at the last Ticknall pottery.[49]

We have evidence of lunacy induced by lead poisoning only in the case of Josiah Marriott. The accounts of the overseers of the poor provide the record, when Jacob Standley was overseer. It started with a payment of 2s to Marriott in March 1767. Two days later the entries suggest that he was seriously ill: 2s was paid for 'going to the doctor for Josiah Marriott', 2s for hire of a horse and 2s 6d for Standley's expenses overnight and 9d for the tollgates on the way, plus 1s for 'refreshment on the road there and back'. Two days later again, Standley recorded 6d spent on the doctor, probably for refreshment, and 1s 6d given to Marriott. At that time it was thought that beer was a strengthening drink, and Standley paid 1s 10d for '22 quarts of beer for a diet drink' for him. A local, Lockett, was paid 5d for attending him, but Tim Beighton clearly took most responsibility for his care; he was paid 7s plus 4d for ale while doing so. The doctor's bill for treating Marriott was £2 18s 4d; it does not record which doctor this was, though it was probably Dr Chadwick from Derby. Marriott apparently recovered for a while, as the next entries are in October 1770: 'Doctor Chaddocks expenses for eating drinking lodging etc when he came to J Marriott 3s 11d', and 'Paid Timothy Beighton for self and sons attending Josi. Marriott in his lunacy 16s 6d'. Dr Chaddock's bill of £1 6s for treating Marriott was paid in February 1771. Marriott appears to have had another bout of lunacy in June 1772: 'Paid three men for attending Josiah Marriott 24 hours 2s each', possibly Beighton and his sons again, attempting to keep him calm as Wilson recommended. In October 1774 Timothy was paid 6s 'for tending Josiah Marriott when ill'. There was a bill from Dr Chaddock 'for drugs', though no total was recorded, and the overseer then, Sam Sheavyn, 'paid a man for going to the doctor and expenses 4s'. The problem was back in July 1776:

> Paid Jos Nichols and George Smith for sitting up one night each with Josiah Marriott 2s
> To John Newbald for fetching the doctor to Josiah Marriott 3s
> For meat to Josiah Marriott 1s
> Coals to Josiah Marriott 1s 10d
> Tim Beighton's bill attending Josiah Marriott 9s 6d
> To George Smith for attending J Marriott 9s
> Gave John Walton when going to Mr Kirkland 5s
> Paid Dr Chadwick a bill on Josiah Marriott in arrears £2 5s

There were no more entries about Marriott's lunacy; he died in 1803. He does not seem to have returned to potting after these attacks which may be why he survived for such a long time. By 1769 Samuel Hill was working at Marriott's pottery and he was still there in 1799.[50]

# References

1 SHC (1916), pp14–15

2 Cox, J. C. (1875–9) p459

3 SHC (1937), pp51, 63

4 Sinar, J. (1979), p153

5 Bulmer, T. (1895), p321

6 D2375m/53/2 DRO

7 D2375m/56/31 DRO

8 SHC (1937), p92

9 *Calendar of Fine Rolls* (1451), vol. 18, p247

10 Jeayes, C. (1906), no. 2295 (1363)

11 Sinar, J. (1979), p154

12 Lysons, W. (1817), p246

13 Bagshaw, S. (1846), pp270–1

14 *Feet of Fines* no. 1326, Westminster 1544; Richard Harpur, Thomas Fynderne esq. and John Porte esq.

15 Sinar, J. (1979), p159

16 Pears, Revd S. R. (1868), pp129–30; Jewitt, L. (1868), pp131–40. The school has the tiles on display, available to the public on request

17 D2375m/25/5/16 and D2375m/25/5/11 both DRO

18 D77 Box 22/5 DRO

19 D1396A/ PI 1/1 DRO

20 TNA: PRO, HO 107/192 folios 1–46; 1851: HO 107/2084 folios 306–52; 1861: RG 9/2268 folios 141–67; 1871: RG 10/3245 folios 330–58; 1881: RG 11/3139 folios 58–83; 1891: RG 12/2509 folios 148–61; also DLSL *The Victoria History of the Counties of England, Derbyshire* (1970) vol. 2, p202

21 Wolley, W. (1712), pp65 rev., 67 rev.

22 Pilkington, J. (1789), vol. 2, p83

23 Pigot, J. (1828), p141

24 Bulmer, T. (1895), p829

25 Wolley, W. (1712), pp65 rev., 67 rev.

26 Pilkington, J. (1789), vol. 2, p77

27 Farey, J. (1811), vol. 3, pp486, 479

28 Scott, W. (1907), p440

29 14 October 1462 and 1 May 1476, both D2375m 25/5 DRO

30 D2375m 286/4/1 DRO

31 D2375m 30/21 DRO

32 Marshall, G., Palmer, M. and Neverson, P. (1992), p147

33 William Hutchinson, 22 September 1670; Sarah Hutchinson, 24 March 1680; both LJRO

34 D165m/95 DRO

35 Usher, H. (1995), p7

36 Rees, A. (1802–20), vol. 21, 'Lime'

37 Usher, H. (1995), pp14–15

38 D2375m/161/2/10 DRO

39 Bruyn Andrews, C. (ed) (1935), pp67–8

40 Farey, J. (1811), vol. 1, p188; Glover, S. (1829), p54

41 26D53/1999 ROLLR

42 D2375m/39/14 DRO

43 Wilson, J. (1771), pp517–26 WIL

44 Kirkland, T. (c.1774), pp138–9 WIL

45 Wilson, J. (1771), pp517–26 WIL

46 Ibid., pp517–26 WIL

47 Percival, T. (1774), pp27–36 WIL

48 Davies, Revd D. P. (1811), p35 DLSL

49 Passmore, R. and Robson, J. S. (eds) (1974), section 37 p7; section 34 p161; section 65 p23; section 34 p37; section 73 p8

50 D2375m/103/103/7 1770 DRO

# 2. The Necessary Elements for a Pottery

Figure 4 (p.20) shows the deposits of boulder and coal measures clays in the area. The most important is the coal measures clay in the area of Ticknall Common, where there was a concentration of potteries. There is a deposit of boulder clay covering the valley of Staunton Harold Reservoir and Derby Hills, where several potters had an agreement to dig clay; it probably refers to the area around Derby Hills Farm where the clay beds are very thick.

The earliest known clay pit was dug on the small deposit of marl west of the church and can still be identified; it was used for marling the land. In 1328 Richard de Newton granted to William de la Ward '5½ acres lying in the Clay puttes' in Ticknall. Documentary evidence shows that these clay pits lay across the boundaries of Knowle Hill Field and Park Field, and this area can be identified today with the damp, dug-out areas at SK346245[1] (see Figure 3, p.17). Marl was recommended by William Harrison in 1587, 'wherewith in many places the inhabitants do compest their soil, and which doth benefit their land in ample manner for many years to come'.[2] There was another marl pit which now forms the pond to the right of the entrance drive for Calke Abbey (SK356237). Before this area was included in the park, it formed part of Little Field and it was described as '½ a rood of the Marle pitt' in 1630, as the 'marl pit mouth' in 1705 and as the 'Marlkin Marlpitt furlong' in 1709.[3] Pilkington noted that red marl was common in the county and added, 'An excellent compost is often formed by the Derbyshire farmers of lime, dung and the soil of which I am speaking. The last is also used alone as a manure'.[4] Ticknall was fortunate to have both marl and lime.

Water was essential to the potters and the main springline runs along the south-western edge of the common clays, reaching into the village itself. Watercourses can be seen on Figure 5. It is possible that the exposed clay along the brooks was being used by the early clay workers. When fieldwalking we found several places where exposed clay has been dug along the banks of brooks in Ticknall. Typically there was a semicircular area which had been dug out and not backfilled, and the clay could still be seen in the bank created by the digging.

Stocks of clay are mentioned in inventories. In 1674 Henry Tetley's 'clay on the common' was valued at £1, Samuel Potter had 8s worth of 'Clay on the comon and in the yard' in 1688 and Edward Long had 'Clay of all sorts' worth £1 9s 6d in 1718. It is possible to get some idea of what sort of quantities these may be by comparing them with clay that the Staffordshire potters had in their inventories, even though the Ticknall references are earlier. In Burslem in 1751, fifty loads of clay were worth £2 10s and clay in the field was worth £1 5s for fifty loads. In 1761 eight loads of common clay were worth £1 and six loads of saggar clay 15s.[5] The 1751 value of 5s for ten loads of 'clay in the field' at Burslem would suggest that Henry Tetley may have had as much as forty loads weathering on the common. Samuel Potter's stock was less, perhaps fifteen loads, whilst Edward Long may have had nearly sixty loads and was obviously using more than one type of clay to make his pots — different varieties of clay were found locally. These references to clay show that these potters were all weathering their clay outdoors to make it easier to use. There is little evidence for the next improvement in preparing the clay, known as blunging. The clay was mixed with water in a large outdoor pit and stirred with poles or paddles. This resulted in the clay particles being more carefully separated and gave the potters greater control in drying the clay. There are no references to paddles in the Ticknall inventories, but John Knifton has two poles valued at 8d with his potting tools so he may have prepared his clay in this way. After 1766 the inventories cease and this type of detail is lost.

In 1588 Gilbert Thacker of Repton esquire leased his clay to Robert Cooke of Ticknall, yeoman. Gilbert was careful to exact all the feudal dues that had previously been owed to the priory. It is the earliest clay lease we have found to date, and it shows that there were already clay pits for potting in commercial use. The lease covered a house in its enclosure in Southwood (which was then part of Repton parish), a piece of waste ground 'latlie enclosed' with the barn recently built on it, rights of common pasture, 'And all manner of Earthe pittes or Pitt mynes and Potters claye whatsoever for the onlie use of potting in or aboute Tickenhall, where the said Gilbert hath anie interest'. Thacker's Ticknall lands were the Spires, Scaddows and Southwood. The lease ran for 21 years and Cooke paid £3 in money twice a year at Lady Day and Michaelmas, but he also had to supply 'upon reasonable requeste' from Thacker or his heirs 'All manner of Tickenhall vessels needful for him or them to be used in the nowe dwelling howse of the said Gilbert att Repingdon aforesaid according to auncient use and custome without anie contradiction whatsoever …'.[6] In effect, part of his rent was to be paid in pots, a custom which may have been operating in Ticknall during monastic times.

An indenture between Thomas Biddulph (Biddle) of Ticknall, gentleman, and John Harpur, 'heir apparent of Sir John Harpur Crewe' was drawn up in 1647. It related to the wood, waste or common land 'known as prince wood or prince fee in Ticknall', identifiable because of the references to the site of the rabbit warren, which is shown on the tithe map of 1843 as the field known as Rabbit Burrow (SK344223).[7] It described a

*cottage or tenement on the said wast or comon called Prince wood or prince fee in Ticknall now or late in the occupation of one Richard Cole als Warren als Harrould als Harrington [with] warren or free warren Conyboroughes and game of Coneys in the said wood princewood also late in the tenure of Richard Cole … Also to digg up any part and to cast up as many conyboroughs to increase the said warren or game of conys … [power to] build any cottage … full power to dig for and gett and to take and carry away any potters clay [or] clay to make any manner of potts or earthen vessels from and out of the usuall pitts and places now used or thought convenient for ye potters use in any part of ye sd wast or common aforesd called princewood or prince fee in Ticknall excepting only the warren and conyboroughs and game of coneys shall bee planted or cast upp, also excepting that cottage or tenement adjoining, also the cottage or lodge house possibly to be built …*[8]

As with Thacker's lease, this shows that the clay on the common already had a recognised monetary value. Clearly, more than one potter was getting it, and the reference to the 'usuall pitts' suggests that they had been doing so for some time. The rabbits were an important commercial consideration too, as the warrens were constantly being maintained by the warrener, Cole. It may be that the cottage which was to be built was for a potter. Unfortunately this indenture does not tell us which potters obtained their clay from Prince Wood.

By the time of the three inventories recording clay, Thomas Pearston, a Ticknall gentleman and a relation of Thomas Biddulph, owned these lands at Prince Wood, and he leased clay to four Ticknall potters. It is clear from the lease that one was already running with the potters at Heath End and this lease, dated 29 December 1690, extended the right to get clay to the new lessees on the same terms. Joseph Potter, Thomas Hanson and John Marriott were all of Ticknall; Thomas Parker was of Calke. They agreed to pay a yearly rent and to abide by the covenants in the lease. Pearston

*… demised granted & sett to farme & Letten … all my clay & sand or Materialls for making earthen potts that are or is to be found in my waist ground of prince wood and Ryallty of Ticknall with full power And authority to gett sinke dig delve & Lay upon heapes and carry away with any maner of Cariages whatsoever the said Materialls for making of potts from any part of the pr[e]cincts above mentioned by themselves workmen or servants or whom the[y] shall appoint or lett unto from the day of the date heareof for and during & until the full end And Tearme of twelve years from henceforth next ensuing to be compleat*

*and ended and that without the lawfull lett suit trouble Interuption & action or disturbance molestation or denial of him the said thomas pearston ... And the said Joseph Potter Thomas Hanson John Marriott and Thomas Parker for the consideration aforesaid for themselves severally and Respectively ... covenant promise grant and agree to & with the said thomas pearston ... by these presents in maner & form following that is to say that the said Joseph Potter Thomas Hanson John Marriott and Thomas Parker ... shall And will yearly & every yeare during the said Tearme of Twelve years well and Truly pay or Cause to be paid unto the said Thomas pearston ... the yearly rent or sum of two pounds eight shillings of good and Lawfull English money at two days of payment in the yeare (that is to say) the five and twentieth day of March and the nine and twentieth day of September by even and equall portions the first payment to begin and to be made at or upon the five and twentieth day of March next ensueing the date hereof And allsoe that the said Joseph Potter Thomas Hanson John Marriott and Thomas Parker ... shall and will from time to time as oft as there shall be occasion fill up or cause or p[repa]re to be filled up all such pitts w[hi]ch the[y] or any of them or any under them shall make or cause to be made in or upon the said Comon or Royallty or any p[ar]t thereof by digging and getting the said Clay or Sand at any time within the said tearme of Twelve years And it is further promised consented and agreed unto by the said Joseph Potter Thomas Hanson John Marriott and Thomas Parker ... that soe many or all of the potters in and about Ticknall and allsoe Edward Stanley & the potters at heathend that are freemen of the potters trade that will observe p[er]forme and keepe the covenants articles and agreements made and agreed upon by the foure Leassees above mentioned wich is for the good of the whole Community of the potters trade, And noe more then the[y] themselves shall p[er]forme and keepe that then the said potters shall have as good privilidge of getting clay and sand for Makeing of potts as the lead takers paying there portion of the annuall rent of fourty eight shillings above mentioned and Likewise paying there proportion of other Costs and paid about Leaseas & artiguels about the concerne and leveling there pitts w[hi]ch the[y] make in the above said precincts In witness whereof the parties first above named to these Indentures Interchangably have put there hands and seals the day and yeare first above written.*

*Memorandum it is further Agreed that we Joseph Potter Thomas Hanson John Marriott and Thomas Parker befor the sealing that if any more set up or a[ny] further bennifet be made more then the sum mentioned for getting of Clay that it then shall be paid to the landlord.*[9]

This lease indicates that the potters could not get free clay from the common, even though the land was 'waste'. Pearston was aware of the value of the clay and sand, and was clearly prepared to encourage all the potters to make use of it for a fee. Edward Stanley and the Heath End potters were the 'lead takers' in the agreement; these four joined it, and the additional memorandum provided for more potters to have access to these deposits on the common. From the comparative values discussed above, clay worth £2 8s could be about ninety-five loads. It is difficult to estimate how much clay the potters might have used in a year but the memorandum does suggest that Pearston thought they would use more and provided for more clay rent to be paid. The provision for the clay pits to be filled in explains why it is so difficult to find the clay sources when fieldwalking.

Joseph Tetley and the Drapers, all of Heath End, were known to be getting clay from Staunton Harold during the first half of the eighteenth century.

In the Melbourne estate records there is an agreement for some of the potters to get clay on Derby Hills.

*Mem. 11th Nov. 1766. Agreed then with David Hide, John Tetley, John Stanley, Richard Knifton, Isaac Hill & Thomas Hide for them to get Potter's Clay (both the White and the Red Sort) upon Derby Hills, paying the Yearly Rent of Twenty Shillings each. The Rents to com-*

*mence at Mich[aelm]as 1765, and to be paid Yearly at the Easter Audit at Melbourne. They are to fill up the Pits again, and if any Person employs more than Five Workmen, in the Pot work, which are called a Set, He is to pay Forty Shillings a Year and so proportionably.*[10]

The initial rents were listed with the agreement, and recorded again in 1767.[11] Lockett suggests the men were 'local brick, tile and coarseware potters presumably from Ticknall'.[12] None of these men was a brick and tile maker; all were potters from Ticknall and Calke. David Hyde is discussed later as working at Heath End, though the pottery may have been run by his cousins; Tetley was also at Heath End. Both were producing better-quality wares than the usual output of the area. Isaac Hill was supplying pots to Foremark Hall. John Knifton, a yeoman potter, had worked on the Harpur Avenue site 3; Richard was his nephew. John Standley or Stanley was from one of the two potting families of that name.

Further information on some of these men is available from other sources. Richard Knifton's settlement examination took place in 1768 when he was 45. He was born at Ticknall but his father George was a certificated man from Ibstock; Richard was baptised at Ticknall on 24 February 1723. He first worked for Susannah Ward of Heath End for a year, being paid weekly. He 'lived several years in this manner of hiring and received 3s, 4s and 5s a week', presumably with board and lodging in addition; even so, it was poor wages. He then hired himself to Joseph Bosworth, a yeoman of Heath End, for the year on weekly wages.[13] From the Melbourne agreements, he must have been doing better after a poor start, apparently working for himself. But the sharp decline in Ticknall's share of the market is reflected in the fact that within two years he had to apply for parish relief.

In 1767 the Melbourne Estate saw another opportunity to exploit the clay.

*'Mem. 3rd January 1767. Agreed then with Mr Mear and Thomas Kirby for them to dig Clay for Bricks and to erect a Kiln and Hovell upon Derby hills with other Conveniences for carrying on the Brickmaking Business for which they are to pay £2 10s a Year commencing at Mich[aelm]as 1766.'*

The rent is recorded for 1767 as well.[14] Mr Mear was probably the source of the finance and Kirby was the brick maker in this venture. In 1756 a man called Hastings from Spilsby in Lincolnshire had been taking six tons of potter's clay each year from Derby Hills.[15] These clays are not suitable for creamware and we discuss imports of clay later.

The Burdett family also exploited the clay on their land. The Derby Pot Company (Cockpit Hill) obtained clay from them, but it has not yet proved possible to identify the site of the diggings. As the Burdetts owned Scaddows, the company could have been using the Scaddow Holes; they were backfilled when no longer used and their exact site is unknown. In their Southwood rental for 1774 and 1778 there is an entry, 'Derby Pot Co for Clay £3 3s 0d'.[16] The company is mentioned again as a Burdett tenant for clay in two deeds of 1766 and 1794;[17] the latter has clearly copied previous entries as the company had finished by then. Jacob Standley (1695–1776) paid clay rent of £1 1s to the Burdetts in 1773, and his clay tenancy was then passed to Joseph Miller for the next year.[18]

Claypits Plantation (SK353231) has been extensively worked for clay and never backfilled. Before enclosure it was part of the Little Field and was used for arable. Potters' clay was dug from the common. It was called Hill Close on the tithe apportionment. Clay from it was used in the last pottery until it closed, when it was abandoned. The nearby Claypits Field was investigated for possible exploitation around 1919 by Wragg's of Swadlincote but they could not get agreement for a large enough area.[19] Ticknall was enclosed in 1766, and in 1789 Pilkington ascribed the entire industry's failure to enclosure. He wrote, 'Formerly a very large quantity of earthen ware was manufactured at this place; but lately the business has very much declined. It is said, that, since the land in the neighbourhood has been enclosed, it has been difficult to meet with proper clay'.[20] It seems likely that Claypits Planta-tion became a major source of clay after enclosure, when the clay from the common was no longer available. If so, the availability of clay here, at Derby Hills, at Staunton Harold and at Southwood seems to contradict his assumption that the potteries declined because they could not get access to clay any more. Subsequent writers have assumed from Pilkington's comments that the potters had free access to the clay on the common before enclosure, but the seventeenth-century leases show that this was not the case.

Someone in the adjoining village of Hartshorne was awarded good clay land in the 1765 enclosure, and hoped to take advantage of Ticknall's reputation. An advertisement was placed in the *Derby Mercury* for the lease of

*TEN, FIFTEEN OR TWENTY ACRES of POTTERS CLAY, which has been experienced at Ticknall for several years, and found to make the very best sort of EARTHEN WARE. Any responsible person desirous of establishing a manufacture there, for making of pots and saggars, may meet with proper encouragement by applying to Gilbert Raven ... There is a navigable river about two miles from the place, and a fresh DELF of coal opened near the premises.*[21]

Gilbert Raven was the landlord of the Bull's Head, the usual place of business in Hartshorne. There is no evidence as to where exactly the clay was, but it is likely that it was on the Ticknall side. There is no evidence that anybody took up the offer, probably because Ticknall's industry was so clearly in retreat by then.

A late claypit was dug at the junction of the Ticknall tramway and the Heath End road (SK359208). It was not there at the time of the 1882 25-inch First Edition of the OS map. It was still in use post-1945.[22]

Three inventories mention kilns: Richard Gardener has 'certayne bords in the chambers about the oven', William Hanbury had 'in his workhouse & upon his oven 41 boards', whilst Samuel Potter's inventory mentions 'potts that was mad & unsould an ovenfull'. The value of the latter and the probable quantity are discussed later. We do not know how many kilns any of the potteries had. Only one site can be shown as having had two kilns together, where they are shown on Larter's map.[23] There are two mentions of fuel in the inventories; John Beighton had 'wood pales & coles xxx$^s$' in the next inventory item after his potting tools in 1620,[24] and Samuel Potter had 'som coles' worth 4s in 1688.[25] A value of £1 10s suggests that Beighton's coal was for the kiln rather than the house, as discussed below. Four other inventories imply that coal was used in the houses because of two mentions of coal picks and one each of an iron coal hammer and a coal riddle.[26] The coal seams of the North-West Leicestershire and South Derbyshire Coalfield run up to Ticknall (see Figure 4, p.00), so there was never any problem in obtaining suitable fuel.

The overseers of the poor paid for coal for the potters where necessary, as they had done for James Blore. In April 1772 they 'paid Richard Knifton's bill for coals', which amounted to £1 5s 5d. The price suggests that the coal was for the kiln, not for the house — a small load of domestic coal was 1s 9d or 1s 10d per load, and large loads of a 'stack' or a ton cost 9s delivered from Newhall or 12s delivered from Coleorton. In December 1792 the overse-ers paid 16s 8d for the 'carriage of 2 tons of coals to William Blore', suggesting a price of 8s 4d per ton; it was probably domestic coal. In November 1795 they paid £1 3s 4d for 'coals and carriage to William Blore by Mr Henson', probably delivering three tons. Coal was also bought from Pisternhill colliery both for the workhouse and for individuals. For example, the workhouse expenses for 1789 included 'Cartload of coals and carriage from Pistern 8s'. It was bought by the stack at the pithead, and this was the measure used for a full load.[27]

The only other documentary evidence we have for the consumption of coal by the potteries comes from a balance sheet drawn up on 7 March 1839 for Sir George Crewe, showing likely income and expenditure if Pistern Hill colliery was reopened. This estimated that the four working brick yards and the Ticknall Potworks would use 1,000 tons per year, about 200 tons each, at 6s 8d per ton or £66 13s 4d per year.[28] There was only one pottery still working by then, at Potworks Farm. It had two kilns, suggesting that a kiln consumed 100 tons per year. This site seems to have had its coal delivered via the Ticknall tramway, which goes out of a direct line to reach the pottery. The 1887 Ordnance Survey map shows a spur from the tramway into the pottery yard and the junction is shown on a photograph.[29]

The potters needed lead for their glazes, but although we have no evidence as to where they bought it, there is evidence for easy access to it — Derbyshire was a major lead mining county. There were long connections with the lead trade through the families who owned Calke. By 1561 Calke had been acquired from the Earl of Warwick and his lessee John Prest by Richard Blackwall, a major lead smelter whose family was heavily involved in the trade.[30] Between 1573 and 1575 Richard Wendsley, a Derbyshire tax collector and lead smelter who was lessee of the Duchy of Lancaster's duties for the Wirksworth mines,[31] acquired the freeholds and leaseholds of Calke Abbey. He not only lived there, but used it as security for his dealings in lead. Calke was mortgaged to Robert Bainbridge, a lawyer and MP for Derby, and eventually sold to him in 1585.[32]

Bainbridge and his father William had been trading lead from the 1550s, and between 1560 and 1590 they were the most important of the Derby lead merchants, selling abroad by the 1580s. By 1578–9 Robert was one of four merchants who controlled the trade in lead through Hull. He also ran a smelting mill between 1576 and 1580 near Higham in mid-Derbyshire, for the Earl of Shrewsbury. An indenture of 4 August 1582 shows that there were close trade links between Wendsley and Robert Bainbridge. A memo to it states, 'provided that Richard Wendesley of Calke esq. to paie to said Robert Bainbrigge at Kingston uppon Hull in the Co. of Kingeston uppon Hull in the weghe howse five skore and fower foothers of peake leade of the usuall [weight]'.[33] Henry (later Sir Henry) Harpur of Swarkestone Hall also had lead smelting interests.[34] He bought Calke Abbey from Bainbridge's son (also Robert) for £5,350 in 1622.[35]

In 1654 Sir John Harpur tried to find workable deposits of lead on his land at Calke. He made an agreement with Robert Day of Hartington, a lead merchant who usually had his lead smelted at the Wirksworth Lower Smelting Mill,[36] 'to permit 6 meeres or parcels of ground in Leadoare Close in Calke to bee begun to be digged & worked to the intent Lead Oare may be there gotten',[37] working to traditional measures and methods with Day and Harpur having half each of the lead. The agreement further stated that a new contract would be required to extend the workings, and allowed each party to work any cross-rakes that were found on their meers for a distance of 13 yards each side of the main rake. Day had to pay one-sixth of the ore from his meers as royalty or rent to Harpur. If he stopped work for a month the agreement would lapse unless he was prevented from working for lack of wind or water power, and Day's interests would revert to Harpur. Day had to make good any damage or loss suffered by the tenants of 'Leadoare Close and other Closes soe to be digged'.

Harpur was clearly trying to find lead to work commercially and sell on a large scale; this is not an agreement primarily intended to supply small quantities of lead to the local potters. Nevertheless the fact that lead was available locally must have been useful to them.

We know lead was mined in Ticknall because a 1686 indenture between Francis Burdett and Walter Burdett described the open-field holdings belonging to a farm in Ticknall. They included 'one half ac at the lead pitts', '3r at the lime kilnes' and 'one $1/2$r at the lime kilnes', all in Knowle Hill Field.[38] A conveyance from the executors of the late Gilbert Hutchinson to Sir Henry Harpur in 1743 contained a reference to a half-acre shooting to the Derby Way near the lead pits,[39] in the same field. Derby Way is probably the old track to Ingleby and thence across the river Trent to Derby — it is the direct route. From documentary references, it is clearly not the modern road going up Stanton Hill. Some lead from Chesterfield, the most important lead market, came overland through Derby to the Trent and passed down the river to Hull on its way to London; it could have been bought at one of the small wharves nearby.

Lead weight was calculated on a local scale. Ore was not weighed but was priced according to the amount of ore which could go into the standard 'dish', kept at the Barmoot Court in Wirksworth. The dish held 60–65lb of ore. Nine dishes made a 'load', which weighed about five hundredweight (5cwt), so there were $3^{1}/_{2}$ to 4 loads per ton. By the late sixteenth century lead was smelted at an ore hearth, producing 'pigs'. They varied because of the difficulty of casting exact weights, but the average for a Derbyshire pig was 2cwt 5qtr 8lb. Larger amounts of lead were reckoned by the 'fother'; in Derbyshire, that was $22^{1}/_{2}$cwt. The ideal weight of a pig was one-eighth of a fother. The weights were standardised by about 1600.[40] Definitions varied at London, Hull and Bawtry but we have used Derbyshire weights.

Most of the lead traded down the river had already been smelted into pigs, and it seems that at least one of the potters in Ticknall may have been doing a little trading as well. Henry Tetley had '3 pigge of Lead and an Iron plate' worth £1 16s in the entry of his house in 1684.[41] The plate could have been used to grind lead on, but the pigs must have been for trade; smelted lead is no practical use to a potter. There would have been between 7cwt and 8cwt of lead there, worth about 11s per pig. This is relatively cheap for lead — it is less than half its price in the 1580s — but prices varied considerably in response to the state of the markets.[42]

The potters needed calcined ore to crush and sprinkle on the wet pots. They used smitham, the fine particles of lead ore which fell through the riddle when larger lumps were knocked off. It gave a soft glaze, which could be scratched off or dissolved by acids such as fruit juice, particularly since the pots were only fired once. Manganese could be added to give a black finish. After about 1660 a better glaze was made, still using calcined lead ore, but ground to a much finer powder and carefully applied to give an even coating. It was absorbed into the clay better than the older type and gave a harder, more shiny glaze. On a white clay, lead glaze gives a yellow finish. These wares like all slipwares were still fired only once. The value of separate biscuit and glost firings seems to have been known during the 1740s though the practice did not come into common use until the 1750s.[43]

By comparing the amount of lead valued in three Ticknall potters' inventories with recorded prices for lead at different periods, it seems likely that these potters had lead ore in store which was intended for glazing. In 1597 Henry Hanbury owed 12s for 'Leide' when his inventory was drawn up. In 1591 lead ore cost 9s per load, and in 1593 it was 8s 8d,[44] suggesting that he had about one load and three dishes of ore. John Coggreave owed Edward Burne 'xix[s] for Leade' in 1626.[45] A load of lead had been 18s in 1616[46] and it seems likely that this purchase was for a load at a slightly higher price. John Standley owed £1 for 'two hundred of Lead' in 1667[47] to an unspecified dealer, and the fact that it is 78lb less than the average pig weight suggests that this 2cwt represented about $3^{1}/_{2}$ dishes of ore, just over one-third of a load. In 1652 a load of ore cost £1 1s,[48] so lead prices must have trebled by 1667 to reach about 5s 8d per dish. In 1724 Joseph Potter's inventory included an entry 'for Lead 13s 6d'.[49] Lead ore had fallen to £3 per ton in 1728;[50] this suggests that Potter had $4^{1}/_{2}$cwt of ore, just under one load. The four inventories together strongly suggest that the potters bought their ore by the load as a standard quantity. The majority of the shards found on the kiln sites in Ticknall have been glazed with lead using increasingly skilful methods.

Even the overseers of the poor at Ticknall recognised that lead was essential to the potters, and were prepared to pay for it in order to keep potting families working and off the poor rates, as discussed in Chapter 3 for James Blore.

Before the introduction of liquid lead glazes, salt glazing had been a popular alternative finish; it was introduced soon after 1700. It gave a transparent glaze and allowed a fashionable white item to be made from white clay. It did not have a glossy finish, however. It was duller, with the appearance of orange peel. It was more difficult to produce, as it required careful control of temperature during firing. Even so, it became very popular between about 1740 and 1760. Salt glazing declined from the 1760s as the fine finish of liquid lead glazes took over.[51] There was an ancient, well-established salt trade from Cheshire and there were long-standing trade connections between the Ticknall potteries and the salt producing areas. Even so, evidence for possible salt-glaze production so far has only been found on two sites in Ticknall. While most sites do yield fragments of brown salt-glazed ware nearly all are of the Nottingham, Denby or Chesterfield types; it seems likely that these were broken pieces of domestic pots. Local salt-glaze production is discussed later.

Lead glazes in liquid form were first specified in Thomas Frye's patent of 1748. The powdered lead was mixed with flint or ball clay and water. With liquid glazes, the ware was biscuit-fired and then dipped in the glaze before a second firing.[52] Liquid glazes were in general use from 1750 and work continued to produce a glaze which was as pale as possible. The eventual result of this development was creamware and pearlware, during and after the 1750s. Liquid glazes were also important for the development of tortoiseshell and mottled ware.[53] Mottled wares were found at sites 11, 20 and 22. Creamwares might have been made at site 24 as well as site 25 (see Fig.5, p.00).

Henry Blest was using ochre, which produced an orange-brown glaze, when he died in 1620. Among the debts owed to him was one from 'Homffrye Tyler' who owed 'xvi[s] the one halfe in money, the other in oker of i[d] of a Stone'.[54] At one penny per stone, Tyler owed him ninety-six stones of ochre, a considerable amount.

Stocks of flints or ball clay are not recorded by name, though they would have been easy to obtain from the river wharves. Calcined and ground flints were available from Kings Mills where the Lloyds ran the calcining kilns and sent flints to Derby and Stoke-on-Trent. In 1770 Arthur Young had described how the flints from the Thames were 'brought rough by sea' to Liverpool or Hull, 'and so by Burton' to Wedgwood's works. 'The flints are bought first by the people about the country, and by them burnt and ground, and sold to the manufacturers by the peck'.[55]

Devon clay fired a true white, unlike the yellow local clays. It is described as ball clay or tobacco pipe clay, and Wetherill notes that it was used for both tobacco pipes and white pottery in London.[56] It was brought up the river in casks for delivery to the china works in Derby. Jewitt stated that he had the surviving weekly bills for the Derby works from 1770 to 1773, and the bill for the first week in December 1770 included a purchase of '2 Tons of fine clay Shipping to Darby [sic] £2 7s'.[57]

We do not know who was supplying the Devon clay used at the Ticknall, Calke and Melbourne sites.

There are thirty-three inventories that list the goods of pot makers from 1587 to 1766. Of these, just three, Henry Hanbury 1597, Joseph Standley 1709 and Anthony Hood 1747, do not list any potting tools, nor was there any mention of tools of the trade in their wills.[58] The rest of the potters' inventories mention working tools of some sort although only the two Thomas Hansons' are so general as to list 'tools belonging to the potting trade £2' in 1725 and 1729 respectively.[59] Although they give us no idea of just what these comprised, there would have been at least some of the tools listed in other local potters' inventories.

Pot wheels feature in the inventories of most of the Ticknall potters. Some were listed simply as 'the pot wheels & other tools belonging to trade £1', as in the inventory of Edward Long, or the 'two wheeles & other necessaries belonging to his trade' which Richard Gardener had. Other inventories listed the wheels with various other pot making tools. The earliest potter's inventory, that of Richard Hanbury 1587 had 'xxx bordes & a pootte whille', Henry Blest had 'one wheele & passe borde wth Ticknall ware' in 1620, John Standley had a pot wheel where he lived and another 'belonging to the potting house at Hanbryes'; none had individual values. William Hanbury had 'his potting wheele pace board his lead bale &

babble tub' in 1672, whilst Henry Tetley had 'two pott wheeles twoe pott grates & other tools' in 1684. John Cox had '1 pott wheel & frame' in 1695 worth 5s, a high sum for Ticknall and one which suggests perhaps a slightly more sophisticated wheel, as does the 'pot wheele & lead pan' valued at £1 that Richard Cox had in 1732. Joseph Potter's 'two pot wey with two pass bords', valued at 15s, may have been scales for weighing clay or pots. No potter seems to have had more than two pot wheels, although Edward Long may have had more. Few individual prices were given and then only towards the end of the inventory period. Robert Draper's 'two pot wheels wth spindles' were worth just 1s 8d in 1742, and John Knifton in 1766 had an old pot wheel worth 3s.[60] Apart from just one entry for a lathe, that of Homfry Makepeace alias Taylor in 1611, there is no documentary evidence for the potters in this area using lathes to improve their wares.[61] This reference is a full century earlier than that noted by Weatherill and may be a wood turning lathe although it is with his potting tools.

The wheels used by the Ticknall potters would have probably have been kick wheels with the power provided by the potter. We have no evidence that people were employed to provide the power for the wheel, although Weatherill points out that treadle mechanisms and adaptations for power provided by people other than the potter were known by the end of the seventeenth century.[62] The low values suggest that few of the wheels belonging to the Ticknall potters would have been technologically sophisticated. Weatherill gives a value of 5s each for four wheels in 1714 for the Burslem potters, and after 1720 pot wheels there were valued around £1. This is in contrast to Ticknall where the wheels still seem to be a much lower value item, the highest being John Knifton's 'old wheel' valued at 3s in 1766 and probably that of Richard Cox in 1732, although it is valued at £1 with his lead pan.[63] Weatherill also suggests that the improved wheel was connected with the making of salt-glazed stoneware. Nearly all the Ticknall wares were thrown during the early period; it was only later that moulds began to be used, and although we have evidence for moulds being used, it is from fieldwork not inventories.

Other necessary items frequently mentioned in the inventories were the boards used to put the ware on whilst drying. These figure in nearly every potter's inventory. William Hanbury had forty-one boards 'very bad and good' worth £1 6s in 1674, giving an average value to each board of 6d. Henry Tetley had 117 boards worth £4 10s in 1684; these were valued at 9d each, a high figure for Ticknall potters. John Cox had forty boards worth £1, another valuation of 6d each. In 1766 John Knifton had twenty boards 'whole & broken' worth 6s 8d, a value of 4d each. From this it is possible to work out probable numbers of boards owned by potters who only had an overall value for their boards, using the average price of 6d. Thus Richard Gardener may have had fifty-five boards, George Hough thirteen, Joseph Potter as many as 130, Richard Cox seventy and Robert Draper twenty-six.[64] The number of boards may also give an idea as to how involved they were with potting. Those potters who had two wheels — Richard Gardener, Thomas Tetley, Henry Tetley, Edward Long and Joseph Potter — also seem to have had the most potting boards. The only exceptions were Robert Draper with an estimated twentysix boards for his two wheels and William Pemberton whose two wheels and 'ould lumber of ould boards' were together worth 6s 6d.[65]

Pass, pace or page boards are also mentioned in several inventories; they were different from the ordinary boards. Robert Fisher had 'pasbordes', Thomas Tetley '2 pageboards', John Cox '1 pass board', William Hanbury a 'pace board', Henry Blest a 'passe borde' and John Knifton 'a passe board'. No values were given apart from the single board worth 8d in John Knifton's 1766 inventory; as his ordinary boards were valued at 4d, this board would seem to be a more substantial item. It is noticeable that the potters do not seem to have had more that one or two. Although it has not proved possible to be certain what they were used for, it is likely that they were the boards that the potters wedged their clay on to remove the air. They would have had to be solid and sturdy pieces of wood.

Many of the potters had tools for grinding lead for glazes. Grinding irons were listed in the inventories of William Hanbury, Tim Beighton (who had two in 1674), John Cox (who had one valued at 6d in 1695) and John Knifton (who had an 'iron to grind lead' valued at 4d and an iron mortar and pestle worth 1s 4d). Iron grates occurred in the inventories of Thomas Tetley, John Cox, Joseph Morley, and John Standley who had three.[66] John Standley had a 'lead ponne', John Cox had a 'leading bowl', Robert Fisher had a 'lead pan' and a 'leading bowle', Tim Beighton a 'lead pond', Richard Cox a lead pan. John Knifton's 'old lead pan' was worth 8d; he also had a 'sive for lead and sherry'. We wonder whether this latter word is supposed to be 'slurry'. His appraisors were not potters and may have thought slip was slurry. Henry Tetley had a 'lead meels', probably a type of sieve for lead; 'meels' was certainly a word for sieving gunpowder and was probably used for lead in this context. Thomas Tetley also had one 'ould sithe', yet another word for sieve. Other tools used in the trade were pokers or prokers for ovens. John Knifton's 'oven poker' was worth 4d and he also had a pair of pincers valued at 2d amongst his potting tools.

The inventories also show that the potters used spades, shovels, mattocks and hackers to obtain and chop the clay. John Cox had '3 ould spades' which with one grate were worth 2s 6d; Richard Cox had spades and shovels worth 4s in 1732; John Knifton had a clay shovel worth 8d and a new spade worth 2s in 1766. Joseph Morley's inventory mentions spades, shovels and 'hasks'; Thomas Tetley had four spades and one shovel; Tim Beighton had a hacker and a spade; John Standley had 'spades, shoules hackers' and Robert Fisher in 1639 had hackers and spades. There were also references to carts which may have been used for carrying the clay. Only one potter, Robert Fisher, included a wheelbarrow amongst his tools.[67]

Specialist buildings are limited to the 'workhouse' in the inventories of Robert Fisher, William Hanbury, Thomas Tetley, Henry Tetley and William Pemberton. Richard Gardener and Robert Draper referred to the 'workshop', whilst John Standley mentioned both his potting house and the potting house at Hanbury's. John Knifton in the last surviving inventory also had 'a pot house'. Again this contrasts with north Staffordshire where an increasingly sophisticated pattern of specialised workshops becomes apparent from the 1720s onwards.[68] The Ticknall sources do not record any dipping houses, but none of the potteries was large enough to have big ranges of workrooms in this way; any part of the existing pottery could have been used.

Although the detail in the Ticknall inventories is good, it shows clearly that there was little or no capital investment in improved tools or methods. Pot making in Ticknall remained on the cottage industry scale.

# References

1 Fraser, W. (1947), p145

2 Edelen, G. (ed) (1994), p364

3 DE2375m/82/63; DE2375m/165/8; DE2375m/67/42; all DRO

4 Pilkington, J. (1789), p286

5 Weatherill, L. (1971), p12

6 TNA: PRO C109/87/77

7 D2360/262B DRO

8 D2375m/56/31 (deeds quoted for properties are not individually numbered) DRO

9 D2375m/82/72 DRO

10 52/8/9 1765 MH

11 52/8/10 1767 MH

12 Lockett, T. (1985), p80

13 D1396 A/PO 422; baptismal register, Ticknall 1723; both DRO

14 52/8/9 1765 and 52/8/10 1767 MH

15 Usher, H. (1989), pp14–15

16 D5054/13/3 DRO

17 Derbyshire Deeds Nos. 2165 and 2166 DLSL

18 D5054/13/3 DRO

19 pers. comm. N. Clarke

20 Pilkington, J. (1789), p83

21 *Derby Mercury*, 11 and 18 July 1766 DLSL

22 pers. comm. N. Clarke.

23 D2375m/170/3 DRO

24 John Beighton 20 October 1620 LJRO

25 Samuel Potter 24 April 1688 LJRO

26 Robert Draper 8 July 1742 ROLLR; Tim Beighton 19 April 1674; Thomas Tetley 10 June 1681; John Coggreave Admon. 5 August 1626; all LJRO

27 Ticknall Overseers of the Poor Accounts, 20 April 1772; 24 April 1773; 2 December 1792; 28 November 1795; 28 April 1789, in private hands

28 D2375m/39/14 DRO

29 Adams, M., Cox, B., Usher, H. and Woodward, S. (1989), p33

30 TNA: PRO PROB 11/50, q7

31 Kirkham, N. (1968–9), pp1108–10; Kiernan, D. (1989), pp179

32 Colvin, H. (1985), p20

33 D2375m 16/4 DRO

34 Kirkham, N. (1968–9), pp1108–10

35 Colvin, H. (1985), p20

36 Kiernan, D. (1989), p138

37 D286/22 DRO

38 D2375m 25/1 DRO

39 D2375m56/36/1 DRO

40 Kiernan, D. (1989), pp149–50

41 Henry Tetley 23 September 1684 ROLLR

42 Kiernan, D. (1989), pp217–18

43 Wetherill, L. (1971), pp28–30, 39

44 Kiernan, D. (1989), p225

45 John Coggreave 5 August 1626 LJRO

46 Kiernan, D. (1989), p225

47 John Standlye 11 December 1667 LJRO

48 Kirkham, N. (1968), p120

49 Joseph Potter 29 May 1724 LJRO

50 Kirkham, N. (1968), p120

51 Wetherill, L. (1971), pp28–30, 39

52 Hughes, B. and T. (1968), pp84–5

53 Wetherill, L. (1971), p30

54 Henry Blest 16 December 1620 LJRO

55 Mingay, G. E. (ed) (1975), pp142–3, quoting Young's *Northern Tour*, vol. 3 (1770), pp306–9

56 Wetherill L. (1971), p15

57 Jewitt, L. (1878), vol. 2, pp70–1

58 Henry Hanbery 23 October 1597, Joseph Standley 29 April 1709 and Anthony Hood 24 April 1744; all LJRO

59 Thomas Henson 28 September 1725 and Thomas Henson 14 November 1729; both LJRO

60 Edward Long 14 June 1718, Richard Gardener 18 July 1614, Richard Hanbery 7 June 1587, Henry Blest 31 May 1620, John Standlye 11 December 1667, William Hanberye 3 March 1672, John Cox 4 October 1695, Richard Cox 14 November 1732, Joseph Potter 29 May 1724, John Knifton 12 April 1766; all LJRO. Henry Tetley 1684 Admon. 45 and 46, and Robert Draper 1742 Admon.; both ROLLR

61 Homfry Makepeace alias Taylor 26 June 1611 LJRO

62 Weatherill, L. (1971), p32

63 ibid., p33

64 George Hough 19 September 1679 LJRO

65 Thomas Tetley 10 June 1681 and William Pemberton 13 April 1724; both LJRO

66 Timothy Beighton 13 October 1674 and Joseph Morley 14 November 1701; both LJRO

67 Robert Fisher 3 January 1639 LJRO

68 Weatherill, L. (1971), p47

# 3. Potteries and Families:
## sites linked to potters

In a small village, many families were inter-related and Ticknall potters were no exception. Although we can never know the full extent of Ticknall's trade, it was extensive — 14 per cent of the wills and inventories prior to 1800 were for potters, not including the potters at Heath End or Calke. This section concentrates on known pot sites and the families who worked them. The sites are shown on Figure 5.

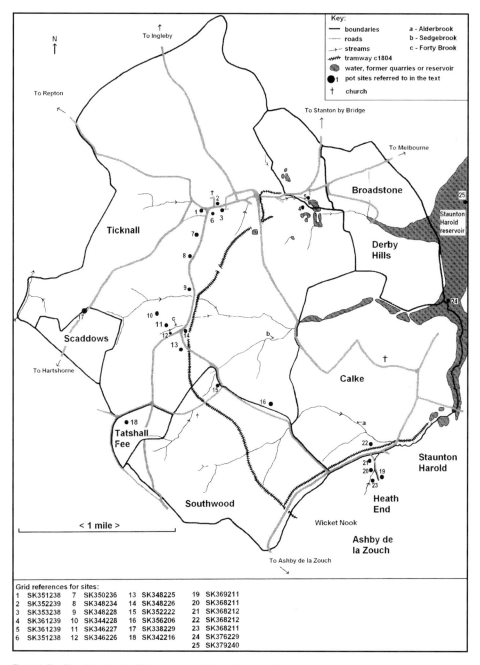

Figure 5 – Pot sites in the Ticknall area with their grid references

The Hough and Pemberton families were related and were working the site to the north of Narrow Lane (**site 1**). This site was probably occupied by the Hough family from the late sixteenth century, as John Hough's will of 1600 divided his property between his sons John and James.[1] The earliest known potter was James's son George who died in 1679. The earliest record of George was in 1630 when he received 12d from his godmother Ales Randall in her will.[2] He was old enough to appear in the muster for 1638[3] and was already married and producing a family around this date. He had one hearth in the Hearth Tax records of 1662[4] and contributed one shilling to the Free and Voluntary Present in the same year.[5] He would therefore have been working from at least the 1630s. His inventory of September 1679 shows a dwelling with four rooms, a 'house' and parlour downstairs, and a chamber over each. The fire irons and cooking utensils, including a spit, were in the 'house' as was usual at that period. The parlour was used for sleeping, although the 'fetherbed' and a 'siled bed' were in the chamber over the 'house', which suggests the best room was upstairs and gained from the heat of the chimney. As corn and apples were stored in the same room there would have been a pleasant musty smell. He had probably retired from potting by the time he died — he described himself as a yeoman in his will and his inventory[6] only lists 'pott boards' worth 6s 6d. Much of his money was tied up in farming, with £2 worth of corn in the barn, 'blendcorne' and wheat worth £1 10s, £1 worth of 'pease' and hay worth £3. Livestock contributed the greatest sum, with his cattle worth £9 10s and his sheep and lambs the same. He had £16 worth of debts owing to him.

His son George inherited the cottage and land. Little is known about the younger George other than the fact that, unusually for the son of a Ticknall potter, he was at school at Repton and went from there to St John's College in Cambridge where he gained his BA in 1668–9 and MA in 1672 — he must have been a bright lad.[7] He may have been the George buried in 1683 as 'George Hough sen'; no will has been found to clarify this, but it is unlikely that he was a potter. It would seem that James Hough, who, together with John Hough, was left one shilling in George Hough the elder's will of 1679, was probably an elder son, and brother of the younger George, who had already received his portion. James was also a potter.

Although we think that this site is the same as where Houghs had previously lived, the earliest deed is from 1694 when James Hough, potter, purchased 'all that their cottage or tenement with thappurtenances in Ticknall where the said James Hough doth now inhabitt & dwell together with the outbuildings, yard ... etc.' from Thomas Pearston for £20.[8] James must have been middle aged by then as he and his wife Dorothy had children baptised between 1674 and 1682; he is probably the James Hough listed with one hearth in the Hearth Tax. He must have been making a successful business of potting to be able to purchase his own house and land. The next deed to mention the site is a 1705 lease between James Hough of Ticknall, pot maker, and Dorothy his wife and William Pemberton of Ticknall, pot maker, and Frances his wife for 'all that cottage or tenement ... wherein the said James Hough doth now inhabit ... together with all houses, outhouses, structures, buildings, barnes, stables, kills (kilns), orchards ... etc.', as well as 2½ acres, 2 roods and 4 butts of land in the open fields of Ticknall. William Pemberton had married Frances the daughter of James and Dorothy Hough the previous year; she was their only surviving child. When James Hough died intestate in 1712,[9] the property had already passed to his son-in-law William Pemberton and his wife Frances. The Pemberton family continued to live at and work the pot site.

William Pemberton and his wife were nonconformists; the only entry in the Ticknall baptism register recorded a son 'born' in 1695. This probably referred to James Hough Pemberton, who was evidently named for his grandfather. At least seven children in total were born, but only four were mentioned when William wrote his will on 18 February 1724,[10] three daughters having died earlier. He described himself as 'sick and weake' and was buried just over a month later on 24 March 1724. William left all his 'bords and pottin tooles' to be divided evenly between his sons James and William. James was to get the 'house and croft' after his mother's death; if he died with no 'ares' (heirs) then the property was to go to his brother William who inherited all the field land. The brothers each had to pay their sister Dorothy the sum of £5 when they had had their inheritance for a year. Dorothy also received one cow, which 'is called hirs', and her sister Ann was left 'two youes and Lambs'. The cottage of 1724 had all the fire implements in the 'house' and the two tables, two cupboards, one form and six chairs in there were all described as 'ould'. The unheated parlour was used for sleeping in, with two beds, one of flock and the other of chaff; the latter must have been rather uncomfortable. There was only one chamber, over the parlour, and it was used for storage. William had both brass and pewter, but his brass consisted of '2 ould Brass potts' and '4 ould Brass Kettles' worth 12s 6d; his ten pewter dishes and five plates ('ould ons') were worth 15s. A workhouse was mentioned for the first time although it did not have much in it that the appraisers thought worth valuing, just 'all ould lumber of ould boards and 2 wheels – 6s 6d, Som more ould and all Lumber besides – 2s, more for things not worth vallueing – 7d'. There was a stable with '2 ould horses' worth £3, '3 ould cows, 3 stirkes and 2 calves' in the croft worth a total of £7 14s, as well as twenty-one sheep and thirteen lambs valued at £3 4s. The total inventory was worth just £20 15s 3d and gives a picture of a potter who was just getting by. The fact that nothing had been spent on household goods for years suggests that trade was not thriving.

There is no indication that either of the brothers married; James Hough Pemberton died in 1729 and never did get his inheritance as his mother Frances survived until 1747, when presumably William inherited. The property descended to their unmarried sister Dorothy on William Pemberton's death in 1764; his will left the property to Dorothy and then to Hannah, the daughter of his unmarried sister Anne.[11] This must also be when potting ceased on this site. There is a neck of a costrel in the local pottery collection at Calke Abbey with a label attached 'from Pemberton & Cooper's works'. This suggests that the Pembertons worked with someone called Cooper in the village. If this is so then the likely candidate would be John Cooper who died intestate in 1729;[12] no occupation was given on his administration so this can only be a suggestion.

When Dorothy Pemberton made her will in 1765,[13] she left all her personal estate to John Taft, a flax dresser and grocer. He was already living on part of the property and was to give Dorothy's neice Hannah Pemberton a home if need be. The property descended to Hannah who sold it in 1776. It was later divided and Sir Henry Harpur bought part in 1806; Sir George Crewe eventually bought the rest in 1843.[14] Number 4 Narrow Lane was almost certainly built on the site of much of the dump in about 1970, as it had to be excavated in large quantities for the foundations.[15]

An extensive dump of pottery was found at Church Lane (**site 2**) when a new house was built in the 1970s; much of this is now in Derby Museum. As yet no potter has been identified for this site.

Another site (3) existed where houses are now. Richard Cox was potting here from 1698, although some of the pottery found may be older. The son of John Cox of the Limeyards (**site 4**), Richard was born in 1674 and died in 1732. The present house on the site, 'Ivy Leigh', may have part of the house of Richard Cox as its core. The 1698 rental shows that Richard Cox paid a half yearly rent of 12s for 'his house and backside purchased of Marriott', indicating that this was land that Sir John Harpur had recently purchased.[16] He continued to pay the same rent throughout his working life until he died intestate in 1732.[17] His inventory shows a three-roomed cottage with a 'house' where the fire was with all his pots and pans for cooking, and a parlour with a featherbed and bed linen, two tables, two chairs and a buffet; the chamber had a feather and a flock bed together with a chest, boxes, three coffers, two tables, two chairs and a joined form. The household economy was helped by five wheels and two reels kept in the chamber, used for spinning and winding thread. There was also a 'seller' with barrels and tubs and a kneading tub. Outside was a workhouse where his potting tools and boards were kept, and a barn where he had corn, peas and hay. His interest in farming was minimal as he had just one cow worth £2 2s — there was nothing in the inventory to indicate that farming played a part in his lifestyle. He had married three times and although he had two known daughters by his first wife, all but one of his six children by his third wife pre-deceased him or died within two years of his death. Richard's third wife was Anne Clearson whom he had married in 1719 at Derby. She remarried the year after Richard's death to John Knifton and it was he who took over the running of this pottery.

The property was listed in the rentals under Richard Cox until after the death of his widow in 1754. This was the only pot works listed as such in the pre-enclosure survey of 1762 which mentions 'house, Pothouses, yard and garden' comprising 1 rood and 4 perches which was valued at £1 5s in the occupation of John Knifton.[18] This is the yearly rent he paid in 1766.[19] Knifton's inventory was taken in April 1766 and shows that the cottage had been extended.[20] The 'house' still had the fire and cooking utensils, although the furniture now included a dresser and a long table. He still had trenchers, although he had nine pewter dishes and thirteen plates. Quite a number of his possessions were described as old. The cellar had gone or was perhaps now called the buttery, with two old barrels and three old tubs, an old treading[?] tub and an old wheel. There were now two chambers, one over the 'house' where two old flock beds, two old chests, a little table and a pair of bedsteads were kept. The other chamber was over the parlour and was used for storing 'half a hundred of Hay' worth 1s 3d. The total of his inventory came to £17 18s 11d and was perhaps another reflection of how the potting trade was decreasing, with many items being described as old. Much of the value of his inventory came from his purse and clothes which were valued at £8, as well as his black horse and 'materials belonging to him' valued at £2 12s 6d.

There was also a pottery in what is now the Limeyards (**site 4**). There is almost no trace left of this, it having nearly all been quarried out, but pieces of pot can still be seen in the dump. This site was run by at least two generations of the Cox family before the quarries extended this far. Four generations of the Cox family were known to be potters, most of them on different sites; a brief guide to their relationship is given here. The family starts with Richard Cox of Ticknall who had a daughter baptised at Castle Donington in Leicester-shire in 1628. His next three known children, Sara (1629–), Maria (1638–) and John (1644–95), were all baptised at Ticknall. Richard's occupation is unknown, but his son John was a potter. John Cox was probably working here from 1665 to his death in 1695, then it was occupied by his son John who died in 1731. Another son, Richard, ran the pottery where Harpur Avenue (**3**) is now. The third brother William does not appear to have been a potter but William's son John (died 1762) was potting at site 24, near Calke Mill. This John's son William Cox (1738–) was potting at The Continent (**site 5**).

John Cox died intestate in 1695 and the administration of his goods was given to his son John Cox of Ticknall, potter.[21] The total value of his inventory came to £9 12s 9d. He was evidently literate as amongst his possessions he had a bible and four little books worth 2s 9d. His potting tools were worth £1 12s. He also had a packsaddle so he may have delivered some of his pots himself. Farming stock did not feature in his inventory apart from one cow worth £2 5s; he evidently made a living from potting. This may explain why some of his furniture is described as 'old' — he had '2 ould sealed Bedds with som little ould furniture to em' worth £1 1s, '2 ould chaires', '2 ould sives and 2 ould settles'. Even his pewter was old — '4 ould pewter dishes' worth just 4s. No rooms were named in the inventory but his cottage cannot have been very large. His two milking gallons were listed in amongst his pot tools with the leading bowl, suggesting he kept them in his workhouse, which does not sound very healthy.

The first deed for this cottage is dated 5 December 1698 when John Cox of Ticknall, potter (son of John who died in 1695), conveyed the 'messuage in Ticknall where the said John Cox lives, a close of Sir John Harpur in the occupation of Philipp Pollard on the east and land of Sir John Harpur in the occupation of the said John Cox on the south', to Gilbert Hutchinson of Ticknall, yeoman, for the sum of £20.[22] Six years later his brother William Cox, a labourer of Calke, bought the cottage and land back from Gilbert Hutchinson for £22 10s. This time it was described as

*'a messuage or tenement in Ticknall where John Cox dwelleth. A close of Sir John Harpur in the occupation of widow Pollard on the east, the land of Sir John Harpur in the occupation of the said Sir John Harpur on the west, abutting on the common belonging to Gilbert Thacker esquire on the north and on the land of the said Sir John Harpur in the occupation of the said John Cox on the south.'*

This places the property firmly on the then parish boundary with the detached part of Repton known as Repton Priory or the Spires (see Fig.3, p.00). The remains of the pot dump were right beside the mill leet; over the other side of the leet was the parish boundary, still visible today.

Nearby, a pottery was started up in the last quarter of the eighteenth century at what is now The Continent (5). This land was also originally in Repton Priory, owned firstly by the priory, then the Thackers and finally the Burdetts, until it was obtained in 1820 by the Harpur Crewe family in an exchange of land.[23] The first mention of a pot site here was in 1778, when William Cox paid 1s for a 'bit of ground at the East End of Ticknall, in the Priory Manor for a Pot Yard'.[24] The rentals are incomplete so it is not clear just how long this site was working; it was an unlikely time to start a new pot site in Ticknall, although it produced a large quantity of waste material. The site can be identified by a deed of 1803 concerning an exchange of land between Sir Francis Burdett of Foremark and William Cox of Ticknall, gentleman.[25] This shows Cox's house, which is the present day Continent. Part of the garden of the property is solid with pot shards and the owner found a large area of burnt earth where the kiln might have been.[26] This William Cox (born 1738) was the eldest son of John Cox, the potter at Calke; William had inherited the property in Ticknall after the death of his father, by his grandfather William's will of 1746.[27] However, he was described elsewhere as a framework knitter so perhaps he built the pot kiln and someone else made the pots.

Another site was in Peats Close (6). From the layout of the medieval village it looks as though an earlier cottage on the site had a croft that extended farther back into the field; this would bring it into line with the other holdings. When the pottery was disbanded and the new house built sometime before 1800, the rough area around the pottery may have been fenced off from the house and become part of the field.

This site is rich in decorated shards of early Cistercian ware; the potter who worked here had considerable skill. The finds are discussed in Chapter 6. It is from this site that some of the original material has been found that matches that found at the Austin Friars excavation in Leicester in a deposit that can be dated to around 1480.[28] This site therefore pre-dates our earliest known pot makers by some 50 years. There is a lot of very fine plain Cistercian ware as well as kiln furniture such as large and small props. Other cruder and more basic ware also appears, but yellow ware is scarce. This site probably finished as a pottery well before the Civil War.

A large dump was found at 38 High Street (**site 7**) when the owner dug out a pit for car maintenance under the garage many years ago.[29] This site can be identified with one of the earliest known Ticknall potters, William Hanbury, who was working in the 1520s. In 1566 William Handbury, citizen and baker of London, bought the property for £23 from Sir George Hastings of Goppeswell (Gopsall) in Leicestershire and his wife Dorothy, daughter of the late Sir John Porte.[30] The property was then described as 'one messuage or tenement in Tycnall in the Countye of Derbye wyth all housies thereupon standing, And wythall lands medowes closes pastures, commodities and other thapperteníces belonging, now in the occupation of Wyllm Handburie potter'.

A 1569 survey described the property as

*One messuage one barne, one lyttell courte, one gardyn & one orchard wythe ij fyshepondes cont[aining] in the whole by estimacon j acr[e] lyeing to the common strete in Tycknall afforesaide ageynst the east to the landes of the quene North and southe & to his owne landes in Skaddowes feld west.*

There were also 24 acres of land in Ticknall's open fields. William Hanbury the potter was described as 'the elder'. In 1593 Robert Bainbridge of Calke, gentleman, leased the property from William Hanbury of London, the lease being for 21 years at a yearly rent of 40s and a £6 fine. In addition Bainbridge was to keep the 'howses buyldynges & walles' repaired as well as 'the sayd pondes stored & replenyshed with plenty of good fyshe of dyvers kyndes'. It was then in the occupation of Edward Hanburye who was probably William the potter's son. William Handbury of London died in 1595 leaving all his other lands, which included this, to his only daughter Elizabeth. By 1609 Elizabeth had married George Sperring, citizen and goldsmith, and they sold the property to Sir John Harpur of Swarkestone for £100. Robert Bainbridge still had some years of his lease to run and this too was to be paid to Harpur. The property was last mentioned as a separate entity in a deed of settlement dated 1617 which lists a large number of properties. The description for this particular one was 'a messuage or tenement in Ticknall and one yardland belonging late in the occupation of Edward Hanbury deceased and bought of George Spering citizen of London and Elizabeth his wife'.[31]

William Hanbury the potter was taxed on wages of 20s in 1524.[32] He was listed in the 1538–9 muster for Ticknall and Calke as an 'archer & horsed & harnesid'.[33] Since he had to provide a decent horse, its tack, and his own armour, this suggests he was doing well. In the tax return shortly afterwards his occupation was given as a potter and he was assessed on goods worth 40s.[34] Still alive in 1569 he was then described as the elder; he was probably the father of William Hanbury of London or possibly a cousin. Edward Hanbury occupied the property after him and died intestate in 1610.[35] His inventory does not indicate an occupation although it did not appear to be farming — he had 'one old mare and one broken legged horse' worth 15s, 'one sowe and seaven pigges' worth 18s and 'one henne foure duckes and a drake' valued at 2s. The total value of his goods only came to £4 8s 6d but he owed money to all sorts of people as the list of debts attached showed. His contacts included a sadler at 'Lughborowe' (Loughborough) to whom he owed 20s, 'one yt dwelleth at Thurcaston' who was owed 9s, Ward of Burton-upon-Trent who was owed 22s, as well as people closer to home. Two of the creditors were pot makers, Humfery Taylor who was owed 13s 4d and Richard Smyth who was owed 20s. Hanbury also owed 3s 4d to Edward Warden who was known to have been involved in distributing pots at that time. It is quite likely that he was a potter although we cannot say for sure.

The description of this site, together with the ponds and pot dump found, suggests that the original site was on the east side of Ticknall High Street which would be the 'common street of Ticknall' in the survey. This, together with the ponds and water obviously flowing through it, suggests that it was Spring Cottage and the area down to 34 High Street. To judge from the 1857[36] map this is 1 acre and 16 perches; it could easily have been one property in the 1500s. The 1857 map also shows a pond at no. 40 High Street; the property shown then has since been demolished and a new house erected on the site. Spring Cottage would have been the cottage where William Hanbury lived — it is certainly old enough.

Another site in the field behind The Green (**site 8**) has a large amount of pottery waste at the back of the cottages, substantial enough to have been the pottery dump from a nearby kiln, probably working during the eighteenth century. We have no name for a potter here as yet, nor a date for when a pottery near here was working. An outbuilding is shown on the early nineteenth-century maps. Part was still there in 1882.

The site at Potworks Farm (**9**) was at the boundary of the open field with the common along the present Ashby Road. It was earlier known as Mireoak, taking its name from a mere or boundary oak nearby. There are references in deeds from the late thirteenth century to a nearby furlong as 'muriok furlong' and 'murichocfurlond'.[37] By the sixteenth and seventeenth centuries there was 'Merrick Close'. It is not to be confused with Mereoak Lane bounding Tatshall Fee, an entirely different area with its own pot site and not part of Ticknall parish at this date; it will be considered separately. This part of Ashby Road was known as Forty Lane during this period, taking its name from the Forty Brook which today is a small stream running behind the cottages on the north-west side of the road. The Mireoak site was later known as Potworks Farm and by 2000 as Potworks Cottage. This was the last pottery to operate and only closed down around 1888. Research has shown that there were two sites, with four families potting here. The Beightons and the Potters were the earliest, followed by the Hyde and the Charvill families; they will be considered in turn.

The earliest known potters in this area were the Beighton family. The surname Beighton has the longest continuity in the parish, from the 1327 Subsidy Roll when 'Ric Beton' was assessed at 30s, through to the 1851 census.[38] John Beighton's 1620 inventory indicates that he was a pot maker.[39] He may already have been working at this site as a deed of 1611 mentions land 'butting upon Forkey Lane near John Beightons house in Ticknall'.[40] His potting tools included 'one whil for his trad wth all bords & other necessaries thereto belonging' worth 20s amongst his goods when he died. Most of his goods show that he was involved with farming. He had four bullocks, four kine and nine young beasts worth a total of £22, fifty sheep worth 50s, a mare and a colt worth £3, as well as corn sown in the field; this with the stored corn and hay was worth £12 13s 4d. He also had husbandry gear worth £5 10s.

His son Henry definitely lived at this site — he already had a family when he was mentioned in his father's 1620 will, and by 1632 rented a 'house and Merrick close' amounting to 2 acres 1 rood; this, with arable land in all three open fields, totalled 10 acres, 1 rood and 12 perches, for which he paid a twice yearly rent of £1 10s.[41] However, we do not know if Henry was a potter, as he left no probate documents. The next known potter was Timothy Beighton, son of another Timothy who in turn was probably a brother or less likely a son of Henry. He had children baptised from 1638 to 1642 and certainly had other children for whom there is no record. He made his will on 17 April 1674,[42] died two days later and was buried the next day as the son of 'old Timothy'. Timothy was also farming as well as making pots; his inventory reveals that he had 12½ acres in the Park Field and Littlefield growing wheat, barley and 'pease' worth in total £12. He also had livestock — his three mares were worth £9, two cows and three yearling calves were worth the same, and he had four ewes and lambs worth £1 6s 8d. He had the necessary husbandry tools such as horse gears, plough irons, ploughs and harrrows to work the land he rented. These, together with his two old carts, were valued at £2 10s 6d. He also had a 'brest of bels' for his horses, the only mention we have of these in Ticknall.

His detailed inventory shows he lived in a cottage with five rooms. Firstly a 'dwelling house' where the fire was with the fire irons and where cooking equipment, such as a 'morter and a pestell', two spits and a 'fringe pann', a 'clever' and a 'beife forke', was kept. Here also was his pewter, a tankard, dishes and porringers as well as an 'ower glasse', with a great and little table with frames, 'twigne cheare', two 'joyned forms' and two 'stoole chears', a little box cupboard for storage and also a little cradle. He kept his 'cole picke' in the same room. The parlour was used for sleeping in and had a 'joyned' as well as a 'trundle' bed that could be easily moved around. Some degree of comfort was enjoyed, as one of the beds was a featherbed and the other was made of flock. A rug, curtains, blankets, pillows, flaxen and holland sheets and other napery ware worth £5 13s were probably kept in either the great chest or the livery cupboard that were also in the same room. The little parlour had a flock bed with the necessary bedclothes but 'course' sheets, much less comfortable. The same room also housed a 'cheife presse' for storage. The kitchen was where the pails, loomes and kneading trough could be found, as well as a little wheel for spinning and a peck for measuring. Here too were his two brass pots and three kettles. The chamber over the kitchen was also used for sleeping and had another 'joyned' bed with a feather mattress, curtains and other furnishings. By the standards of Ticknall potters, this was a comfortable home for the times and social status, although it is only the degree of detail in the inventory that lets us see this.

In 1681 Joseph Beighton, Timothy's son and also a potter, was renting 'a mess the miryoake close stoking close & half a yard land' for £3 1s payable at Michaelmas and Lady Day. In 1708 he was paying additional rent of £1 13s 4d for '1 yardland and 7 roods meadow'. A yardland in Ticknall seems to have been around 24 acres[43] so Joseph Beighton was farming more than 36 acres. Farming was obviously important to his economy but his inventory of 1720[44] is brief. He was growing barley, wheat, peas and hay worth £6, and his only husbandry tool was an old cart. His livestock consisted of just three horses with a yearling foal worth £4 and a cow and a yearling calf worth £1 17s. There is no detail of his household goods, just a brief mention of two rooms, the parlour and kitchen, with goods in them worth just 18s. Like William Pemberton's, Joseph Beighton's inventory suggests that he was not doing so well. However it may be that only part of the house was his and much was not therefore recorded. After his death, his son Joseph continued to rent the land until he died in 1745. He was described as a husbandman on his father's administration bond, but it is not known whether he was a potter, although it is likely. His brothers Gilbert and Timothy both married and had children. Of these it is Gilbert, born in 1725, the youngest son of Timothy (1680–), who was the next known potter, and his two sons Joseph born 1759 and Gilbert (1763–30) who followed him. By the nineteenth century the Beighton family was involved in selling pots rather than making them.

Also at Mireoak, and adjacent to the Beighton site, was the messuage where the appropriately named Potter family were tenants during the seventeenth and much of the eighteenth century; it is this that is the best known and only site to be marked on the Ordnance Survey maps. The Potter family first appears in the Ticknall records with Edward Potter who was raising a family when the parish registers start in 1626. He had at least six children and was of sufficient status to act as an appraiser for the inventories of two neighbours. However, he omitted to leave a will himself. Of his children, only Samuel is known to have been a pot maker; he died in 1688. None of the Potter family was listed in the 1638 muster — Samuel must have been under eighteen at that time. His brothers Abraham and Isaac married Frances and Susanna Basford in 1657 and 1660 respectively; their wives were sisters and were likely to have been related to Henry Basford or Berrisford, a Ticknall-based pot seller who had died in 1626.

Samuel married twice, firstly at Church Gresley in 1651 to Rachel Beighton, one of the daughters of Henry Beighton already mentioned. This suggests that Samuel was working for or with the Beightons. However, as the Potter family only ever paid rent for a 'mess & Tenemte' with a rent of 15s half yearly from at least 1681 until the 1750s, it is apparent that they were not so involved in farming as the Beightons.[45] After his wife Rachel died in 1658, Samuel Potter married Sarah Holland, a member of another Ticknall potting family. Samuel had three known children and when he made his will in 1686, his son John was then of

'Pinkson' (Pinxton) and left £5. It was a younger son, Joseph, who inherited the pottery.

Samuel Potter's inventory of 1688[46] shows a six-roomed building. The rooms included a 'house', a buttery, a kitchen and a parlour where two feather beds, their curtains and blankets were kept, as well as chests, coffers and a cupboard. There were two chambers, one over the 'house' and the other over the parlour. The chamber over the parlour had 16s worth of malt stored there, suggesting that Potter did his own brewing; there were also 'barells' in the buttery. The fire irons were listed separately at the end of the inventory so presumably the fire was in the 'house' as he was only assessed on one hearth in 1662. His reliance on pastoral farming for part of his income is shown by a 'hors £2 10s, 2 ould cows £3 10s' and forty sheep worth £6 6s. There was little in the way of agricultural implements or tools, although he had three lands of 'pays and barley on the ground' worth £1 5s as well as 20s worth of stored hay. It was April when his inventory was taken, so this would have been the crop sown the previous autumn, probably with the help of his neighbours. His potting tools were worth more than those of the majority of local potters, being described as 'boardes wheales grates spades matthookes Leadpan with all tooles belonging to the potting trade' and were valued at £3 6s. He also had 8s worth of 'Clay on the comon and in the yard', 'potts that was made and unsould an ovenfull' worth £3 and book debts of £9 10s.

His son Joseph continued to work the pottery and was one of the signatories to the deed to get clay from the common just outside the works in 1690.[47] His will was written in September 1721 when he was described as a 'pottmaker' and signed with a very shaky signature.[48] His inventory was appraised by his near neighbours and fellow pot makers 'Jos Marriot', Joseph Tetley, and his son Samuel Potter; it listed goods worth £34 8s 10d. No indication of the rooms in his house was given, though he was reasonably comfortably off with his featherbed and two flockbeds, pewter dishes, brass pots and kettles, chest of drawers, table, chairs and buffets. He evidently made his own cheese as he had a cheese press and there was cheese, malt and bacon in the house worth 9s. He also had a cow worth £2, a heifer worth £1 10s and twenty-four sheep worth £3 10s. Crops were peas growing and one 'lant' of wheat. His potting tools were probably included in the 'tooles' that were worth £1 5s 6d. He also had £3 9s 4d worth of boards (for potting), 13s 6d worth of lead, and 7s 6d was allowed for 'Margens'. He evidently weighed his clay before making the pots as he had two 'pot wey' which together with two 'pass bords' were worth 15s 6d; he also had saddles worth £3 3s 6d.

The surviving Suit Rolls showing who should have attended the manor courts for each property give the continuity of the family on the site.[49] Thomas, Joseph's elder son, continued to pot on the site and he appeared in the suit rolls until his death in 1758. His widow Sarah then continued to be listed in the suit rolls, being described as old in 1769. There was no entry for her from April 1774. She was buried in January 1776 and the property was described as 'void' in May of that year. She was allowed two half levies at 2d in December by the overseer of the poor.[50] In December 1773 the roof was repaired as 6s 8d was paid for '40 thack sheaves to potters house' and Robert Doman was paid 4s 6d for 'three days thacking at potters house at his own board'. From October 1773 to February 1774 the overseers paid William Cartlidge 1s a week for rent of 'potters house', and again from April 1775 to April 1776, but this time only 10d per week. As the same accounts also record 4s paid for 'the carriage of Astles goods to potters house' in October 1773 it seems likely that there was an agreement to house one of the poor; Edward Astle received a load of coals in January of the following year. William Cartlidge had married Rachel, the daughter of Thomas and Sarah Potter, in 1745. It seems that they still lived there and were subletting part of the cottage. It is possible that pot making ceased during this period, although members of the Beighton family may have worked the pottery.

Joseph Hyde had taken over by April 1777 when he appeared in the suit rolls for the same property. In 1825 his son Joseph was paying a half yearly rent of £6; both were potters. The

Hydes supplied pots to a wide range of people, including the Harpur family at Calke for the kitchen, dairy and kennels, and also chimney pots and garden pots worth 14s to the Burdetts at Foremark.[51] The Ticknall parish officers bought pots from Joseph Hyde 1784–92, some of which were for the use of the workhouse.[52] By 1800 there were only two potteries working in the Ticknall area of which this survived the longest. Three generations of the Hyde family tenanted the property — Joseph (1744–1811), his son Joseph (1770–1833) and his grandson John (1802–1860s). Joseph junior's widow Ann evidently carried on the business as she was described as a manufacturer of coarse earthenware in 1838.[53] When her will was proved in 1847 she was described as a widow and late potter.[54] Her estate was valued at under £100 and she was able to leave her daughters a variety of goods including silver spoons, a dressing table and two sets of china. Although we have little information about the family, it is during the period of Hyde tenancy that we get the first map evidence of the layout of the pottery, as shown in Figure 6.

The earliest is the map by Larter, thought to have been drawn in the late 1830s. It is so similar to the tithe map of 1843 that it was probably used as the base for it; the numbering of fields and houses is almost identical, with a few sub-divisions appearing on the later tithe map. However, there are differences: Larter shows a T-shaped building with a round building either side, presumably the kilns; the tithe map of only a few years later shows a similar layout but no kilns. The estate was surveyed in great detail by John Shaw in 1857, by which time the layout of the pottery had changed. The T-shaped building had changed shape and now had a semicircular structure at the southern end, probably the kiln. John Hyde was running the pottery at this time and was listed as a 'brown ware manufacturer'. The 1851 census gives him as a 'master potter employing 7 men'.[55] The 1882 25-inch First Edition Ordnance Survey[56] shows yet another change, with the kiln on the south side of a building that now ran west–east and the outline of another, perhaps older or demolished kiln. This gives a picture of the layout of the pot works that were here towards the very end of their life. A replacement building on the site of the west–east building was built as a cow shed and, when we visited, it showed no signs of ever having being used for anything other than agriculture; it has now been converted into a dwelling.

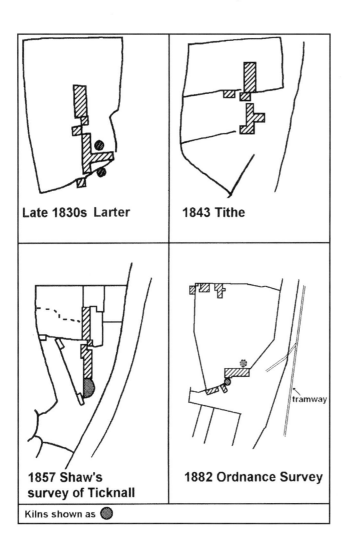

Late 1830s Larter

1843 Tithe

1857 Shaw's survey of Ticknall

1882 Ordnance Survey

tramway

Kilns shown as ●

Figure 6 – Changes to the layout of Potworks Farm

The house itself was rebuilt around 1859 and has since been extended.[57]

Sometime between 1857 and 1861 the Charvill family took over the pot works. The 1861 census lists Ann Charvill as an earthenware manufacturer, running the business with her 27 year old son Thomas and employing six men and five boys; her husband Thomas was not at home that night.[58] In 1851 Thomas Charvill was a coachman to Sir John Harpur Crewe at Calke Abbey and the family was living at the Dog Kennels on Derby Hills. By 1871 Thomas Charvill the younger was running a rather reduced business, with three men and three boys; he was occupying four acres of land.[59] The last reference we have to the pottery working is in the Trade Directory of 1888.[60] By 1891 Charvill was listed as a farmer and deputy agent living at Basford Hill and a long established Ticknall industry had come to an end.[61]

At the top of Hazard Hill there is a large area full of ploughed potshards, now down to grass. This was the pottery run by the Marriott family and later by Samuel Hill (**site 10**). The 1843 tithe map shows a cottage that later became the isolation hospital after the First World War. It was demolished sometime after the end of the Second World War. The Marriott family was living on the common from at least the 1670s when John Marriott (1646–99) of the common had children baptised; we know from his son John's will that he too had been a potter. These two were son and grandson of yet another John Marriott 'the elder' who died intestate in 1679.[62] This first John Marriott was described either as a husbandman or yeoman and he was assessed on one hearth in 1662. He was a witness of several wills in Ticknall as well as appraising others, including that of William King, a Ticknall pot seller, in 1670 and William Hanbury, potter, in 1674. Although we have no mention of him being a potter, the family's substantial involvement in the trade makes it a possibility. He had at least four children. His inventory shows that he had debts of £11 owed to him when he died in 1679. It is difficult to see why he was described as a husbandman, unless he had retired, as there were no indications of farming in the inventory that was taken, just a few goods in the two parlours, suggesting that perhaps he was living in part of a house.

It was his son John (1649–99) who was living on the common when he had his children baptised during the period 1674–93. He died in 1699 without leaving any will. Four of his sons, John (1674–1708), Samuel (1679–1718), Josiah (1683–1740) and Joseph (1693–1759) were potters. The next to run the business was his eldest son John who died young at around 34 years old; it is his will[63] that tells us that both he and his parents were potters. John Marriott left his wife Elizabeth '*halfe the trade with my mother as I had before painge halfe the cost and charges of it & if my wife will not hold up trade with my mother that my mother or brother shall pay to my wife for my part of roome & tools the soume of 15 shillins every yeare & fifteene for my part of the close every year according to Covenant.*'

This latter phase is very significant as it makes it plain that potting in Ticknall was a family affair and that women were very much involved, something that is all too often hidden by the surviving records. It also shows that a formal written contract about the business had been drawn up amongst members of the family. John had time to realise the consequences that his early death might have for his widow, so he mentioned it in his will, thus making sure that she was able to play her part in the family business if she so wished. It was the working man's way of providing for his wife after his death. He had married Elizabeth Morley only eleven years earlier and had two young children; another was born after his burial. John Marriott and his brothers had enough workers within the family to run their business.

John Marriott was buried in July 1708. His inventory was fuller than that of his grandfather in 1680, 81 per cent of whose value consisted of debts. The 1708 inventory indicates a house with three rooms, comprising a 'house', parlour and chamber. The fire and cooking utensils were in the 'house'. The parlour had a little table and was used for storing goods, as there was a chest, 'cubord' and a 'cofer'. The family evidently slept in the chamber where the beds were. He was clearly involved in farming as he had three head of cattle, a score of sheep, twelve lambs and a pig. He also had half an acre each of wheat and barley in the 'cornefilde' and 3 roods of 'pease' in the 'pease fild'.

It was either his mother or widow that was the widow Marriott in the earliest surviving deed to the property in 1711. This describes it as 'cottage in Ticknall at a place called Prince Wood or Prince Fee,[64] a close to the said cottage adjoining called Intake close containing about two acres, also the working house, oven and hovells to the said tenement which said cottage or tenement are in the occupation of Widow Marriott'.[65] Thomas Pearston of Ticknall, gentleman, sold the property to Joseph Tetley of Heath End in the parish of Ashby de la Zouch, potter, who was obviously looking to invest in a potting property, perhaps to ensure the trade survived. In 1730 Joseph Tetley's son and heir Joseph sold the property to John Bryan of Smisby, husbandman. By now Josiah Marriott the brother of John was given as the occupier. John's widow Elizabeth was still alive at this time so it looks as if she had given up running the pottery by then; she died in 1734. In 1767 John Bryan assigned the property to his son William Bryan; the occupier was now Josiah Marriott nephew of Josiah Marriott deceased, who had died in 1740. This hides the fact that there must have been another Marriott running the pottery as Josiah the nephew named in the 1767 deed would have only been twelve. The most likely candidate is his father Joseph Marriott (1694–1759). He was the youngest of the Marriott brothers, his elder brother Samuel having died in 1718. Josiah Marriott (1728–1803) the nephew continued to run the pottery until 1769–70 when he became ill, suffering from the effects of lead poisoning as described in Chapter 1. Pot making continued. By 1770 Samuel Hill was bracketed along with Josiah Marriott in the suit rolls and it was he who no doubt ran the works when Josiah was incapable. The 1780 Land Tax has only Samuel Hill as the occupier of land owned by William Bryan in Ticknall;[66] Hill seemed to have taken over completely by then, although Josiah lived until 1803. A 1799 Certificate for Land Tax Redemption in the deeds states 'potworks at Ticknall in occupation of Samuel Hill'. Samuel Hill was born in 1754, the son of Thomas Hill (1707–76). He is the only one of Thomas's five sons whose occupation is known; his uncle Isaac Hill (1712–71) was another potter. Earlier members of the Hill family lived at Scaddows where a number of potters also lived. It is quite possible that other members of the family were potters too.

This pottery was the second to last pottery to close. It evidently provided a living in a declining market. However, the business was dealt a blow when Samuel and his son Thomas both died in 1816. Thomas was the second son of Samuel. He had married in 1800 and had a family of six children. He was only thirty-eight when he died in January 1816. His will left his wife Jane as the sole executor of his estate.[67] Four years later she married William Blore, a widower. Samuel Hill his father died in August of the same year. His will mentions just his son Samuel to whom he left his silver watch and clothes, and his wife Martha who was executrix and who received the rest of his goods;[68] she carried on the pottery business. In 1822 there were two 'pottkilns' with details about this and other land belonging to the Bryan family in Ticknall and Smisby.[69] The land was sold to Sarah Salisbury of Ashby de la Zouch in 1826, when it was described as 'houses and potworks at Ticknall ... formerly in the occupation of Widow Marriott but now or late of Widow Hill'. Martha Hill, pot maker, died in 1832, her estate being valued at under £100. Potting at this site must have ceased at this time, leaving one working pottery.

Further down Hazard Hill, towards the Ashby Road, was another pot site (11). Thomas Hanson was one of the potters named in the 1690 clay agreement. This site can be identified with Thomas Hanson's 'New Intake', which contained 1¹/₂ acres.[70] This was leased for fifty-one years by Hanson from Thomas Pearston, at a rent of 7s a year. In 1695 it was described as 3 acres and adjoining a cottage known as the warren house in the tenure of Widow Cole. In 1711 Thomas Pearston sold the land to Sir John Harpur, and the description included 'a mault kill (kiln) and pump belonging to the said kill adjoining to a house of the said Sir John Harpur where Thomas Henson inhabits'. From 1693 Hanson had been paying a rent of £11 5s to Sir John Harpur for 'his house and Southwood Close'. This was an earlier house at Top Farm, which lay alongside the road; the present farm was rebuilt in the late 1820s to 1830s. In 1707–8 Hanson paid £1 4s 'for Clay Pitts and wast ground called Princewood' and 18s 6d 'for the intake on the said waste and the house and croft late Coles'.[71] The rental remained unchanged until 1716–17 when he paid an additional 12s for the right to graze three animals on nearby 'Gilborow Leys'. Two years later this had increased to five animals. When he died in 1724 his inventory[72] showed that not only was he a potter, with potting tools worth £2, but that he was heavily involved in farming and malting, with malt worth £120 in a chamber. His dwelling was simply furnished with only brief details given; he had a 'house', parlour, two chambers and another room. His wagon, carts and other husbandry items were worth £10. He had horses and mares worth £20, cattle worth £25 and sheep worth £20. Eighteen acres of growing crops were worth £26. He was also owed £196 14s 2d in bonds, bills and debts. His total inventory came to £449 14s 2d, the highest sum for a Ticknall farmer and potter. It shows how well some did at this period. As well as the land he rented, he also had feehold messuages and other lands in Ashby de la Zouch and Hartshorne. He also had a messuage nearby that was occupied by Joseph Marriott and may have potted in partnership with him until the latter took over the Marriott pottery further up the hill. Thomas Hanson seems to have been responsible for the lease of the clay from 1707 onwards and maybe before. Controlling the clay would have been economically important.

The pottery and farm were taken over by his son Thomas, who died only five years after his father in 1729; he too was farming. His inventory,[73] although not very detailed, showed a dwelling with a 'house', parlour, chamber over the 'house place', a cellar and two little rooms as well as a garret. Otherwise his inventory was similar to his father's, with the emphasis on farming, but only a small debt of £6 17s was owed. The whole was valued at £232 19s, which like his father's was a substantial sum. Once again the rentals were not updated with his brother Joseph's name until 1751, but Joseph took over the pottery and farming after Thomas died until his own death in 1758. By 1735–6 Joseph Hanson rented a total of 12 acres, 12 roods and 16 perches in 'Gilborrow Leys' and paid a total rent of £17 14s half yearly. In 1747 he took over a copyhold in Atherstone, Warwickshire, in lieu of an outstanding debt of £140 from Joseph Steel.[74] He left this to his wife when he died.[75] After Joseph's death the first surviving rental is that of 1766, which showed his widow paid a yearly rental of £78, double what had been paid in the past, probably due to the costs and increased values after enclosure. The 1762 survey shows that she rented the same land as her late husband. This surely must have had an impact on the availability of clay and may be behind Pilkington's statement blaming enclosure for the lack of available clay.[76] With Joseph's death in 1758, potting ceased in the Hanson family and they concentrated on farming, becoming one of the more successful farming families in the village.

It is this site, known by the name of Booths Close on the Tithe Award of 1843[77] and as Minions Close in 1857,[78] which was drained in 1862.[79] This was the time when Matilda Lovell was staying at Calke. She found pots where drains were being laid 'in Calke', and much of the Ticknall pottery at Calke Abbey comes from her finds.[80] We believe that it was from this site that Miss Lovell found her pots. We have similar rims and bases from this site, as well as fourteen little heads used as the knobs on chafing dishes. It indicates that this site was in use from at least the late Tudor period and it must be associated with one of the earliest potters. There were two or three large heaps of pots still there after the Second World War. However, subsequent ploughing has reduced these to an extensive area of ploughed potshards and kiln waste, with a large orange patch of burnt earth where the kiln must have been. The site is now down to pasture and some of it has been sold.

By the side of the Ashby Road, opposite Top Farm and on an intake from the common, was the pottery run by the Blore family (**site 12**). The first mention of this family in Ticknall was when Richard Blore's eldest son Oliver was baptised in 1680. Although Richard had land in two of the open fields of Ticknall in 1686,[81] he was not renting this from the Harpurs. In 1719 Richard Blore of Ticknall, yeoman, paid £16 for the property he bought from Robert Shevin of Ticknall, mercer. It was described as 'All that pott workhouse and three bays of building scituate and being in a certain place in Ticknall called the Prince wood and halfe an acre of land by estimation to be the same more or less upon which the said pott workhouse and premises stand now or late in the possession of one Stephen Ridgeley'.[82]

Richard Blore died in 1727 leaving no will or administration of his goods. It is possible that he was involved in potting but much more likely that he invested in the property for his younger son Richard (1690–1760). It has not been possible to ascertain whether Richard Blore the younger was farming. After Richard died in 1760, his son James (1718–) took over the running of the pottery. James and his wife Mary had eight children, two of whom, William (1747–) and Thomas (1762–), were potters.

By the 1760s, and perhaps before, things began to get difficult for this particular potting family. The 1762 survey of Ticknall[83] shows that James Blore's house, workhouse and garden consisted of 38 perches and were valued at a yearly rate of £1 5s; there was no evidence of any farming land. It may have been the total dependence on the declining pottery trade that made the fall in the family fortunes inevitable. In 1766 James mortgaged the property for £26 from George Orton, the miller at Calke Mill.[84] He still had a young family — three of his children were born in the 1750s and the youngest, Thomas, was only four when his father took this step. It is possible, using entries from the overseers of the poor accounts that date from 1762[85], to gain some insight into the Blore family. On 5 January 1765 John Byard the overseer of the poor went to a local justice of the peace, Sir Robert Burdett, to see about James Blore, probably to ascertain where his settlement was; no record of this has survived. Blore subsequently received regular payments of between 1s and 4s a week during January and February of that year. In October of the following year he received a bushel of barley worth 3s. Possibly the parish officers had suggested that he mortgaged his property to obtain a loan. It is interesting to note that the original mortgage was taken out in 1766, the year after the agreement to enclose the open fields of Ticknall was made. Enclosure may have hit Blore hard, making it difficult for him to obtain adequate clay supplies. He was evidently still potting in 1771 as in February the overseer of the poor gave him £2 4s 8d 'at several times to buy lead and coals and bread'. In December he received 2s to buy medicines. Perhaps it was the shortage of money that got his sons John and James into trouble. They were prosecuted for taking a load of hay from a barn in Newton Solney on their way home from selling pots in March 1772. They told their father they had paid 8d for it.[86]

In 1774 Blore borrowed a further £30 from Orton on an additional part of the property, an old part of the house at the south end of buildings, and a new part or bay of building at the north end of the said buildings, and the other half of the garden in the possession of the said James Blore, and to have and hold likewise the land beyond the old buildings at the south end to the full extremity of his property that way.

The loan was never paid back. In 1782 the sum of £45 14s 10d was outstanding and the buildings were 'so ruinous and out of repair as not to be worth the money'. They were sold for a mere £10, a sum voluntarily paid by Orton. By 1830 the property had been replaced by three cottages and was sold to Sir George Crewe. Following the sale of his ruinous pottery, James Blore turned to selling pots; even then he found it difficult to make a living. The parish officers gave him 2s to buy pots with in 1787, and in 1789 he received a further 5s. He and his wife Mary received fairly regular relief for bouts of illness, and the parish looked after Mary in her last illness in 1792. James continued to receive relief into the 1790s, by which time he would have been in his seventies. No burial record for him has been found.

Misfortune also followed some of James's children — his daughter Ann (1752–), received money from the parish in 1774. In April 1775 she was pregnant, and the parish officers spent time and money in chasing the father and making him marry her. The child died of smallpox two years later and she continued to receive help after that. Her sister Mary was ill during 1774; she too received money and the parish officers went to much trouble to find where her settlement was to save Ticknall paying for her. She was sent to Bretby as she had worked there as a servant.[87]

Their brother William was also a potter, and he too had a struggle to make ends meet. In 1774 he was at Melbourne to work at the pottery at Furnace Farm, as discussed in Chapter 6. By October 1778 the family lodged with Timothy Beighton who ran one of the public houses in Ticknall, the parish paying for this. Their rent was paid in December and in January 1779 William was given a total of 6s when he was lame. His lodgings continued to be paid for by the parish during the rest of the year. By October of that year he had deserted his wife for at least three months, and she received money to keep the family of six children going. This happened again in August 1790. In October 1780 he was ill and receiving money. The family continued to need assistance from the parish to get by, their rent was frequently paid and attempts to help them support themselves were made. In 1789 William was given 10s 6d to buy an ass; the ass was a favoured animal for pot hawkers.[88] In 1792 'Blore's lad' was given 1s to buy pots. Later that year William was given 10s for the same and in 1794 he was given another 3s. In 1795 his brother Thomas Blore, wife and daughter appear in the accounts. He had been brought up as a potter and had been hired by Sam Hill in 1779,[89] but by the time he received relief he was probably selling pots rather than making them.

The Blores show some of the hardships suffered by one family following enclosure — with no land to fall back on, their reliance on the potting trade was total. When that began to decline severely they suffered too, getting into debt, mortgaging then selling their property and eventually being dependent on the parish to keep them. They were not alone in this but it does illustrate what could happen. William Blore's settlement examination also shows why so little has been found about apprenticeships — many of our potters simply learnt their trade from their fathers.

Near to Top Farm the pasture on Staunton Lane (**site 13**) was reported to be covered with potshards when ploughed,[90] suggesting another site. A ditch at the side has potshards embedded in both sides to a depth of around 2 feet.

The garden at the cottage at Staunton Lane End (**site 14**) contains a large number of pot wasters, many now in Derby Museum. Amongst them are a large number of Martincamp flask shards. This property was sold by Thomas Pearston in 1711 to Robert Shevin of Ticknall, mercer.[91] At that time Elizabeth Marriott widow was the occupier. In 1792 it was owned by Thomas Bucknall and sold to Josiah Robinson. Shortly after Robinson bought the property the ancient messuage 'having been injured by fire' was taken down. The present property was built on another part of the croft. Elizabeth Marriott would be the widow of one of the John Marriotts, either the father who died in 1699 or his son who died in 1708; both their wives were called Elizabeth.

**Site 15** was the cottage at the bottom of White Hollow Lane. This was the pottery run by John Smallwood during the period c.1700–43. John Smallwood was probably born in the 1680s, the son of Richard Smallwood alias Weaver and his wife Sarah, also of Whitehollow. He married Elizabeth Parker in 1707. She was probably one of the daughters of Thomas Parker of Calke, another potter. They had just two daughters before Elizabeth died in 1712. In his will of 1743,[92] John left 'all working tools of trade as a pottmaker' to his friend John Marriott. He was probably the John Marriott baptised in 1710 at Ticknall as the son of Samuel and Elizabeth. Elizabeth was John Smallwood's sister and had married Samuel by licence in 1702; he too was a pot maker. John Smallwood also had a freehold messuage in Stapenhill, which he left to his son-in-law Samuel Mason who had married his daughter Catherine. His other daughter Elizabeth had married Joseph Woodward of Southwood, just along the lane. She and her children were left one shilling each, her family being 'already provided for'. Smallwood's inventory was brief and had a total value of £17. His money and clothing came to one pound, whilst his 'household goods' were worth just £2. Most of the value came from his livestock — three mares, a cow and some sheep, which together were valued at £12, with another £2 for his 'Implements of Husbandry'. If he had not made a will stating his occupation it would have been impossible to know that he was a potter.

Further along the lane is Standleys Barn (**site 16**). We believe that this was another pot site, although no pottery has been found here, the farmhouse has been rebuilt and the farm-yard concreted over. The Standley family was renting land in this part of the parish from the Harpurs from the 1640s through to the 1750s, which is how the name originated.

Francis Standley died in 1638 and his will proved in the same year showed that he was a husbandman.[93] His son John was to have the lease of the house when he was out of his apprenticeship and he was executor to his father. Only a kitchen and parlour were men-tioned although the inventory was quite detailed. Much of the value of £50 0s 4d was from his livestock, crops and farming implements; these came to £32 13s, well over half the value of the total inventory.

His son John Standley had evidently been apprenticed to a pot maker as his nuncupative will of 1667 showed; he had a sudden short illness although he survived long enough to dictate his wishes.[94] He had evidently done quite well and was able to leave his children substantial sums — his daughters Elizabeth, Ann and Jane were to receive £50 each, Hellin the youngest was left £60 and was also 'to be put and kept to the schoole to learne to read and sowe untill shee be able to get her living by that callinge'. If his wife Sara remarried and changed her name then their son Joseph was to pay her £30; if not then she and Joseph were to share all the residue of the estate, with Joseph eventually inheriting it after his mother's death.

The inventory is a good example of a well-off farming potter, with a total value of £333 18s 0d, although £226 16s 9d of this was 'in monies, bondes and debts', sadly not detailed. The building consisted of a six-roomed dwelling with the 'house' where the fire, fire irons, table, form and chairs were kept. The parlour had a bed with its associated furniture as well as a table. Next to the parlour was a dairy, with three barrels, boards and a safe. There was another little parlour next to the 'Intry' with a flock bed. Standley made his own cheese as there was also a cheese press as well as a 'presse' and a 'kneading trowe'. Upstairs there were two chambers, over the 'house' and the parlour. The chamber over the 'house' had another flockbed and bedclothes, two 'coulfers' that were presumably coffers for storage, one 'bas-ket to lay clothes in', and also two wheels. The chamber over the parlour was used for storage, with 3st of wool to be spun into yarn using the wheels in the other room; bacon, malt and cheese were also stored there. He had a pair of flax (linen) sheets and seven and a half pairs of 'canvice' (canvas) sheets, napkins and 'pillowbeeres'. He had dishes and spoons, a cup and candlesticks made of pewter, brass kettles for cooking, as well as three iron pots and other implements. He was comfortably off. His farming goods show that this too was important in the economy of the family. He had 28 quarters of winter corn, barley and peas in store worth £26, as well as ten loads of hay valued at £6 13s 4d. Two ploughs with their irons, two harrows and two carts were valued at £7. He also had sawn timber and other wood around the place; this together with the manure was worth another £5. He had four draught horses for ploughing; these with a yearling colt were worth £10 5s. He was breed-ing cattle as he had a bull and twelve other cattle of various ages valued at £14 5s, as well as fifty-seven sheep which came to another £10 17s 6d.

He also had a potting house valued at £5 14s 6d, containing a pot wheel, two grates, a lead pan with boards, spades, shovels, hackers and 'pots fired and unfired' in it. Interest-ingly this inventory shows that he was also potting on another site as well — at 'Hanbryes House' he had another pot wheel, a loom, a grate and 'bords belonging to the potting trade' worth £2 11s 6d, as well as 'two Hundred of lead' worth £1. He also had goods in three of the rooms there. The parlour had a bedstead and a 'chafe' (chaff) bed in it, most uncomfortable. At this date, this was probably the house at Scaddows of William Hanbury, another potter.

Joseph Standley, John's son, died intestate in 1709. His inventory[95] shows that he too was a potter, although not on the same scale as his father. He evidently lived in a different cottage as only a 'house', parlour and one chamber were mentioned. As was usual at this period the inventory was less detailed. Even so it is apparent that Joseph was affected by the decline in the pottery trade and the competition from Stoke-on-Trent. His inventory was valued at just £22 19s 2d. He was still farming although only livestock was mentioned. His five cows were valued at £10 2s 6d, five heifers and a bull were worth £3 17s 6d, two stirks and three calves came to £3 5s 6d, and there were just two sheep worth 5s 6d. The goods in the 'house' were rather sparse, with a value of just £4 18s 10d. No potting tools were listed and this suggests that perhaps he might have been working for another potter rather than running his own pottery. His widow Mary also died intestate in 1718.[96] Her inventory is very similar and the house the same. The administration bond shows that their son Jacob Standley (1695–1776) was also a potter. Jacob was still the tenant of the area around Standleys Barn in 1762, but we do not know whether he was running his own pottery. He probably was as he paid £1 1s for clay rent from the Burdetts in 1773.[97] This was taken over in 1774 by Joseph Miller who only paid for that year. His grandson Jacob was probably a pot maker at Heath End in 1776.[98]

The Scaddows (**site 17**) on the Hartshorne to Ticknall road is another area that had several potters. It originally belonged to the Francis family of Ticknall and went to the Burdett family when Sir John Francis of Foremark died with no male heir in 1603.[99] There are two areas called Scaddows in Ticknall. The one nearest the village is now known as Little Scaddows, and was always in Ticknall, whilst Scaddows Farm is further away from the village and was originally on Burdett land. As all our references to the potters at Scaddows are in the Burdett papers we are fairly certain that their pot kilns were in this area. There is a kiln site on the opposite side of the road on the land of what is now Foremark Park Farm, but there may have been more elsewhere in the immediate area. The 1857 map of Ticknall,[100] drawn up just before the present Scaddows Farm was built, shows the old farmhouse by the roadside. With the modern road being wider, some of this site is almost certainly under the present road.

The earliest known potter here was Richard Hanbery 'pootter' who died around 1587.[101] He left Richard Gardener 'my pooter whille and the one halfe of my bordes'. He also owed Gardener 15s out of a total of £1 1s 8d worth of debts owing. His 'xxx bordes and a pootte whille' were worth 5s, he had two 'kine' and two 'coultes' which together were worth £5 6s 8d, just about half of the value of his total of £10 17s 4d. The rest comprised his household goods. There was no mention of who the other half of potting boards were left to but he did have a servant, Anne Broune, to whom he generously left a number of household goods and a calf, presumably so she would be better enabled to get married. This suggests that she was perhaps a relative, especially since his wife was still alive. His widow Marie died five years later and she left more goods to Richard Gardener and his wife Anne. Richard Gardener had married Anne, who was probably the daughter of Richard and Marie Hanbury, although no relationship was given in the will; Gardener was also the executor of Marie Hanbury's will.[102] One of the appraisers of her inventory was Edward Hanbury.

Two years later in 1597 Richard Hanbury's brother Henry died. Henry was also of the Scaddows and another potter. Although his inventory does not mention any potting tools, he owed 12s for 'Leiade'; perhaps he had already passed on the majority of his tools. His inventory totalled £15 12s 10d but out of that had to come £3 16s of debts that he owed. The reversion of the lease of his house came to £5 of the total; he paid 10s a year in rent. He had three 'kyne' and a mare worth £6 13s 4d, together with corn and hay valued at 13s 4d. His household goods came to just over £4, including a spinning wheel. Deeds of 1613[103] show that he had been renting two closes called Scaddowe Closes, each containing two acres. In 1631 the description was 'a shread one hemp place and a garden at the Scaddowe yate, late in the tenure of one Henry Hanbury'.[104]

Another potter at Scaddows, working before the death of Henry Hanbury was Humfrey Taylor alias Makepeace. He was of sufficient status and maturity to have acted as an appraiser for Henry's goods in 1595. In 1604 'a parcel of ground in the Scaddowes lane alonge by the lytle Scaddowes hedge & adjoining to the same towards the west with th'appurtenances' was leased by Richard Francis to Humphrey Taylor or Makepeace of Scaddowes, in the parish of Ticknall, potter;[105] the lease was for four score years.[106] A later deed of 1631 gave the description 'one cottage or tenement called by the name of the White House lately erected by one Humphrey Taylor alias Mackpeece and the buildings belonging and a little close adjoining to said cottage lately inclosed forth of Scaddowe lane by the said Humphrey Taylor'.[107]

Humphrey Makepeace alias Taylor died intestate in 1611.[108] He was described as a potter, of the Scaddowe yard, and his inventory gives some idea of his 'White House'. Apart from its name it was in many ways similar to others of the time. The dwelling had a hall with a table, three forms and two chairs, the fire irons and a spit. The parlour had a standing bed with its furniture and also a servant's bed with a small cupboard, a chest and two coffers. The chamber over the parlour had a bed for servants, four yards of russet cloth, three strike of rye, eight strike of dredge (mixed grain) and four strike of oats as well as two old wheels, sives and a shelf with wool and yarn. The chamber over the hall only had six strikes of wheat in it. The milkhouse had shelves, forms, a churne and 'powdringe trowe', as well as four flitches of bacon stored there. There was also a buttery. Taylor had two pairs of flaxen and seven pairs of canvas sheets, as well as towels, napkins and four table cloths. His pewter and brass was appraised separately. He had ten pewter dishes, two salts, a cup and twelve spoons worth 10s; his brass consisted of two brass pots, a pan, three 'cettels', a frying pan and a 'scimmer', worth 33s 4d. The total of his household goods was £9 16s 8d. Outside there was a barn which had corn and hay in it that was unthreshed, valued at £6 13s 4d. Presumably he had a workhouse for his lathe, 'bordes and formes' and the other implements belonging to his trade, but it is not mentioned separately. He must also have had hovels for his 'One Oulde Carte w[i]th Carte geares harrowes plowes ploweyrons Axes hatchet mattock spade w[i]th other implements belonging to husbandry'; these were valued at 20s. However, he was more involved in farming than the Hanburys. His cattle were worth £25 6s 8d, and his sheep, five horses and a foal were valued at £20. He also had eight small store pigs worth 30s and 2s worth of poultry running around. His inventory included the lease of the house at £15 and a close that still had three years of the lease to come worth £10. There were unspecified good debts owing to him worth £2 10s and another £2 4s worth of 'desperate' debts that he was unlikely to get. The whole inventory totalled £106 5s 4d.

Humphrey Page who owed twenty 'fats' (casks) of ware to Edward Warden[109] in 1614 may have been working here; he was probably a nephew of Humphrey Makepeace and can be identified as 'Homffrye Tyler' who owed 16s to Henry Blest in 1620 for supplying him with ochre.[110] Anna Page alias Tyler, widow, was buried in 1637 and the name Taylor appears as Tyler in connection with other members of the family at Scaddows, who were at there until the 1670s.

Richard Gardener also rented land at the Scaddows. In 1613 a deed describes 'one great close of land called Great Scaddowe or Scaddowe holes now divided in part lying in the lordship of Ticknall and Repton and the houses, late in the holding of one Richard Gardner'.[111] He may have potted on the same site as Richard Hanbury (died 1587) and certainly was closely associated with him. He had also bought 11 acres of land called Petchers

Close in Ticknall.[112] Richard Gardener was an archer in the 1585 muster for the parishes of Ticknall and Calke.[113] He was described as a husbandman when he was executor to Robert Barrow of Ticknall in 1609[114] and he acted as an appraiser to his neighbour Humphrey Makepeace alias Taylor in 1611.[115] In his will[116] he left his wife Elizabeth his land called Petchers Close and this was still in her possession in 1627–8 as the wife of Edward Squire whom she had married not long after the death of Richard;[117] they lived at Gosley Leys in Ticknall. Anne Barrow who was under age was to have £5; she was the daughter of Richard Barrow and presumably the only child not yet provided for in the discharge of his duty as executor to her father. Trothe Webster the wife of Richard was left 40s and a black heifer. The poor of Ticknall were not forgotten, with 40s to be distributed 'where most need is' and the churchwardens were given 5s for the repair of the seats in the church. He also had two servants, Peter Sibley and Elizabeth Holland, who were each left 10s.

Richard Gardener's home was comfortably furnished and had a 'house' with the fireplace and cooking items, table, a bench with a 'peece of seeling to itt' (carving), joined forms, a 'dishborde', cushions and a salt box. He slept in the parlour which must have been quite crowded as there were two standing beds with testers and five chests, a small trunk and a desk; his bedcoverings alone came to £3 10s. Upstairs the chamber ran over both the 'house' and parlour. A wool bed was here with its coverings. Amongst his linen he had three pairs of flaxen sheets, three pairs of middling sheets and no less than 'therteene paye of camvace sheets' as well as other linen. He was well provided with brass — he had two pans, three pots, three kettles, two brass candlesticks as well as a chafing dish and a 'scummer'. He also had pewter dishes, saucers, a pewter candlestick and a nest of salts, as well as eight spoons. His pewter and brass was valued at £3 11s 8d. In the buttery and milkhouse were two dozen trenchers and a wooden platter as well as costrels, bowls, barrels, piggins, pails and an 'ould kimnell'. There were 'two wheeles and other necessaryes belonging to his trade' worth 3s 4d as well as 'certayne bords in the chambers about the oven and in the Barne' valued at 27s 8d. This latter entry suggests that he had at least one workhouse attached to his kiln. Richard Gardener did not rely on potting alone for his income as he had 4 stone of wool stored worth 53s 4d; he also made cheese as he had a cheese press. But most of all he was farming — his 'croppe of corne in the feild and closes of all sortes' was worth £33 6s 8d. His leases were valued at £60 and he had four 'melche kyne' worth £9 6s 8d as well as four each of young beasts and weaning calves. He had three mares, a gelding, forty-four old sheep and twelve lambs. He was owed a total of £10 12s 8d in debts. His debtors included another Ticknall potter, William Madeley, who owed 8s, and John Wardyn a known pot seller of Griffydam who owed 26s 8d, presumably for pots that he had taken to sell. Gardener's inventory totalled £188 7s 10d.

The last known potter at the Scaddows was William Hanbury who died in 1674. His relationship to the earlier Richard and Henry is not known but there must be one. Another Richard Hanbury was of Scaddows when he was buried in 1658 and he may be the father of William. William Hanbury was listed on the 1638 muster and by 1648 was paying £1 14s 2d in rent for 'Schaddowes holes'.[118] The Hearth Tax shows he had one hearth; this was the norm for most Ticknall houses at that time. His inventory came to just £14 15s 7d when it was taken in 1672.[119] The contents of the 'house' included the fire and cooking implements, three 'very bad cubboards' fastened in the walls, as well as a bacon 'cubboard', a table with a frame, a little falling table and four little chairs. He slept in the parlour where he had a sealed bed with a featherbed and coverings; there was another bed as well as three coffers and a 'kneatinge trowe' (kneading trough). In a chamber was 'a very sorry bed that Bullocks (a family) lyeth in, 2 blankets a very bad bolster, a little cofer and a small forme' worth 6s 2d. His buttery had two old churns, a flasket and benches in it while another chamber had just two short boards in it. His kitchen appears to have been used for potting, as he kept his mattock, spade, grinding iron and lead pan in there. His workhouse had 'his potting wheele paceboard his lead bale and babble tub' worth 8s and he also had '41 boards very bad and good' in his workhouse and 'upon his oven'; these were worth £1 6s 6d. There was a 'bucket, windes a chaine' for the well. There was some livestock around — he had 14 sheep worth 4s each, together with a cow and a young calf worth £2 10s; he also had hay worth £1. The picture of a run down pottery is completed with the description of his linen — he had just '3 paire of very bad sheets'.

There was another pottery on the hillside at Tatshall Fee (**site 18**). This site was probably in production from the 1690s to around the 1760s. Though strictly speaking this area was part of Breedon manor, its inhabitants often baptised their children at the nearby churches such as Hartshorne or Calke. The earliest potter known here was Edward Standley who was the lead taker for the clay lease on Ticknall common in 1690. He is mentioned as the occupier of a cottage in Tatshall Fee in a lease of 1702.[120] It is likely he was related to the Standley family of Standleys Barn, but the records are incomplete. Edward was probably the father of John 'Stanly' of Tatshall Fee whose son John was baptised at Hartshorne in 1719. The younger John was also a potter here, and had children baptised at Hartshorne during the period 1745–65. He is probably the same John Standley who was a signatory to the Derby Hills clay agreement in 1766. In 1784 when he was buried he was described as a pauper so had been receiving parish relief to make ends meet. His son Edward, born in 1748, was also a potter; he worked for the potters at Heath End. In the 1780s Edward was still living at Tatshall Fee. He too was described as a pauper in 1787, by which time this pot site had probably ceased operation.

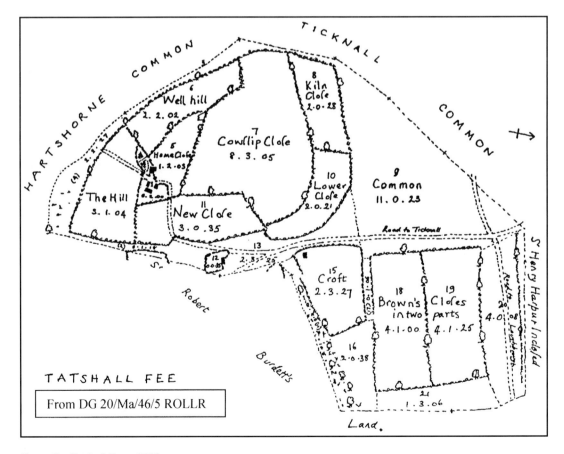

Figure 7 – Tatshall Fee c.1760

The kiln site can be clearly seen when the field has been newly ploughed as a very dark patch on the hillside which, when examined, is full of kiln debris and potshards. There are faint traces of the harder surface of a track leading into the next field and there is a spring nearby for water. Figure 7 shows the area and is redrawn from a map of the 1760s.[121] The kiln was about half way up the close marked 'Kiln Close'. Today there are no buildings left associated with the site. There is a field barn and milking yard lower down the hill; this barn is purely agricultural and has never been used for potting.

The history of the potteries at Heath End is complex. Heath End is where the parishes of Ashby de la Zouch and Staunton Harold (part of Breedon parish), both in Leicestershire, and Calke in Derbyshire all meet. To complicate matters still further, the land in these three parishes was owned by different landowners, the Earl of Huntingdon, Earl Ferrers and the Harpurs respectively. Today little remains of the industrial past — there are three houses on the Ashby side, one former pub The Saracen's Head on the Staunton side and nothing on the Calke side. In former times things were very different. Figure 8 shows the area in more detail in 1904, with the sites added.

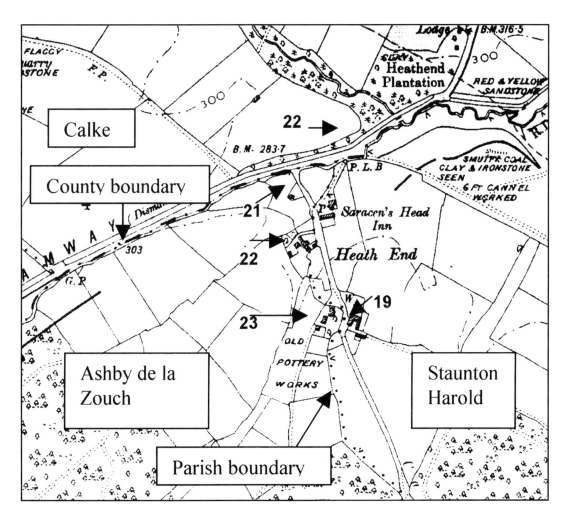

Figure 8 – The Heath End area showing pot sites (Geological Survey of England and Wales, 2nd Edition 1904, Derbyshire LXI NW)

On the Staunton Harold side, **site 19** was the pottery run by the Draper family and their descendants. Roger Draper, who had been living on the Staunton side of Heath End since 1654, inherited a property in Ashby from his elder brother John in 1673, but we have no further mention of this property and presumably it was later sold. He appeared in the first surviving Ferrers rental of 1674, when he and others rented Calves Close for a half yearly rent of £4; he also paid 1s 6d for a cottage.[122] By Michaelmas 1677 the rentals showed an additional half yearly rent of 10s for his 'pott house and digging clay'. This was unpaid by Michaelmas when his son John (1652–1721) was responsible for the payment of the pot house rent, although Roger Draper's other rent was paid on time. John Draper did not pay his rent for the pottery either, apart from a period from Michaelmas 1683 to Lady Day 1687 when he paid 10s each time; none of the arrears was paid. From Michaelmas 1687 until the rental ends at Michaelmas 1692 he was behind with the rent again.

In 1691 John Draper purchased a messuage or tenement in Ticknall 'wherein John Varnham then lately dwelt', together with land in the three fields of Ticknall from Ralph Holland of Ticknall, potter, for which he paid £95. The deeds show that he was already farming the land, which consisted of 7½ acres.[123] This was passed down through his family for several generations until it was finally sold in 1824 to Thomas Sheffield and bought by Sir George Crewe in that same year. Draper bought another cottage with land from Ralph Holland (potter) in 1698 [footnote D2375m/173/3DRO], this was aquired by the Harpur Crewe Estate in 1849, having been a bakery; it is now the site of the Staff of Life pub. He also inherited a freehold messuage in Ticknall from Anne Varnham[124] with the proviso that he paid certain legacies out of it; he left this to his daughter Elizabeth in his will.[125] By the time the next surviving rental starts in 1718 he was paying his rent regularly. Evidently any other land that he rented was included in the overall sum. At Michaelmas 1720 he paid 'in full for a yrs rent & Potthouse & taxes pd' for £6 16s 6d.[126] He evidently did quite well out of potting if he could afford to buy property and although no inventory survives we know that he also farmed. The 1719 rental showed that he paid £1 10s for three mares and a filly to be in Staunton grounds as well as the land that he farmed in Ticknall. His will left his household goods to be divided between his daughter Elizabeth who inherited the land and his son Robert who was the executor. When the will was proved in 1721 it stated that he too was of Staunton Harold in the parish of Breedon, potter.

After the death of his father in 1721, Robert Draper appears in the rentals, paying a lesser half yearly rent of between £2 12s and £2 2s 6d. The pothouse was not mentioned but he carried on the business as well as farming — he had potting tools in his inventory.[127] In 1724 he paid £3 for 'the Ley of 5 cows in the Heath'. From 1730 to 1735 he paid no rent until Michaelmas of the latter year when the entry 'recd Robert Draper in part £20 0s 0d' was recorded. Evidently he was behind with his rent and this payment was to catch up. At over £4 per year this would be about right. In 1729 he had mortgaged the land in Ticknall his father had bought for £20 1s; by 1738 there was £28 outstanding including the interest. The same deed showed that Robert Draper had also borrowed a further £77 by this date from Nicholas Joyce, the Ashby apothecary from whom Draper had the mortgage; presumably some of this money enabled him to pay the rent that he owed. This suggests that both the potting business and the farming were difficult at this time. Robert was buried in 1742 and was described as a husbandman in his inventory which was valued at £34 15s 9¼d. There was no mention of his debts. His inventory shows a reasonably large dwelling with a 'house' with the fire and cooking utensils. There were also two parlours, a buttery, kitchen and two chambers, one of which was over the kitchen. Outside there was the fold yard with the well, a barn, a workshop which contained his potting tools, a stable and a cart hovel.

Besides the fire and cooking items, the 'house' was furnished with two tables, one round and the other square, six ash chairs, a dresser, shelves, some old books, a lantern and also a pair of 'garding sheers' with a 'goss bill' and a hatchet worth 2s 6d; he also kept his brass and pewter here. He slept in the parlour in some comfort, on his featherbed, with two pillows which weighed a total of 95lb, worth £2 7s 6d; the other bed clothes were of far less value. Small luxuries included a clock, an old close stool and a small looking glass. The little parlour also had a bed, as did the 'first' chamber. The kitchen had the cheese press and brewing utensils, as well as an old copper, a pad and a pair of scales and beams. The kitchen chamber was used for storing lumber.

Outside he had three horses, one old gelding and two mares worth £6 6d in the stable, collars, gears and harnesses for the horses and a cart saddle. His two carts were kept in the hovel together with harrows and the plough. He was possibly living on the wealth generated by the previous generation, or had used the money he borrowed to make sure he could be comfortable.

The next tenant of the property was Robert Draper's sister Elizabeth. At this time she was the widow of Robert Richards her second husband. She also made pots — in June 1746 the steward's account notes 'pd Widdow Richards for Garden Potts £2 18s 9d'.[128] In 1751 Elizabeth Richards finally paid off the debt owed by her late brother Robert, now £140, but only by taking a loan from John Bodle of Ashby de la Zouch, butcher.

Elizabeth Richards was succeeded by her son-in-law Joseph Bosworth and his wife Isabel. Isabel was Elizabeth's only child by her first husband Nathaniel Green. Joseph Bosworth described himself as a yeoman in his will of 1773[129] in which he left his wife Isabel all the household implements which included 'stock in trade, tools and all utensils belonging'. Presumably this included potting tools as he was mentioned three times in the Ferrers accounts for supplying pots. In 1748 he supplied £1 2s 6d worth of 'Garden Pots'. In 1751 the accounts record 'pd Joseph Bosworth for Garden Potts and Earthenware £2 7s 9d'.[130] The third mention was in the rental for Michaelmas 1761 when he was allowed 'a bill for potts and barley £6 18s 0½d' out of his half yearly rent of £9 7s 6d.[131] A survey of the Staunton Harold Estate taken in 1778 shows that all the tenants could claim against their rent for goods supplied or work done.[132] However, the balance of the economy had clearly shifted to farming; potting was playing a lesser part. The Ferrers family seem to have bought quite a large quantity of pots for the garden; they would all be of low value. This contrasts with the much more upmarket 'Earthenware' they purchased in 1747 from Thomas Wheildon, for which £7 6s 6d was paid. Wheildon was one of the foremost producers of the fashionable products being made in The Potteries area at that time.

After Joseph's death his widow was 'allowed a Bill for Potts' for £3 5s 6½d at the Lady Day rent in 1763, 'allowed a bill for pans and pots' worth £1 14s 3d at Lady Day 1764, £8 0s 11½d worth of 'pots and chimney pipes' at Michaelmas of the same year, 'allowed for carriage and potts' £3 7d at Michaelmas 1765, 'allowed a half years window tax £3 3s and a bill for pots for 12s 1d' at Michaelmas 1766. The last two bills she was allowed were for just 11s 7d and 6s at Michaelmas 1768 and 1769 respectively. This coincides with the decline of other potteries in the area. During these last few years she had taken out another loan from Thomas Godkin of Melbourne, gentleman, for £200 to pay off the amount owing to John Bodle in 1767. In 1768 she repaid Thomas Godkin £208 which included interest. She continued to use the Ticknall property as security for further loans and by 1778 had debts of £130 on it. However, by this time she had moved to Lichfield. By 1824 when the property was sold to Sir George Crewe, all the debts had been paid off.

After Isabel Bosworth moved the pottery was taken over by George Richards. He too supplied the Ferrers family with garden pots, which were offset against his Lady Day rent for the years 1774–6. In 1776 Jacob Standley was potting here;[133] perhaps he was making the pots for Richards. This is the last reference we have to the pottery on this site. There would appear to have only been this one pottery on the Staunton side of the boundary. The field behind where Drapers farm was is uneven and shows signs of clay having been dug out of it and backfilled.

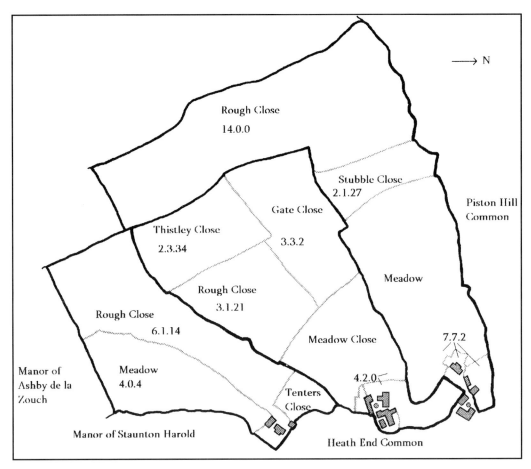

Figure 9 – Heath End in Ashby parish, 1735

Figure 9 shows three properties in Ashby parish at Heath End. Two have a pot kiln.[134] That at Ley Farm (**site 20**) was working at the same time as that on the Staunton side and probably earlier. The Tetley family first appeared in Breedon parish where Henry Tetley had five children baptised between 1606 and 1623. Henry was buried at Breedon in 1658 and he was also renting in the adjacent parish of Calke as he appeared on the jury for the Calke Court in 1640 and was later fined one shilling for failing to appear at the court in 1643.[135] We do not know whether he was a potter, but both of his sons Thomas (1610–81) and James (1612–78) were. Thomas worked in Ticknall and James was at Heath End from at least 1667 when his wife was buried at Ashby de la Zouch as 'of Southwood'. James was described as a potter at his burial in 1678 although he had been described as a labourer at the baptisms of his children during the period 1639–43. He may have been employed at one of the less skilled jobs earlier, maybe even getting clay. James and his wife had four sons. James the eldest became a butcher in Ashby, Henry the second son (1637–84) was also a potter, and the fate of the two youngest sons Thomas and John remains unknown. Henry Tetley married in 1670 and had at least three children before he died in 1684.

In his inventory[136] he was described as being of 'Inner Southwood', which was the area on the Ashby side of Southwood.[137] His inventory gives a clear picture of a potter farmer. His cottage had a 'house' where, as was usual, the fire and cooking implements were found. It also had a buttery, a little parlour and a 'Farr' parlour, which, together with the chamber over the latter, contained four beds. There was a kitchen with brewing utensils in it. Upstairs was the chamber over the 'house' where he slept which was warmed from the fire in the room below, the 'new' chamber with wool in and the 'storr' chamber where his cheese and bacon were kept. There was also the entry where he kept '3 pigge of lead'. His work-house was where his potting tools such as boards, raw pots and two pot wheels were to be found. He had clay worth £1 weathering on the common. As well as potting, Tetley was very much involved in farming. His carts, ploughs and husbandry gear were worth £9 10s alone, which was a large amount for his status and the area. He had eleven horses worth £48 10s; he was breeding these as he had a stoned horse (an uncastrated stallion). His 148 sheep were worth £29 and he also had eighteen assorted cattle including a bull calf. These were spread around the area. He rented land in Ashby Old Park, Smisby Park, in 'Ashby Grounds' and Oakthorpe, as well as at Calke. The Calke rental for 1682 shows that he paid £7 5s for the land he rented there.[138] He must have been making a comfortable living in order to do this and his inventory came to a total value of £270 0s 6d, of which £20 were 'sperate' debts which had some chance of being paid, whilst another £20 was owing in 'desperate' debts which had little chance of being recovered.

The rooms mentioned in his inventory match the layout of the present Ley Farm, a prop-erty which has been largely unaltered since the seventeenth century and which we were fortunate to survey before the present owners moved in. The stream that runs alongside the road and forms the parish boundary was found to be full of potshards.

After Henry Tetley died his cousin Thomas Tetley ran the pottery until Henry's eldest son Joseph was capable of running it. The Staunton Harold rentals show that Thomas Tetley paid 1s in 1675.[139] Later entries make it clear that this was for an encroachment. This would explain the kiln waste across the stream onto the Staunton Harold side.[140] Joseph Tetley was evidently reasonably successful as a potter to start with — in 1711 he bought the property tenanted by John Marriott's widow on Ticknall common for £40 from Thomas Pearston of Ticknall. In July 1728 he raised £40 on a mortgage on this property, to be repaid with interest on 1 July 1729; this was unpaid at his death in November of the same year. He also got some of his clay from the Staunton Harold area and paid 2s for getting clay at Michaelmas 1728.[141] He died intestate and his inventory shows that he was much less in-volved in farming than his father.[142] As was usual at this time, the inventory was much less detailed, but the farming had been scaled down so much that he only had one old horse worth £1, four beasts and four sheep worth £6 16s. All his goods were only valued at £19 15s.[143] The inventory also described where he lived as 'Inner Southwood' but the burial register at Ashby de la Zouch gave 'Heath End', confirmation that the two were the same place.

His son Joseph took over the pottery after his father's death. In 1730 he sold the Ticknall property for £80 and paid off his father's debt, which had grown to £44 14s. He too got some of his clay from the Staunton Harold area — in the 1750 Michaelmas rental he paid 1s 6d for 'getting Clay on the waste' and he paid the same amount at Michaelmas 1751–3. He was still getting clay from the same place until 1761.[144] The 1735 map of Ashby manor shows that the tenant of Ley Farm also rented several adjacent closes — clay may have been taken from there and the holes backfilled. Joseph's brother John was also a potter and was a party to the lease to dig for clay on Derby Hills in 1766.[145] We do not know how much longer after this the pottery operated. Robert Hough married Joseph's daughter or grand-daughter Mary in 1793 and the Houghs were the subsequent tenants.

The other property shown as a pottery on the 1735 estate map (site 21) has undergone considerable alteration. There would seem to be no buildings left from this period and comparison of the maps suggests the present cottage was built over the site of the kiln. The adjacent field is very uneven, suggesting previous industrial use. It has been much more difficult to work out who was potting there. The most likely candidate is William Hyde (1699–1755).

The Hyde family can be traced back to William's father David (died 1749) who was married at Peckleton in Leicestershire in 1696 to Elizabeth Newton. David appeared in the Calke rentals paying for a 'house and close late Newtons', which suggests that his wife came from Calke. His origins are unknown. It may be that he came from outside the area, or perhaps, as there are scattered references to the surname in the previous century, he may have been born locally. Like so many families in this area at this time, many baptisms, marriages and burials seem to be unrecorded. The Hyde family became more involved with potting than any other, despite coming to the industry at a time when it was declining. David Hyde had two sons who survived to adulthood. Henry (c.1698–1760) the eldest married Anne Hanson the daughter of Thomas, another Ticknall potter. Their son David (1721–1802) was a party to the lease for getting clay from Derby Hills in 1766, and it was David's son Joseph (1744–1811) who took over the running of Potworks Farm at Myreoak in the 1770s.

William, David's second son, was also a potter and the baptism entry for his youngest child Mary in 1753 at Calke states that he was of Heath End in Ashby liberty. In 1735 the Ashby Town Book records that 'Wm Hide shew'd his Indenture in the Vestry and allow'd to be an Inhabitant of this Parish'.[146] In his will of 1755, William left his potting tools and the trade to be equally divided between his two sons Henry and Thomas.[147] Of Henry nothing more is known. Thomas evidently took over the pot site at Heath End. He is described as a potter of Ashby de la Zouch on his marriage bond of 1758 and we know that he employed Edward Standley by the year at his Heath End pottery from 1768–71.[148] Thomas's cousin David Hyde (1721–92) also worked at this site and he too employed Edward Standley in 1767. Both David and Thomas appear to have been potting on two sites. By 1750 David Hyde was renting land in Ticknall as well as Calke. In Ticknall his land and cottage was at Whitelees and he eventually retired from pot making and continued to farm the Ticknall land. By 1761 he was paying £11 rent for Whitelees. He is a good example of the way potting and farming could be combined.

On the Calke side of Heath End was the farm rented by George Vernon, a carpenter. This was also a pottery, **site 22**, which we believe was 'David Hydes ... potworks in the township of Caulke'. Edward Standley was also hired to work here in 1766. This site was definitely finished by 1787 when the buildings were demolished after the death of George Vernon.

The third cottage on the Ashby side (**site 23**) also appears to have been a pottery; the geological map of 1904 marks it as the 'site of old pottery'. This may have been the site worked by William Coxon and his son William who were pot making on the Ashby side.[149] The Coxons were probably there during the period 1760–1806. Edward Standley was hired to work for William Coxon in 1765. It is likely that William Coxon junior was the William Coxon who came from Polesworth to marry at Ashby de la Zouch in 1805 and who was running a pottery in Chilvers Coton 1807–38.[150]

So far all the known sites at Heath End have been covered. There may be sites not yet found. Other potters are known to have been working at Heath End although these may be men working in the potteries as part of the 'set' of six men. Jonathan Shaw was a potter whose settlement certificate of 1742 allowed him to move from Ashby de la Zouch to Ticknall where he had a child baptised in 1745. He was later back at Heath End, when he had another three children baptised at Calke in the period 1743–51. He died in 1786. Thomas Jones was born in Ticknall and married in 1701 at Ashby; he too was a potter at Heath End.[151] His daughter probably married William Hyde in 1726.

Calke, too, is problematic. We believe that **site 22** was where David Hyde worked and it is counted in the Heath End group. But we have other potters in the parish, notably John Cox who rented land right on the parish boundary down near Calke Mill. This is now under Staunton Harold Reservoir. Cox was not potting where he lived. When the reservoir was very low in 1994–5, there were virtually no potshards to be seen on the site of his house.

However, there were a substantial number on the other side of this arm of the reservoir, which at this point is just a few yards away. Cox had a moiety or half of a cottage on the Melbourne side of the boundary and **site 24** was the location of his pottery. Potshards from there were dragged up when the banks of the reservoir were graded. There may have been a pottery here earlier. The changes in the layout in this area are shown in Figure 10. It is now all under Staunton Harold Reservoir.

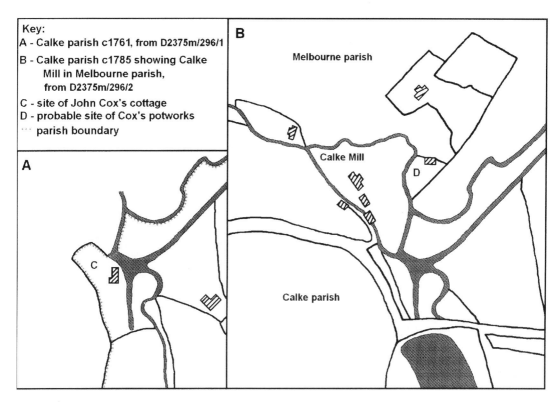

Key:
A - Calke parish c1761, from D2375m/296/1

B - Calke parish c1785 showing Calke
    Mill in Melbourne parish,
    from D2375m/296/2

C - site of John Cox's cottage
D - probable site of Cox's potworks
   parish boundary

Melbourne parish

Calke Mill

Calke parish

Figure 10 – The changing layout at site 24, 1760s–1780s

John Cox died in 1762. In his will, written in November 1761[152], Cox left half his cottage in the parish of Melbourne to his daughter Elizabeth; the cottage was tenanted by Thomas Hyde. Hyde had been born at Heath End in the parish of Ashby de la Zouch, and his 1762 settlement examination stated that he had lived there 'until last Lady Day then removed to the parish of Melbourne and Newton where he now lives'[153], suggesting that he had moved to this site between one and two years previously. He still rented property at Heath End. Two other potters may have worked here. Thomas Parker was a potter of Calke, and was a signatory to the 1690 clay agreement. John Varnum, a pot maker, came to Melbourne from Chilvers Coton in 1700[154]. It is possible that he was a local returning to the area, as the name is common around Calke. The pottery at Furnace Farm, Melbourne (**site 25**), is dealt with in Chapter 6.

# References

1 John Hough 9 November 1602 LJRO
2 Ales Randall 9 November 1635 LJRO
3 TNA: PRO SP 16/405
4 Edwards, D. G. (ed.) (1982), p121
5 TNA: PRO E179/245/6
6 George Hough 19 September 1679 LJRO
7 Venn, J. and Venn, J. A. (eds) (1922) part 1 vol. 2, p413
8 D2375m/165/8 DRO
9 James Hough 2 October 1712 LJRO
10 William Pemberton 13 April 1724 LJRO
11 William Pemberton's will is mentioned in the deeds but it does not appear to have
   been proved at Lichfield or in the Prerogative Court of Canterbury. It is probable that
   it was never proved and a copy has not survived
12 John Cooper 14 October 1729 LJRO
13 Dorothy Pemberton 13 September 1765 LJRO
14 D2375m/165/8 and 68/6 DRO
15 pers. comm. J. Illsley
16 D2375m/171/76 DRO
17 Richard Cox 14 November 1732 LJRO
18 D2375m/63/62 DRO
19 D2375m/54/20 DRO
20 John Knifton 12 April 1766 LJRO
21 John Cox 4 October 1695 LJRO
22 D2375m/174/7 DRO
23 D2375m/299/44 DRO
24 D5054/13/3 DRO
25 Deeds 1886 DLSL
26 pers. comm. I. Bird
27 William Cox 19 May 1747 LJRO
28 pers. comm. A. MacCormick
29 pers. comm. S. Woodward
30 D2375m/28/12 DRO
31 D2375m/145/20 DRO
32 TNA: PRO E179/94/407
33 TNA: PRO E101/59/7
34 D77 Box 22/5 DRO
35 Edward Hanbury 21 June 1610 LJRO
36 D2375m/170/4 DRO
37 D2375m/25/5/7 and 25/5/84 DRO
38 Cox, J. C. (1908), p47. Cox ascribes this village whose name is missing to 'Repton?'
   as the first name is the Prior of Repton. However, most of the men also listed are
   those who feature in the Ticknall deeds of the late 13th and early 14th centuries and it

is clearly referring to Ticknall; Repton surnames of the same period are not the same. We would suggest that the Prior of Repton was living at Ticknall, perhaps at a house on his grange there; TNA: PRO HO 107/2084

39 John Beighton 6 February 1620/1 LJRO

40 D2375m/47/26 DRO

41 D2375m/63/53 and 94/6 DRO

42 Timothy Beighton 13 October 1674 LJRO

43 D2375m/145/20 and 28/12 DRO

44 Joseph Beighton 29 March 1720 LJRO

45 Rentals in D2375m/277/2 1681–82, 171/50 1691–92, 54/20 1695–94, 171/76 1698–99, 171/21 1707–08, 264/12 1708–09, 162/2 1713–14, 171/16 1716–17, 162/18 1718–19, 171/19 1736–37, 103/70 1743–44, 63/14 1751, 103/74 1752–53, DRO

46 Samuel Potter 24 April 1688 LJRO

47 D2375m/56/31 DRO

48 Joseph Potter 29 May 1724 LJRO

49 D2375m/103/103/1–4, 6–9 1727–1807 DRO

50 Ticknall Overseers of the Poor, Account Book 1762–96, in private hands

51 D2375/m/119/3 DRO; D5054/13/5/2 DRO

52 Ticknall Overseers of the Poor, Account Book 1762–96, in private hands

53 Pigot, J. (1857) p387

54 Ann Hyde 20 April 1847 LJRO

55 White, F. (1857) p387

56 Derbyshire sheet LVIII, 13 DRO

57 D2375m/71/144 DRO

58 TNA: PRO RG9/2268

59 TNA: PRO RG10/3245

60 Kelly, E. R. (1888) p297

61 Kelly and Co. (1891) p373

62 John Marriott 5 October 1680 LJRO

63 John Marriott 28 April 1709 LJRO

64 So called because it belonged to the Black Prince in the fourteenth century

65 D2375m/164/14 DRO

66 QRL microfilm XMI/211–216 DRO

67 Thomas Hill 16 April 1816 LJRO

68 Samuel Hill 15 October 1816 LJRO

69 D2375m/164/14 DRO

70 D2375m/56/31 DRO

71 D2375m/56/31 DRO

72 Thomas Henson 28 September 1724 LJRO

73 Thomas Henson 14 November 1729 LJRO

74 L2/2 WRO

75 Joseph Hanson 1 December 1758 LJRO

76 Pilkington, J. (1789), vol. 2, p83

77 D2360/262b DRO

78 D2375m/288/2 DRO

79 D2375m/94/90 DRO

80 Usher, H. (1989), p2

81 D2375m/25/1 DRO

82 D2375m/164/2 DRO

83 D2375m/63/62 DRO

84 D2375m/163/2 DRO

85 Ticknall Overseers of the Poor, Account Book 1762–96, in private hands

86 Q/SB2/1159 DRO

87 D1396 A/PO 431 DRO

88 Farey, J. (1817), vol. 3, p161

89 DE 179/103 ROLLR

90 pers. comm. Russell Brown

91 D2375m/164/6 DRO

92 John Smallwood 4 October 1743 LJRO

93 Francis Stanlye 25 May 1638 LJRO

94 John Standlye 11 December 1667 LJRO

95 Joseph Standley 29 April 1709 LRJO

96 Mary Standley 10 November 1718 LJRO

97 D5054/13/3 DRO

98 D655A/PO 625 DRO

99 Sir John Frances 14 July 1603 LJRO

100 D2375m/170/4 DRO

101 Richard Hanbery, 7 June 1587 LJRO

102 Marie Hanburey, 30 May 1594 LRJO

103 D 156m/13 DRO

104 D 156m/13, 36 and 37 DRO

105 D 156m/35 DRO

106 D156m/37 DRO

107 D 156m/14 DRO

108 Homfry Makepeace, alias Taylor, 28 June 1611 LJRO

109 Edward Warden 1611–1615 ROLLR

110 Henry Blest 31 May 1621 LJRO

111 D156m/13 DRO

112 D2375m/25/1 DRO

113 DAJ (1895), vol. 17 p19

114 Robert Barrow 22 June 1609 LJRO

115 Homfry Makepeace alias Taylor, 28 June 1611 LJRO

116 Richard Gardener 18 July 1614 LJRO

117 D2375m/25/1 DRO

118 TNA: PRO SP16/405; D5054/3/4 DRO

119 William Hanberye 3 March 1672 LJRO; the inventory was totalled to £15 15s 11d,
    the corrected total is £14 15s 7d

120 DE 41/1/28/3 ROLLR

121 DG 20/Ma/46/5 ROLLR

122 26 D 53/2197 ROLLR

123 D2375m/164/12 DRO

124 Ann Varnham 1702 18 ROLLR

125 John Draper 14 March 1721 ROLLR

126 26 D 53/2200 ROLLR

127 Robert Draper 8 July 1742 ROLLR

128 26 D 53/2408 ROLLR

129 Joseph Bosworth PR/T/1778/31/1–2 ROLLR

130 26 D 53/2410 ROLLR

131 26 D 53/2226 ROLLR

132 26 D 53/1984 ROLLR

133 D655A/PO 625 DRO

134 DG 30/MA/9/4 ROLLR

135 D2375m/82/72 DRO

136 Henry Tetley 1684 Admon. 45 and 46 ROLLR

137 The area called Southwood was a detached portion of Repton parish; the adjacent area in Ashby de la Zouch parish was also called Southwood

138 D2375m/277/2 DRO

139 26D 58/2197 ROLLR

140 Deirdre O'Sullivan and Leicester University excavated this site in 1998

141 26 D 53/2213 ROLLR

142 Joseph Tetley, 1730 Admon. ROLLR

143 corrected total

144 26 D 53/2226 ROLLR

145 94/3/3 MH

146 DE 432/1 Ashby Town Book, ROLLR

147 William Hide 28 July 1756 ROLLR

148 D1396A/PO 437 DRO

149 Land Tax MF 94 ROLLR

150 Gooder, E. A. p9

151 Thomas Jones 1734 ROLLR

152 John Cox 23 November 1793 LJRO

153 D655 A/PO/374 DRO

154 D655 A/PO/158 DRO

# 4. Potteries and Families:
## potters from unidentified sites

Many of our potters and their families can be ascribed to particular sites. However, there are also some families and potters, mainly in the pre-1700 period, whose potting activities cannot be linked to a particular site. This chapter looks at what we know about them.

Some of our earliest known potters are those who are the most elusive. Richard Knight senior was assessed on goods worth 40s and Richard Knight junior on goods worth £3 in the tax list of 1538–47; one of them was still alive in the 1570s. Two Turners, Thomas and Richard, were assessed on £3 and 20s worth of goods respectively; Richard Turner was a 'bilman' in the 1538–9 muster.[1] He was also an appraiser of the goods of John Beighton who died in 1541, whilst Thomas Turner was Beighton's son-in-law and executor. Two Cunweys, John and Richard, were both assessed on 40s worth of goods in 1538–47. John was also listed as an archer in the 1538–9 muster and he may have been the John Cunwey listed as running an alehouse in 1577.[2] Together with William Hanbury, these seven potters listed in 1538–47 suggest that at that date at least four pot sites were running and possibly seven. At present we know of four, possibly five, which could have been running by then. At least three may have been running in the 1520s when Richard Turner and Richard Knight were both assessed on goods worth 40s, Richard Cunway on goods worth £4 and William Hanbury on wages of 20s.[3] This list does not give occupations. By 1588 Robert Cook, who held the first known clay lease from Gilbert Thacker as mentioned in Chapter 2, was probably potting in Southwood. In 1614 Thomas Cooke, with John Holland, owed £5 worth of ware to Edward Warden.[4] John Holland was still alive in 1640 when he witnessed a riot on Derby Hills.[5]

Other members of the Holland family were also potters although some of the relationships are uncertain. John Holland of Ticknall, 'the poter there', was owed 8d in an account of 1539,[6] although he did not appear on the 1538–47 tax list. Richard Holland, a former parish clerk, gave evidence about tithes in 1628[7] when he was 'nowe lying very sicke, upon his bed'; this was six days after he had made his will.[8] His will left his son William 'all the bords belonging to ye trade of potting' and 'his mother shall have ye use of halfe of them whilst she liveth'. This was another potting family which involved the women, and provision was made for the wife to continue to have a say in the running of the business if she so wished. Jone Holland, Richard's widow, died in 1645. Richard Holland lived in a cottage with a 'house place', parlour, chamber, buttery and kitchen. He was also farming, as he had cattle, horses, sheep, pigs and poultry, as well as three roods of corn growing and corn and hay stored in the barn. The value of his inventory came to £42 14s 8d. It is possible that he is the same Richard Holland 'of the Forty' that owed money to Edward Warden in 1614. This may have been either site 11 or 12.

Three of Richard's sons were also potters. Robert the eldest received 12d from his father's will and died in 1667. In 1613 Robert Holland, potter, bought 'all that cottage with appurtenances where the said Robert Holland dwells, and one croft adjoining containing one rood in Ticknall' in 1613. He leased another for 13s 4d half yearly rent in 1617.[9] Together with his brother Raph he was renting 'Whiteleees and Cloisters' in the earliest Calke rental of 1621; their first half year's rent was £8 but they were already behind by 25s.[10] Another brother, Thomas, potter, bought a horse at the Derby horse fair in 1658.[11] William Holland still lived or worked with his mother as a list of the lands belonging to Sir Henry Harpur made in 1630 noted 'Jone Hollande widdow and hir two sonnes Willm and Frauncis Holland' and 'one cottage house in the occupation of Widdow Hollande with garden and backside'.[12] William died in 1663 and in his will left 'all that belongs to the trade of making potts to Daniel'.[13] Like his father, William had an interest in farming though on a smaller scale. He had a pig, two cows and a calf, two horses and half a score of bad sheep, as well as a quarter of wheat and rye sown. The value of his inventory was £23 15s. His son Daniel was the eldest of a large family of four boys and five girls; so far as is known he was the only one to continue the family potting business.

There was also Ralph Holland (1639–1700), the son of Samuel, who was a potter. It is not known how he is related to the other Holland family. His sister Sarah married Samuel Potter in 1658. Ralph sold a 'messuage or tenement in Ticknall wherin John Varnham then lately dwelt', as well as land in the three common fields in Ticknall, in 1691 and a further cottage with land to John Draper, potter, of Heath End in 1698.[14]

There were a number of different Fisher families in Ticknall, two of whom were potters. Richard Fisher, potter, owed 22s to John Dericke in 1613, as well as being a witness to his will and appraiser.[15] Robert Fisher, who may have been Richard's son, died intestate in 1639.[16] His goods were valued at £27 10s 4d. However, he left debts totalling £48 9s 4d, and it is doubtful whether some of his creditors ever got paid. Only one of these creditors was a known potter — George Hough, to whom he owed 20s. His home had a parlour, chamber and buttery as well as his workhouse. No pewter or brass was mentioned in the inventory — he had iron pots for cooking and wooden trenchers for plates. He also had fourteen sheep and two cows. His potting tools in the workhouse were valued at 10s; they included a lead pan, hackers, spades, pass boards, wheels and a leading bowl. He may well have delivered his own pots to the pot sellers or taken them to local markets himself as he had four horses and packsaddles as well as a cart.

Two more potters in the first half of the seventeenth century were William Madeley and Henry Blest. William Madeley was the son of Francis; he was mentioned in his father's will of 1606[17]. He was a tenant in a deed of 1611–12[18] and he owed Richard Gardener a debt of 8s in 1614. He was listed in the 1638 muster and died sometime after 1647 when he bought a horse at Derby horse fair.[19] Henry Blest died in 1620 and his will and brief inventory[20] give us information that has not been available elsewhere. He shared his house with his mother and paid half the lease of 10s a year. He had three cows and seventeen sheep. His potting goods were 'one wheele and passe bord with Ticknall ware' worth 7s. However, amongst the debts that he owed was 37s 5d to John Pegg as well as 'one fatt and a hundred of ware'. John Pegg was evidently selling the pots he made. Henry Blest was also owed £9 2s 6d in debts and of those 'Homffrye Tyler' owed 'xvjs the one halfe in moneye, the other in oker of jd of a stone'.

Joseph Morley was another potter, the son of Thomas who died in 1658. He was left 'one pounde and all my cloathes and all my boardes except foure to make a dore'. Thomas Morley gave his occupation as a labourer in his will, but this reference to boards suggests that he too may have been a potter, though we cannot say positively. Joseph Morley died in 1701 and in his will[21] he left small legacies to his relations Elizabeth Marriott and William Pemberton. His inventory gave a 'dwelling house', 'nether house', chamber and barn. He had potting tools — a pot wheel, iron grate, boards, spades, shovels, 'hasks' and 'all things belonging to ye potting trade' valued at £3 2s 6d. In his barn was corn to the value of 15s; he had hay worth £7 and one cow. The whole was valued at £17 10s 2d.[22]

John Coggreave who died in 1626 was another potter who owed money to ten people, including 19s to Edward Burne for lead. He owed a total of £13 15s 6d, whilst his goods were only valued at £4 3s 6d. His potting wheel was valued with two score of hemp 'in ye roughe' and a spinning wheel; these came to 3s. He also left 'rawe pots' but these were included with a pig and three hens, the manure and two chairs, giving a value of 14s. Even less is known about Samuel Clare. He was old enough for the muster in 1638, and said to be under twenty-one in his father's will of 1639[23] when he was left a small amount of land. He also bought a horse in 1649 at Derby fair;[24] he died in 1677.

Some of the numerous Smith families in Ticknall were potters. Richard Smith was working from at least 1632 to 1670 and in 1653 bought a tenement in Ticknall in the occupation of George Garratt for which he paid £15.[25] He, together with his sons Richard and John, both potters, sold this property in 1670 to Frances Banton of Castle Donington for £10 5s. In 1826 it was sold to Sir George Crewe, by which time it had become four cottages. Nothing more is known about the younger Richard, but his brother John was raising a family during the period 1672–88.

The other potting family still unplaced during the seventeenth century is that of Thomas Tetley who died in 1681. He was the uncle of Henry Tetley who potted at Heath End. Thomas Tetley's will[26] left the house and land in Repton that he owned to his eldest son John; another house and land in Hartshorne was left to his youngest son Thomas who had run the Tetley potworks at Heath End when his cousin Henry died. The elder Thomas also left his son Thomas 'all tooles belonging to the potting trade'. His home, which he leased, was not on Harpur land, as he did not appear in the rentals. The building was quite substantial, with the ground floor containing a 'house', two parlours, a 'booting house' and a buttery. Upstairs were two chambers, one over the 'house' and the other over one of the parlours. There was also an upper loft. His home was comfortably furnished, with two feather-beds and two flock beds. The inventory gives a detailed picture of his brass and pewter for cooking and eating, although he still had a dozen trenchers in the buttery. Signs of comfort include a warming pan, chamber pot, two 'glases' and a looking glass. The inventory also suggests that the women of the house were spinning to help the household economy as there was wool, a woollen wheel, linen, long and little wheels. The 'booting' house suggests that he made his own bread, as it contained a 'kneadinge' trough and a 'meale' sieve; he also had a cheese press. His livestock included a flock of sheep worth £22, three mares, two cows with a heifer and a calf. His plough and cart would have been used on the farm — he had £2 10s worth of corn growing on the ground. Outside was his workhouse with fifty-five boards, a trestle, two 'pageboards', two pot wheels, four spades and a shovel, a lead pan, grinding iron, 'proker', hacker, an iron mortar, a lead 'meels' and an old sieve, together worth £2 8s 6d. His inventory totalled £82 8s 10d.

A few potters remain unplaced during the eighteenth century. Samuel Shaw was almost certainly working on one of the Marriott sites, probably at the top of Hazard Hill. He had married Mary Marriott in 1732 at Calke. His father had a small croft near to the Marriott pottery and he was the administrator for his mother-in-law's goods when she died in 1734. Anthony Hood was a pot maker of Broadstone, in Repton liberty, when he died in 1744. His inventory listed goods to the value of £18 5s.[27] He had married Sara Tetley in 1720 at Repton. She was probably related to the family of Thomas Tetley mentioned above.

Edward and Samuel Long came from Polesworth in Warwickshire twelve miles away, another pot making centre. Edward was born in 1694, the son of Robert Long, a potter there. He was married at Ticknall to Anne Hanson in 1716, but died just two years later in 1718. His administration showed that he had his own site and workhouse.[28] The inventory indicated that he depended mostly on potting for his income. His workhouse contained '55 potting boards and 11 long boards £2, the pot wheels and other tools belonging to the trade £1, clay of all sorts £1 9s 6d, fired pots ready for sale 10s, Book Debts £11 0s 2d'. His interest in farming was slight — two 'melch' cows for milk, a 'stirk' heifer, a horse and a store pig, worth £10 8s 0d out of a total value for the inventory of £38 3s 6d. His cottage was small, with a 'house', parlour and chamber. He had pewter dishes, plates and porringers but still had his trenchers. His furniture included a dresser with shelves, a table, two 'joyn't' chairs and three flag chairs in the 'house', where the fire was. The parlour had four black chairs, two tables and a looking glass. He also had a chest of drawers and a trunk in the chamber where his bed was, as well as a bacon flitch. By the 1750s his nephew Samuel Long had come to work in Ticknall, hired initially by Thomas Potter. Samuel married in Ticknall in 1757 and had at least three children baptised there, but we have been unable to pin down where exactly he was potting. He did not appear on the suit rolls or any of the rentals although he had his own pottery as the Burdett accounts show, for they bought garden pots from him in 1767–71.[29] He was still in Ticknall in 1776 when there was an examination into the place of his settlement.[30] Later the overseers were paying relief to the Long family at Polesworth which suggests that he had moved back when his pottery finished. Another son of Robert Long also had Ticknall connections — Benjamin Long married Mary Banton in 1725 at Ticknall, but it is not known whether he was a potter or worked in Ticknall.

We have not yet been able confidently to assign a site to the remaining potting family — that of Isaac Hill (1712–71) and his descendants. Isaac was the son of John Hill and his wife Margaret of Ticknall. He was stated to be a pot maker on his administration in 1771.[31] He had had a large family of nine children, of whom five survived to adulthood. Isaac was the uncle of Samuel Hill of Hazard Hill. Isaac Hill was succeeded by his son Isaac (1743–1800), who continued the family business. One of the two Isaacs was a party to the agreement to obtain clay from Derby Hills in 1766. Isaac junior was a Baptist and he and his wife Dorothy had the births of five children registered at Melbourne Baptist Chapel between 1764 and 1774. Presumably he worked the same site as his father and he sold 'pots and sawsers' worth £2 3s to the Burdett steward in 1774.[32] In 1781 his apprentice Thomas Cartledge ran away and the local Baptist Minute Book agreed that he should be inquired after.[33] In 1787 the same Minute Books showed that Cartledge had returned, and told them that he had 'sold a quantity of his masters goods, imbezeld the money and absconded. In about six years after returned, being a soldier, when talked with respecting his evil conduct, said he was not to blame, and stood to it'. Thomas Cartledge had joined the Marines in Yorkshire in 1782 and he was discharged by Admiralty Order in 1788.[34] Presumably he was home before that as he met the local Baptist elders in 1787. Isaac Hill junior was mentioned as the tenant of a cottage in 1772 in Ticknall.[35] He was also mentioned as a tenant in Ann Simms' will of 1780.[36] The will of Robert Orme Sheavyn in 1791[37] again mentioned Isaac Hill's premises as bounding some of the property he owned and this suggests that by then Isaac Hill was somewhere along the south side of Main Street, but exactly where has not yet been ascertained. It is possible that at that date he was continuing to work the pottery at site 3. In 1792 the Ticknall parish officers bought a small number of pots from him.[38]

Many of the potting families mentioned in this chapter and the previous one were involved in farming, but just how important was farming to their economy? Most potters had some animals. It is noticeable that the potters who did not seem to have some involvement in farming ended up in debt. Only Henry Blest (probate 1620) and James Blore seem to have had no involvement whatsoever, whilst John Coggreave (1626) just had the pig in the yard and hens. Coggreave and Blest died with more debts than their goods were worth, Blore had to mortgage and finally sell his pot site and rely on parish relief. When things got tight, he had nothing to fall back on.

Most potters had a few animals — a flock of sheep or several cattle. They must also have had a close or access to land where they could graze their animals. Quite a number of potters were more involved, however, and had land to be tilled as well as more animals. This would have provided a cushion against lean times in the pottery industry. The potters who died in the second half of the seventeenth century who were quite involved in both arable and pastoral farming, such as Timothy Beighton (1674), George Hough (1679) and Samuel Potter (1688), had inventories that showed a relatively comfortable standard of living. The next generation who inherited, however, were obviously not doing nearly as well. Joseph Beighton (1720), Joseph Potter (1724) and William Pemberton (1724) all had much poorer inventories, in terms of total value, their farming stock and their household goods. They were not farming on such a large scale. This may reflect farming in general at this time, or it may show that Ticknall's share of the pot trade was declining.

At the top end of the scale were those who were successful farmers. These include

Humphrey Makepeace alias Taylor (1611), Richard Gardener (1614), John Standley (1663), Thomas Tetley (1681), Henry Tetley (1684) and the two Thomas Hansons (1724 and 1729). They not only had more land and livestock, but they also often owned ploughs, harrows and other husbandry tools. Some such as Richard Gardener and John Standley made cheese. Thomas Tetley had a flock of sheep and four spinning wheels to process the wool produced. Humphrey Makepeace alias Taylor also had spinning wheels, wool and yarn in his inventory, as did John Standley who had 3 stone of wool and two wheels. Richard Gardener had 4 stone of wool, a flock of sheep, and also leased land worth £60. His crop of corn was worth over £33. Henry Tetley brewed his own ale or beer, whilst both Thomas Hansons were involved in malting as well as potting and farming. Humphrey Makepeace had one servant and Richard Gardener had two. Profit was put back into stock; their inventories show few luxuries. Although some had large debts owing to them, most were loans to be repaid with interest. A few also bought land elsewhere — Thomas Tetley had freehold land in Hartshorne and Repton, as did the elder Thomas Hanson. The Hansons also held the clay lease from the Harpurs. Others were breeding animals — Henry Tetley had a stallion and a bull calf, and John Standley also had a bull. The value of livestock in proportion to household goods was much greater at this time. The Ticknall potters were typical examples of the dual-occupation economy.

The social standing of the potters is harder to judge. It is difficult to assess how they were seen in the eyes of their fellow villagers and those who ran the local affairs. Mostly their status was referred to in terms of their occupation. Substantial farmers like Richard Gardener (1614), John Standley (1666), Thomas Tetley (1681), the two Thomas Hansons (1724 and 1729), as well as George Hough (1679), John Draper (1721) and John Knifton (1766) were described as yeomen, men who had some freehold land, however little. Others such as John Beighton (1620) and Robert Draper (1742) were described as husbandmen, men who rented their land. However, sometimes the descriptions vary.

Another way of ascertaining status is to look at the appraisers of inventories. These would have been neighbours, reliable and honest men. Several of the potters, like most of the husbandmen and craftsmen in the village, were appraisers once. Just two, John Beighton (1620) and Thomas Tetley (1682), were appraisers four and six times respectively during the seventeenth century. However this is nothing by the side of the dominance of Nicholas and Gilbert Illsley who appraised sixteen and seventeen inventories respectively and who were, with the Hutchinsons, one of the main farming families in the village.

The same sort of men who were appraisers would have often been members of the vestry, which ran parish affairs. Members of the vestry served the parish offices of churchwardens, overseers of the poor and surveyors of the highways. Villagers had also to nominate parish constables. The constable's accounts are the earliest to survive. They run from 1708 and show that Thomas Hanson, Joseph Potter and Jacob Standley were members of the vestry who signed the accounts. Jacob Standley is known to have been churchwarden at least twice, as well as constable. The office of constable had the least status; it was a time-consuming job and the net was spread widely amongst the eligible men. William Pemberton, Josiah Marriott, Joseph Beighton, Joseph Hanson and David Hyde all served their turn as parish constable. They may have held other parish offices but the records are incomplete.

The presence of so many families involved in the pot making trade raises the question as to whether Ticknall was attracting potters from outside or whether all the families were already established in the village. To answer this question a survey of the core names in Ticknall at different periods was taken — the tax list of 1538–47, the 1638 muster, the Hearth Tax and the Free and Voluntary Present, both in the 1660s, as well as other documentary evidence. Although it is not intended to be exhaustive, it shows that the potting families of Turner, Conway, Fisher, Knight, Holland, Hanbury and Beighton were all present by the 1530–40s. By 1638 they had been joined by the Hill, Tetley, Morley, Clare, Madeley,

Hough, Hanson and Cox families, who were amongst thirty-four families whose surnames appeared for the first time. Another twenty-three new surnames appear in the 1660s, amongst them Standley, Marriott, Potter and Hough. Although all of these had appeared in the registers from the late 1620s, it is possible that they were not on the muster list because there was no one of the required age. Families that appeared later include Smallwood, Blore and Pemberton towards the end of the seventeenth century. All the names mentioned so far occur in the immediate vicinity of Ticknall during this period and before. The Longs from Polesworth and Vernon from Chilvers Coton who came in the early eighteenth century are the only potters who can be shown to come from another potting community, although the name Vernon was very common locally. Alone amongst the potting families, the Hyde family first appeared in Calke in 1699 and although there are a few sparse references to the name in the preceding century, there is not enough evidence to ascertain where they came from.

Many of the later potting families were related. The earlier ones probably were, but the evidence no longer exists. The relationship between the families of Potter and Beighton has already been mentioned; they were also related to the Holland, Tetley and Hood families. The Hanson family was connected to a large network including the Hyde, Long and Parker families; they were related to the Marriott family through the marriage of Elizabeth Smallwood and Samuel Marriott in 1702.[39] The Marriott family was also related to the Hough, Pemberton, Blore, Shaw and Morley families. Many of these marriages took place during the period 1680–1730, before Ticknall's population really started to increase rapidly, and when pot making was still an important part of the village economy.

# References

1 TNA: PRO E101/59/7

2 Hart, W. H. (1879), vol. 1, p73

3 TNA: PRO E179/94/407

4 Edward Warden 1611–1615 ROLLR

5 94/58 MH

6 D2375m/82/63 DRO

7 D2375m/53/2 DRO

8 Richard Holland 28 March 1628/9 LJRO

9 D2375m/81/2 and 82/22 DRO

10 D2375m/63/72 DRO

11 Derby Fair Book 1658 DLSL

12 D2375m/82/63 DRO

13 William Holland 9 June 1663 LJRO

14 D2375m/164/12 DRO

15 John Dericke 7 December 1613 LJRO

16 Robert Fisher 3 January 1639 LJRO

17 Francis Madeley February 13 1606/7 LJRO

18 D2375m/25/1 DRO

19 Derby Fair Book 1647 DLSL

20 Henry Blest 31May 1621 LJRO

21 Joseph Morley 14 November 1701 LJRO

22 corrected total

23 Richard Clare 13 March 1639/0 LJRO

24 Derby Fair Book 1649 DLSL

25 D2375m/164/13 DRO

26 Thomas Tetley 10 June 1681 LJRO

27 Anthony Hood 24 April 1744 LJRO

28 Edward Long 14 June 1718 LJRO

29 D5054/13/5/2 DRO

30 D1396 A/PO 434 DRO

31 Isaac Hill 23 December 1771 LJRO

32 D5054/13/3 DRO

33 pers. comm. D. Bell

34 TNA: PRO ADM 158/4 and ADM 158/5

35 D2375m/164/1 DRO

36 Ann Simms 3 April 1782 LJRO

37 Robert Orme Sheavyn 24 April 1792 LJRO

38 Ticknall Overseers of the Poor, Account Book 1762–96, in private hands

39 BIC/6,7 1702 LJRO

The documentary sources and the fieldwalking collections provide most of our information on Ticknall's products. They have been analysed for details on the pots and their date ranges, and the documentary evidence has been compared by county.

In Leicestershire, the inventories list cressets, mugs, jugs, bottles, chafing dishes, porringers, pippin pots, saucers (these were jugs), cans, chamber pots, dripping pans, steans, posset pots, plates, platters, all sizes of dishes and cooking pots, kettles, bowls, basins and salts. Porringers and posset pots are particularly interesting, as they indicate that the potters were not out of touch with fashion. The dates for these items are 1675 and 1677 for the three posset pots, and 1675 for the four porringers mentioned in Leicestershire;[1] another two are listed in 1683 in Warwickshire.[2] They came into fashionable use following the Restoration in 1660, and in better-off households they might be made of silver. The potters made items such as candlesticks, cups or chalices echoing the forms used for silverware. There were painted dishes, plates, platters and a chamber pot (these were slipwares). Butter pots were listed for dairy use, with pancheons, milk bowls and milk pans for setting milk, and cream pots to hold the cream collected for butter and cheese. Butter and cream pots were almost invariably dark bodied and lead glazed.

Outside Leicestershire, the recorded variety of pots was even greater. The inventories list cans, mugs, chamber pots, pudding pots, jugs, frying pans, flower vases, steans, dripping pans, cressets, basins-and-ewers, kettles, porringers, colanders, salts, platters, pitchers, bottles, dublers, dog bowls, chicken feeders, outdoor pots for plants and trees, from small to very large, with saucers to stand them in, flowerpots for the garden, waterplates and covers also for the garden, chimney pots and ridge tiles. They listed all the basic kitchen and dairy ware as well, usually grouped by room. Joseph Hyde's bill, discussed in Chapter 6, named pots he supplied but which were not listed in other sources: venison pots, soup pots and half a dozen 'bird pots', which could be for seed or water for cage birds, or for cooking a bird in.

The Calke Abbey collection has examples of painted platters, candlesticks, egg cups heated by hot water, moneyboxes, and bird feeders for small birds or cage birds, in addition to pots, dishes, cans and tygs. Chimney pots made in Ticknall can still be seen on houses locally and in neighbouring villages. From the deposit in Derby Museum, it is clear that the pottery at site 14 specialised in making Martincamp flasks.

During fieldwalking on the sites where we have found pottery we have systematically collected rims, bases, handles and any decorated body shards made from the variety of local clays[3]. We found only one complete piece. These shards take the production history back further than the written sources. There are shards from costrels and candlesticks in various sizes, plus pots for grease. We found fragments of fine-bodied Cistercian ware cups and other decorated Cistercian wares. There are tygs, cans and tall handled mugs in various sizes. Examples have been found of little female heads as knobs and supports for mugs and chafing dishes, and a very early English figurine in Stuart dress. These items are discussed in Chapter 6, together with the evidence for later, better-quality ware. Ridge and floor tile shards have been found, and bricks from the sites of local brick kilns.

The variety of named types of Ticknall pottery was limited in the sixteenth century but it gradually expanded, as can be seen in Figures 11 to 15. It is infrequent in Leicestershire after 1729. Other areas recorded items until 1739; after this there are only occasional mentions, mainly in local estate records. The date range for mentions of different types of Ticknall pottery from all sources is shown in the following tables, compiled from inventories and estate accounts.

| Type | <1553 | 1580 | 1590 | 1600 | 1610 | 1620 | 1630 | 1640 | 1650 | 1660 | 1670 | 1680 | 1690 | 1700 | 1710 | 1720 | 1730 | ... | 1780 |
|---|---|---|---|---|---|---|---|---|---|---|---|---|---|---|---|---|---|---|---|
| Salt | * | | | | | | * | | * | * | * | | | | | | | | |
| Mug | | | * | * | | | | | * | * | | | * | * | | | | | * |
| Stean | | | | | | * | * | | | * | | | | | | * | | | |
| Can | | * | | * | * | * | * | * | | | * | | | | | | | | |
| Plate | | | | | | * | | | | * | * | * | * | * | * | * | | | |
| Porringer | | | | | | | | | | * | * | | | | | | | | |

Figure 11 – Tablewares <1553–1789

| Type | 1580 | 1590 | 1600 | 1610 | 1620 | 1630 | 1640 | 1650 | 1660 | 1670 | 1680 | 1690 | 1700 | 1710 | 1720 | 1730 |
|---|---|---|---|---|---|---|---|---|---|---|---|---|---|---|---|---|
| Bottle | * | | | | | | | | | * | | | | * | | |
| Frying pan | | * | | | | | | | | | | | | | | |
| Dripping pan | | | | * | * | * | * | | | * | * | | | | | |
| Pan | | | | * | | | | | | | | | * | * | | |
| Kettle | | * | | | | | | | | | | | | | | |
| Bowl/Basin | | | * | * | | * | | | | | | | * | * | | * |
| Dish | | | * | * | * | * | * | * | * | * | * | * | | * | * | |
| Pudding pot | | | | | | | | | * | | | * | | | | |
| Pipkin | | | | | * | | | | | * | * | * | | | | |
| Jug | | | | | | * | | * | * | * | * | | | | | |
| Saucer | | | | | | * | | | * | | | | | | | |
| Dubler | | | | | | * | | | | | | | | | | |
| Pitcher | | | | | | | | | | | | * | | | | |
| Chafing dish | | | * | | * | | | | | | | | | | | |
| Colander | | | | | | * | | | | | | | | | | |

Figure 12 – Kitchen or buttery wares 1580–1739

| Type | 1580 | 1590 | 1600 | 1610 | 1620 | 1630 | 1640 | 1650 | 1660 | 1670 | 1680 | 1690 | 1700 | 1710 | ... | 1780 |
|---|---|---|---|---|---|---|---|---|---|---|---|---|---|---|---|---|
| Pancheon | | * | * | * | * | * | * | * | * | * | * | * | * | | | * |
| Milk pan | | * | * | | * | * | * | * | * | * | * | * | | * | | |
| Milk vessel | | | | | * | * | | | * | | | | | | | |
| Butter pot | | | | * | * | * | * | | | * | * | | | | | |
| Butter dish | | | | | | * | | | | | | | | | | |
| Cream pot | | | | | | | * | | | | | * | | | | * |

Figure 13 – Dairy wares 1580–1789

| Type | 1760 | 1770 | 1780 |
|---|---|---|---|
| Garden Pots | * | * | * |
| Dog Bowls | | * | |
| Chicken Feeders | | * | |
| Building Items | * | * | * |

Figure 14 – Outdoor pots and building materials 1760–1789

| Decade→ Type↓ | 16 00 | 16 10 | 16 20 | 16 30 | 16 40 | 16 50 | 16 60 | 16 70 | 16 80 | 16 90 | 17 00 | 17 10 | 17 20 | 17 30 |
|---|---|---|---|---|---|---|---|---|---|---|---|---|---|---|
| Platter | * | * | * | * | * | | * | * | * | * | * | * | | * |
| Painted dish | | | | * | * | | | | | | | | | |
| Painted plate | | | | | | | | | | * | | | | |
| Painted chamberpot | | | | * | | | | | | | | | | |
| Cressit | * | * | | | | | | | | | | | | |

Figure 15 – Decorative wares 1600–1730

The tables show that the trade concentrated on cheap, useful household, kitchen and dairy ware. Ticknall ware in the dairy is easily the most frequent reference in the probate inventories, though much was listed in kitchens and butteries. The better pieces could be found in the hall, parlour or closet, while chamber pots were usually in the bedrooms. In William Martin's inventory in 1683,[4] the contents of the cellar include a typical reference to Ticknall ware: 'It. One Dish-bench with Ticknall Ware 00-01-06'.

The inventory sources provide a comparison of pottery types over the same period as the evidence for Ticknall and from the same sources. These inventory entries give no information as to where the pottery was made, and all other named types of pottery are discussed later. These are the 'generic' references to wares made in England. They often describe simply 'earthenware', but equally often they give a type description for the pots. Many are the same as the descriptions of the Ticknall pots and a minority extends the range. In addition to the types of pots made in Ticknall there were covered cups, cruses, a pan to marinade fish, water pots or bowls, pitchers, piggins, earthenware trenchers (plates), noggins, galley pots, 'poupotes', mustard pots, spout pots or syllabub spouts or syllabub cups, a voyder (jug), watering pots for the garden, a pasty plate, cheese platters or plates and egg plates. The sugar dish, earthen fruit dishes, tea pots and tea cups, punch bowl and 'crackil' (crackle) dish would all have been better-quality ware, perhaps imported china. There was a 'monteth and bason' too; a monteth was a vessel with a notch in the rim so that a wine glass could be hung in cold water to cool the bowl.

The types of pottery produced in Ticknall and recorded in the inventories were clearly the common everyday wares in use in most ordinary households. They are the kind of wares described generally as 'coarse' wares. In Staffordshire, Weatherill suggests that they were made for local not fashionable markets and for 'country' sale. The local markets 'probably did not extend much beyond the county boundary to the north and west and not as far as the county boundary in the south and east'.[5] This points to an interesting contrast with the market range for Ticknall's comparable coarse wares, also for country sale; the Ticknall products were sold over the whole of the midlands (discussed in detail in Chapter 7). There may be a clue here to suggest that Ticknall had captured a larger country market, but Staffordshire produced better-quality wares for a more fashionable market, as well as country wares, into the eighteenth century.

Ticknall's output reflects the analysis given by Brears for the introduction of new types of domestic ware from the late fifteenth to the early sixteenth century, particularly cups of various forms, influenced by trade with the Continent. The types of pottery Brears describes fit very well with the Ticknall fieldwalking potshard evidence in various fabrics including yellow wares and black wares. The cups, tygs and cans he illustrates all have their Ticknall counterparts.[6]

Ticknall's only ornamental figure, the lady in Stuart dress dating from about 1620, appears some fifty years before there is any evidence of pottery ornaments in the inventories. Though it is very early, the idea of making realistic figures does not seem to have been promoted. There are no inventory references specifically to Ticknall figures. The inventories give an insight into the growing popularity of purely ornamental pottery, and the ability to afford it. In general, it seems that the use of the term 'figures' referred to stone wares or home-produced ornaments, and 'images' to china. 'Toys' was an alternative description for ornaments. The earliest reference is to 'ornaments' in the best parlour of a house in Belgrave, Leicester, in 1675 but with no more details. There are twelve references in other inventories.

Tall butter pots to store butter for transport and sale were a major item. These were made for use in the dairy in huge numbers and were the only type of pottery regulated by law. By tradition, a butter pot should weigh 20lb: 14lb of butter in a pot weighing 6lb, sealed with wax and salted to preserve it. Walter Moseley's inventory recorded an example: 'In the buttery one pott of Butter being 20 pound'.[7] By 1662, however, so many potters and farmers were cheating buyers that a law was passed to regulate the trade. The Act stated the problem and laid down the solution:

*... the Pott of Butter ought to weigh Twenty pounds viz Fourteen pounds of good and Merchantable Butter Neat and the Pott Six pounds And whereas great Complaint hath been made by the Traders in Butter and Cheese That by the fraudulent dealing and practice of several Farmers Owners and Packers of Butter and by theire irregular manner of weighing with Stones Iron Wedges Bricks and other unwarrantable Weights the same quantities of Butter are not put up into the respective Cask and Pots aforesaid ... and the Pots [are] made generally to weigh Seven pounds and some of them Eight pounds or Nine pounds weight ... from and after the first day of June which shall be in the Yeare of our Lord One thousand six hundred sixty and two ... every Pot of Butter do and shall contain fourteen pounds Neat or above besides the weight of the Pott of good and merchantable butter ...*[8]

It must have been easy to make the pot overweight and cheat on the quantity of butter in it; the buyer would not know the truth until the pot was unpacked. The buyer then had the problem of identifying the source of the underweight butter. For the London buyers who came, for example, to Uttoxeter and Ashbourne markets and spent large sums at a time on butter from many sources, it would have been impossible. The Act tried to ensure that the potters could be identified, by fining them 1s if they did not put their initials and the weight of the pot on the base. Farmers were to be fined 2s if they sold butter in unmarked pots.[9] This Act may not have been enforced very well, as it was necessary to pass further acts in the eighteenth century. We have not seen any evidence of marked pots in all the material collected by fieldwalking, though butter pot shards are frequently found. It may simply be that we have not been fortunate enough to find the right shards, though we have found complete bases, all unmarked. Weatherill quotes four cases in Staffordshire where people were accused of selling butter in unmarked pots but we have no evidence of this for Derbyshire.[10] The extensive trade in butter meant that large numbers of butter pots would have been needed. Weatherill's research suggests that butter pots made in Burslem were sold in a 15- to 20-mile radius, with Uttoxeter as the chief market; it was Ticknall's chief market too. Both places supplied local farmers over a wide area. Derbyshire may have sent approaching 2,000 tons of cheese and butter to London via local markets and the east coast ports, and the Staffordshire Moorlands also supplied Uttoxeter and Ashbourne. Uttoxeter had been established as a major market for butter and cheese since the Middle Ages,[11] and London buyers could spend £1,500 at a time there. Defoe noted the importance of the Trent to the cheese trade from Cheshire, Staffordshire and Warwickshire to York, London and the eastern parts of the country. He stated that about 4,000 tons of Cheshire cheese passed down the Trent each year[12] for York and the county produced about 22,000 tons annually.[13] Ticknall dairy wares were sold in all three counties.

The Leicestershire inventories show the trade in butter pots and other dairy wares continuing throughout the entire series, but most of the references are to unspecified Ticknall ware grouped with other items in dairies. However, between 1606 and 1682 there are inventories which detail the contents of Leicestershire dairies and these are helpful in understanding the trade. There are many references just to Ticknall 'pots', 'vessels' or 'ware', but enough to named types to show how dairies were equipped. Pancheons were the commonest named item, the wide bowls with sloping sides and internal glazing, used for cooling and setting milk. Ezabell Brimingham had 'won kooler of Ticknall mettell' in 1606, which was probably an alternative description for a pancheon.[14] Cans and bowls, butter pots, cream pots and platters were mentioned as being in the dairy. Butter and cheese were stored there, waiting for sale. Other necessary items in dairies were churns, scales and butter weights; cratches for maturing the cheese and shelves for storing pots; wooden pails, loomes, tubs, firkins, kimnells and barrels; cheese fatts and cheese presses, and standard gallon measures. Selected Leicestershire examples are quoted to illustrate the dairies, and similar examples could be quoted from other counties.

William Foxe of Claxton had 'a Chourne & ix Ticknall Cannes' worth 4s in 1616.[15] John Thame's dairy had 'Two potts of salt butter, Twelve Ticknell butter potts, eleaven Panchins three wooden kimnills, Twelve shelves, and two paire of butter scales wth waights and other implements' worth £2 3s 10d in 1635.[16] So he had 28lb of butter packed, and expected to pack another 168lb. Two years later Marie Croft had two churns in her dairy, along with 'seaven milke kimnells, nyne panchens, eleaven creame & butter potts, two old kimnells, six ticknell potts, a cheeseloome, tenn chesefatts, a gallon ...' among other items, worth £2 in total.[17] John Massie was another who must have been making butter for sale, possibly to London as most of the butter that went out by river was packed in firkins or pots: he had '4 panchings 2 ticknall platters 2 barrells a little firkin a Churne 2 butter potts other odd things' worth 6s 8d.[18] The essential nature of Ticknall ware for the farmers is shown in the wording of John Smalley's inventory: 'Item nessesries for darie as tecknall in the buttrie 0-2-0'.[19]

During this period the Hull port books frequently list butter in pots passing through the port. Even though most of it went in firkins or casks, there was still a demand for butter packed in smaller quantities. There is no direct evidence that any of the butter pots in the trade were made in Ticknall though it is likely that Ticknall was the source for the dairying areas along the upper navigable reaches of the Trent. The Stoke-on-Trent area was also making butter pots, probably to supply the upper Trent valley and the numerous dairies around Leek. Examples of entries in the Outwards books give a flavour of the trade.

In 1633–4 eight Hull vessels carried butter in pots to London as part of their cargo. In September 1633 the *John and Roger* carried twenty-three pots and in December the *Elizabeth* carried 300 pots. In January 1634 the *Content* carried 500 pots and the *Gift of God* took sixty. In November the *Antony* carried '200 potts of butter cont[aining] one Tonn xii cwt' and the *Joseph* took another ton of butter in pots. In December the *Truelove* carried 4$\frac{1}{2}$ tons of butter in 210 pots, while two days later the *Andorothie* sailed with '560 potts of butter of 12 tons; Also 820 firkins of butter'. Edward Tocke was the trader who consigned the latter two large cargoes.[20] The butter would have been bought in bulk at markets such as Uttoxeter and others along the Trent; it was a valuable trade. It shows how important the manufacture of butter pots was, particularly as we have no evidence for a return trade in empties. The same traders were shipping large quantities of cheese to London on these vessels.

Butter was still being sent in pots in 1663–4. In January 1664 the *Seaflower* took 194 pots and some firkins to London. In February the *Tallent* sailed with '1 tonn of butter in potts' and in March the *Endeavour* of York took forty-nine pots and ten firkins. In July the *Peregrine* had two pots on board for Newcastle. In November the *Unity* sailed for London with 120 pots.[21] But the use of pots was declining and all butter was sent in firkins by 1666–7.[22]

Ticknall pottery had sufficient recognition to attract comment by contemporary writers, who could safely assume knowledge of the ware, and recognition of the name, among their readers. Philip Kinder's well-known comment on Ticknall pots, made in about 1650, has intrigued many historians of the pottery trade. He wrote, 'Here are your best Fictilias made you; earthern vessels, potts, pancions, at Tycknall, and carried all East England through'.[23] Fictilias are any type of clay pots, and Kinder here seems to be making the sweeping claim that Ticknall's output is better than that of the Stoke-on-Trent area and other established potteries. He must have felt there was a general truth in his statement, though allowing for his local links it should be taken with a pinch of salt. About twenty years later William Wolley in his *History of Derbyshire* also acknowledged the importance of Ticknall pottery in a more factual way and without the claims for superiority: 'It is mostly a sandy clay soil proper for making coarse earthen ware, for which it is famous … [at Calke] Here also is made pots as at Ticknall …'.[24]

The reputation of both Ticknall pottery and the potters' skills had gone much further afield. In 1670 Samuel Newton of Newlands in Alfreton, Derbyshire, sent instructions to his English agent from his plantation in Barbados. One was 'That you send over artificers and tradesmen such as may be fit for our plantation by the first especially Taylers and Smiths and when you are a[t] leasure in Derbyshire goe to Tickner and procure a potter and allow him wages. Pray send over one that is a workman'.[25] We have not been able to identify a Ticknall potter who went to Barbados as yet. It may be that Ticknall pottery had been taken out to the plantation, or sent since its founding; clearly though it would be in Newton's interests to have a potter on site. He obviously needed locally made pottery and was well aware of Ticknall's reputation.

In *The Academy of Armory*, written in 1688, Randle Holme described the coat of arms of 'the *Potters*, or sellers of *Earthen* or *Tickney Ware*' as 'He beareth Gules, a Potter sitting on a Stoole, working at his Wheele, Or; Cap and shift, Argent; Apron, Vert; Breeches and Hose, Azure'.[26] It is clear that he assumes that his readers will equate pottery with Ticknall ware even at this date, when the Stoke-on-Trent area was producing luxury items like the decorated platters, as well as everyday wares. In discussing household goods Holme provided our earliest contemporary list of Ticknall products, all of which appear in the inventory sources.

*Of these kinds of clay or earthen weare called Tickney weare there are diuers kinds as china, counterfet china white dickney [sic] and mugen ware both red and black and yellowe: whereof are made seuerall things usefull for an house service, as potts pitchers pipkins candle sticks platters dishes pudding pans piss pots mugs juggs and drinking cups Bottles & most things made of peuter.*

Holme supplied details on other Ticknall products which appear in the inventories but not in his list. In his descriptions of family coats of arms immediately prior to this list of pots he described a flower pot as 'a jugge with two eares, or a pott double handled … These Kind of double eared bottles are much used to keepe flowers fresh in chambers, and windows, haveing water put into them'. Writing about a chamber pot in another coat of arms he commented, 'But there is nothing never so usefull, but it may be abused, so is this when it is called by such persons a Rogue with one eare, and a pisse pot'.[27] Later he described another coat of arms where 'In the sinister cheife is a drinking Jugg, or a Tickney Jugge: and such an one eare Jugg gules in a field Argent, is borne by Hafner van Suntheim, a Germane family'. The dripping pan which appeared on the Scullion arms was described as oval, made either of earthenware or iron; 'some are guttered at both ends, others at but one: these serve to set under meate, while it is roasting at the fire', but other dripping pans were 'square … with handles'. Possett pots were also called 'wassell cups' or a 'sallibube pott, having 2 handle, with a pipe on the side … this kind of vessel is made either of earth, or mettle, according to the greatnesse and riches of the person'. Watering pots formed part of another coat of arms, described as 'a round bottle' with handles.[28]

John Morton, writing in 1712, compared the output of Potterspury in Northamptonshire unfavourably with that of Ticknall. Having described the local yellow clay he comments, 'Yet notwithstanding its density, the ware made of it is of a brittler and less enduring nature than that of Ticknall in Derbyshire; tho' equal care and skill have been used in the managing [of] it …'. It may be significant that he uses the comparison with Ticknall not the Stoke-on-Trent area; Ticknall rather than Stoke-on-Trent may have been associated in the minds of contemporaries with yellow ware. He noted that both places were sending their wares into Northamptonshire, and selling it cheaper than the local potters could make it, a fact which he ascribed in part to the higher cost of living in Northamptonshire.[29]

Nowadays Ticknall seems an unlikely place for a thriving pottery industry. By the end of Ticknall's productive life in the 1880s its long history as a manufacturing area was recognised by Llewellyn Jewitt as dating from 'as early, at all events, as the reign of Queen Elizabeth; probably much earlier', proved by 'remains which have from time to time been exhumed on the spot'.[30] But its reputation rapidly declined and was forgotten. In 1903 Chaffers described it as 'supposed to have been established as early as the sixteenth century',[31] a rather dismissive comment. Forty years later Honey, keeper of ceramics at the Victoria and Albert Museum, confidently reassigned Ticknall wares to Staffordshire,[32] effectively erasing Ticknall's reputation. Detailed study of the evidence, however, reinstates its significance.

When Kinder was writing, the Stoke-on-Trent area had outpaced Ticknall but it is clear that Ticknall's reputation was still high and its products were widely recognised. The importance of the early Ticknall potteries is reflected in this recognition, as Ticknall's output was known by name across the midlands. Its reputation seems to have been gained initially because of the high-quality decorated wares produced on a few sites in the late 1400s and early 1500s, and from one in particular. They were backed up by large-scale production of cheap domestic wares and pots for use in the dairy by several other potteries. Ticknall did not mass produce decorated wares in the same way that Stoke-on-Trent did by the late 1600s, but it is clear that decorated pieces were produced, probably to order, throughout the industry's life. By the mid-seventeenth century the Ticknall potteries were falling behind those in Staffordshire, yet the pottery continued to be recognised by name in probate inventories, until these ceased to be taken. The range of other named pottery types in probate inventories confirms that appraisers could recognise pottery from different sources.

All the early Ticknall potters produced Cistercian wares such as the three-handled cups called tygs. In 1924 Rackham and Read recognised the closeness in style and manufacture of Ticknall ware and the Cistercian wares of unknown origin they had seen from Kirkstall Abbey in Leeds, Fountains Abbey near Harrogate, and from Cambridge (in the British Museum). Though the Ticknall ware decoration was described as crude and the wares as 'rather insignificant slipwares', they acknowledged that 'they are the nearest in type to what we know of Cistercian shapes, and though they are cruder in design, this is easily explained if we are to regard slipware as a survival carried on with some difficulty after the dissolution of the monasteries'.[33] They noted that two-handled cylindrical mugs were commonly made, and illustrated two examples (their figures 28 and 29) from the Yorkshire Museum in York, both covered with a dark treacle glaze and having applied pads of white clay. Shards of many such examples have been found when fieldwalking the sites in Ticknall.[34]

Like many crafts in the Middle Ages, the potters had a guild organisation to regulate and protect the trade. It covered matters such as apprenticeships and skills training, and a potter had to go through a recognised apprenticeship, become a journeyman and work for a series of master potters to gain experience before finally being recognised as a master potter and a freeman of the Potters' Guild. A fee had to be paid for a child to become an apprentice. The

Elizabethan Statute of Apprentices provided the legal framework for the system. In the early modern period, when the Ticknall and Staffordshire potteries were making their names, the system does still seem to have been in force, even though many of the early potters were not working full-time in the trade, but had other part-time occupations, most notably farming. In this peasant stage of potting, the work was carried on as a family concern and children learned the trade from their parents, possibly by an informal apprenticeship. All the family worked at potting during the periods when the pottery was made. The mention in Pearston's clay lease of 1690 quoted above of 'soe many or all of the potters in and about Ticknall and allsoe Edward Stanley & the potters at heathend that are freemen of the potters trade' is the only suggestion we have that there was any form of guild operating locally and that the potters saw themselves as freemen of the Potters' Guild. They would have trained in a period when the potteries here were thriving and still maintaining a good reputation.

By the early eighteenth century it was less common. In Staffordshire there is evidence that the apprenticeship system continued well into the eighteenth century after specialisation had become common. Indentures specified which skills were to be taught so that the apprentice could graduate to becoming a highly skilled and therefore highly paid worker in a particular aspect such as handling. By then, apprentices were likely to come from higher-status families, with the expectation that they would become master potters. They were a minority, however; most pottery workers were not formally trained like this.[35] There are no Ticknall pottery apprentices on the National Index of Apprentices. In Ticknall, there is a mention of three boys as apprentices. John Standley was still apprenticed to an unnamed potter in 1638 when his father died (discussed in Chapter 3). No record has been found for the apprenticeship of Thomas Smith who was described as Josiah Marriott's apprentice when he was buried in Ticknall in 1734. Thomas Cartlidge was apprenticed to Isaac Hill by 1781 (discussed in Chapter 4).

In general, the Ticknall potting families appear to have trained their own children and run their potteries within the family. William Blore was clearly trained this way — his Melbourne settlement examination in 1774 specifically states that he was never formally apprenticed.

The number of potteries in and around Ticknall grew until 1689 and declined after that. Numbers of potteries can be estimated from documentary sources and fieldwalking, but it is

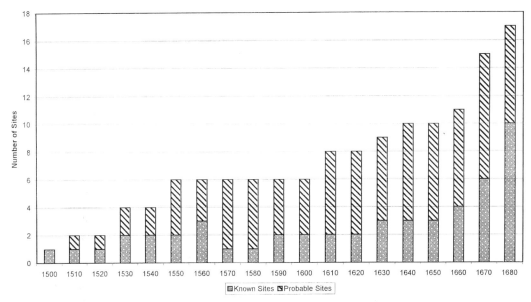

Figure 16 – The rise of the Ticknall potteries 1500–1689

not always possible to be certain of the working dates for a site. We have classified them in Figure 16 as 'definite' or 'probable' sites. Probable sites are those for which we have good reason to think there was one but no documentary proof; they have been counted in the totals.

In north Staffordshire, there were two potteries known at Sneyd Green, Burslem, in the thirteenth century and one at Tunstall in the fourteenth. In the late fifteenth century there is good archaeological evidence for pottery production at site 6 in Ticknall and there were two known sites in Staffordshire, at Penkhull and Burslem. At this date site 6 was producing very high-quality decorated and Cistercian wares, and it seems likely that the long-lasting brand recognition of 'Tickney ware' derived from the reputation of this site. Its wares may have sold better then than the Staffordshire output; certainly it was doing something which gave Ticknall an unusually persistent reputation. Site 7 was probably working after 1520.

Between 1530 and 1559 Ticknall had these two definite sites but there must have been more as seven potters were liable for tax in the 1540s, when sites 1 and 17 may also have been working; site 17 was definitely working in the 1560s. In the 1550s sites 9 and 11 were probably working, and these six sites continued through to the 1590s. During this century there was at least one in Tunstall and two in Burslem. Even if this is an underestimate and the numbers were doubled to six, the two areas were still comparable.

While the two areas started the seventeenth century at a comparable level, north Staffordshire had become more important by 1630. It had three potteries at Penkhull around 1600, one at Tunstall in 1603 and three at Burslem. Two of the latter were the families established in the previous century[36] and the third was Gilbert Wedgwood from 1612.[37] These seven potteries before 1629 were competing with Ticknall's six sites in the 1600s, and eight in both the next two decades. Over the four decades to 1669 Ticknall's numbers were nine, ten, ten and eleven potteries, a slow rate of growth compared to Staffordshire's — Wetherill gives figures of around thirty-eight in the district by 1660 (twenty-eight were in Burslem). Ticknall then had fewer than a third of the number of potteries in Staffordshire. Ticknall acquired a further six sites over the following two decades to a maximum of seventeen by 1689, while Staffordshire's increase accelerated to about forty-eight (thirty-five in Burslem) in the 1670s, forty-two (thirty-two) in the 1680s and thirty-nine (thirty-four) in the 1690s. When Wedgwood drew up his list of potteries in Staffordshire some time between 1710 and 1715, he listed forty-seven potteries and Wetherill suggests that the true figure was probably sixty-seven.[38] Ticknall by then had fifteen, and whatever competitive edge it had had in the early period was comprehensively lost to Staffordshire's innovative, high-quality potters such as the Elers in the late seventeenth century.

Figure 17 shows the numbers of known potters working in Ticknall during the period of growth up to 1689. Comparing numbers of known potters with numbers of known sites is not very informative. We do not always know who was working each site so it is difficult to link them firmly, and we do not know whether we have located every working site. In the 1660s north Staffordshire employed ninety-two men; Ticknall had reached its peak of twenty-seven known men. In the next four decades the figures for north Staffordshire were 150, 200, 268 and 406.[39] This suggests that Ticknall still had typical pre-industrial family concerns, which were no longer competitive.

| Decade | 1520 | 1530 | 1540 | 1550 | 1560 | 1570 | 1580 | 1590 | 1600 | 1610 | 1620 | 1630 | 1640 | 1650 | 1660 | 1670 | 1680 |
|---|---|---|---|---|---|---|---|---|---|---|---|---|---|---|---|---|---|
| Known Potters | 3 | 3 | 7 | 1? | 1? | 1 +1? | 5 +1? | 6 | 5 | 12 | 17 | 19 | 22 | 22 | 27 | 24 | 19 |

Figure 17 – Numbers of known potters working in Ticknall, 1500–1689

# References

1 William Henson 3 August 1675; John Beeby 17 December 1677; Robert Groves 21 November 1675; all ROLLR

2 Isaac Carter 17 October 1683 LJRO

3 The authors would be pleased to make this collection available to researchers

4 William Martin 26 April 1683 LJRO

5 Weatherill, L. (1971), pp76–77

6 Brears, P. C. D. (1971), chapters 1 and 2

7 Walter Moseley 11 March 1632 LJRO

8 13 and 14 Charles II, cap. 26 (1662), quoted in Mountford A. R. and Celoria F. (1968), pp8–9

9 ibid., pp8–9

10 Weatherill, L. (1971), p77

11 Fussell, G. E. (1966), p274

12 Defoe, D. (1983), p11

13 ibid., vol. 2, p209

14 Ezabell Brimingham 26 December 1606 ROLLR

15 William Foxe 7 November 1616 ROLLR

16 John Thame 23 February 1634 ROLLR

17 Marie Croft 5 July 1637 ROLLR

18 John Massie 23 January 1648 ROLLR

19 John Smalley 16 September 1665 ROLLR

20 TNA: PRO E190/317/5

21 TNA: PRO E190/319/13

22 TNA: PRO E190/320/7

23 Kinder P., MSS *History of Derbyshire* (1663) with Notes and Observations by J. J. Briggs FRSL (1870) DLSL

24 Wolley, W. (1712) MSS, DLSL

25 Johnson, R. (1968), p139. We are indebted to Adrian Henstock for this reference

26 Holme, R. (1688) p113 BL

27 ibid., Bk 3, all p2

28 ibid., Bk 3, pp7–9, 246

29 Morton, J., *Natural History of Northamptonshire* (1712), quoted in Brears, P. C. D. (1971), pp41–2

30 Jewitt, L. (1878), p151

31 Chaffers, W. (1903), p791

32 Honey, W. B. (1945), pp23–7

33 Rackham, B. and Read, H. (1924), pp22–3

34 A study of the Ticknall Cistercian wares has been undertaken by A. L. Irving as part of her PhD thesis, and should be published by the Medieval Pottery Research Group as 'The Cistercian Ware Products of Ticknall, South Derbyshire' in 2005

35 Weatherill, L. (1971), pp59–60, 96–97, 103
36 Figures for Staffordshire from VCH reprints: *History of Stoke-on-Trent* p. 202, *History of Tunstall* p99, *History of Burslem* p131–2
37 Smiles, S. (1897), p9
38 Weatherill, L. (1971), p5
39 Weatherill, L. (1983), p41

# 6. Design and Prices for Ticknall Pots

The decoration discussed here relates to the period up to about 1750 for the Ticknall potteries in general, and for the basic domestic and dairy ware potters up to the end of production. The potteries which responded to new developments in Stoke-on-Trent from about 1750 are dealt with separately later.

Large quantities of Midland Purple wares were found on sites 1, 6, 11 and 17. Most of the Ticknall ware shards are undecorated, as would be expected for strictly utilitarian items, and undecorated wares form the vast majority of our finds. Many products were for the kitchen. The potters also made chimney pots, ridge tiles (see Figure 18) and land drains; a good example of the latter is illustrated in Figure 19.

Above: Figure 18 – Ticknall ridge tiles from site 6
Below: Figure 19 – Land drain found near site 11

There is also kiln furniture, mostly very crude, though site 6 has nicely potted kiln props in varying sizes. Some of the tygs and cans were decorated with double bands of the body clay at the foot and close to the top of the vessel, in imitation of the laths which bound wooden cans in earlier times. There is a good, undamaged example of a can in the Calke Abbey collection and an almost complete tyg in the Victoria and Albert Museum collection. We found shards of both on the pot sites. A few of the utilitarian vessels in the Calke Abbey collection have had the names or initials of their intended owners incised in the clay: 'W. Cooke' on a pitcher, 'W O' on a large costrel and 'C. M. B. Ticknall 1843' around the base of a delightful child's money box. The upper part of the money box is decorated with models of animals clustering around a tree — there is a dog, a cow, a chicken, a fox, a cat and what is probably intended to be a goose. During fieldwalking we found identical animal and bird heads on site 11. Where applied decoration is used it takes several forms.

The incised patterns shown in Figure 20 are found mainly on the Midland Yellow or Ticknall white wares. It is clear that the potters made tools for decorating their pots, probably by carving wood to the desired shape. They were found on sites 6, 10, 11 and 24.

There are many examples of feathered patterns, both brown slip feathered on yellow and yellow on brown. Where the shards are from the rim of a pot, piecrust edging is usually associated with this pattern. A complete white ware candlestick in the Calke Abbey collection uses the piecrust edge for decoration round the rim, as bands of decoration, at the foot of the stick and on the corners of the square-section vertical. Feathered patterns (Figure 21) were found on sites 9, 10, 11, 22 and 24.[1]

Slip-trailed patterns are equally common; these were done freehand so the patterns vary more than the feathered ones. An elaborate piece found on site 18 (Figure 22) has a bold squiggle of white slip under the base, making it one of only two pieces with a possible maker's mark of any sort; the other is from site 24 and has a double circle mark impressed on the base of a red shard. Site 11 had a possible foot or handle in the form of a ball-and-claw foot (Figure 23). It cannot have been made before about 1710, when ball-and-claw feet for chairs were introduced.[2]

Figure 20 – Incised wares from site 24

Above: Figure 21 – Feathered patterns from site 24

Below: Figure 22 – Slip-trailed ware from site 18

The Calke Abbey collection has the only certain Ticknall platter or dish with slip-trailed decoration. Two other platters, one in Northampton Central Museum and the other in Manchester City Art Gallery, have good provenance since they were sourced through a respected local collector, John Joseph Briggs of King's Newton, for William Bemrose, the Derby historian, in about 1894. Bemrose's own label, still with it, states that 'This authentic specimen was bought from a retainer on the Earl Ferrers estate near Tickenhall in whose family it had been for several generations'.[3] The Manchester example has the appearance of naive art. Bemrose's label states that it was bought locally 'from an old servant of [J.J. Briggs] in whose family it had been for many years, and had been known to [Briggs] for some years'.[4] The Calke Abbey collection has a reddish candlestick decorated with bands of white slip on the stick and arcs of slip on the base.

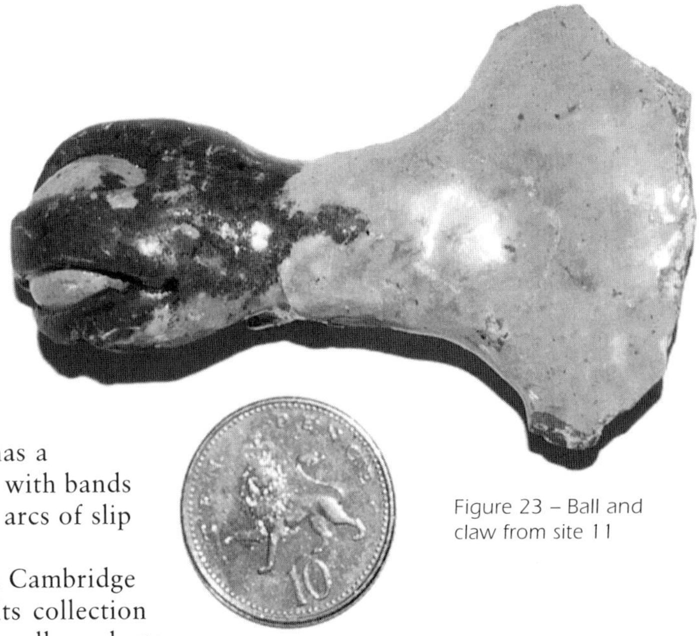

Figure 23 – Ball and claw from site 11

The Fitzwilliam Museum in Cambridge has several large platters in its collection which are believed to be Ticknall products. They came from the Glaisher Collection, were not acquired in the immediate vicinity of Ticknall as Bemrose's pieces were, and there is no firm written provenance. One dish was said to have been bought from a Baslow family called Penistone. We know that Ticknall ware was going to north Derbyshire in that area. The largest item is an impressive posset pot inscribed 'A Present for Thomas Bryan's Wife April 16th 1817'. Glaisher's description of it only states that it was found 'at Burton-upon-Trent, quite near the Ticknall pottery', in use for flowers. There could be other items from Ticknall there but it is impossible to prove. The more basic designs could equally well have been made elsewhere.[5]

Other museums have items which are stylistically similar to Ticknall platters and dishes, but which have no direct provenance. There is a dish with a cockerel and the date 1793 in Leicester Museum.[6] Norwich, York and Ipswich museums may also have Ticknall products, and the British Museum has a piece dated 1643.[7] Slip-trailed patterns were found on sites 6, 10, 11, 18 and 24. Output from site 6 is discussed separately below.

Another common form of decoration is the use of applied pads of white clay on a dark body. The pads are sometimes plain, but more often they have been impressed with a decorative or symbolic device (see Figure 24). There is an IHC stamp from site 1 and two from site 6 (see Figure 25); the letters stand for 'Jhesus Christus' (the letters I and J were interchangeable then, often written with the 'h' in this order). An alternative stamp has IHS, which derives from the first three letters of the Greek spelling of 'Jesus'. Over time, this became associated with the Greek *ichthus*, fish, a common Christian symbol. IHS is often seen on gravestones. This use of IHC should not be confused with the IHC letters stamped on the products of the estate brickyard — they are the initials of John Harpur Crewe, owner of Calke between 1844 and 1886.

White clay was frequently applied in the form of oak leaves.[8] The Potteries Museum at Stoke-on-Trent has a shard with a dark body, white applied leaf decoration, and an applied dot in dark clay on each leaf, which might be intended to be a berry. Its origin is not known, but it bears a strong resemblance to Ticknall products. A similar applied leaf decoration was found in the excavations of the medieval defences of Newark.[9] Applied clay decoration was found on sites 1, 2, 6 and 11; Figure 26 shows an example.

Figure 24 – Applied, stamped pad decorations from sites 6 and 11

Figure 25 – IHC stamps from site 6

Site 6 is by far
the most interesting
in terms of artistic
quality. The archaeo-
logical evidence from
Full Street (Derby) in
1972 and Austin Friars
(Leicester) in 1981[10]
indicate that the site
was working in the last
quarter of the fifteenth
century, and it continued during the

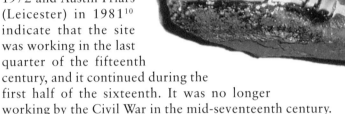

Figure 26 – Applied clay decoration from site 6

first half of the sixteenth. It was no longer
working by the Civil War in the mid-seventeenth century.
The quality of the ware is so good and its decoration so accom-
plished that we are inclined to suggest that Ticknall's name and its persistent 'brand recognition' rested from an early date on the high reputation of this site. At some point, someone
with a fertile visual imagination worked here, and was able to translate ideas into form with
a sophisticated skill which does not seem to be matched anywhere else at the time. From
fingerprint evidence, Irving makes the interesting suggestion that the potter here, or at least
the decorator, may have been a woman.[11] Certainly whoever did the applied decoration
would have needed dexterity and a steady hand for the tiny details.

Some of the decoration from this site has been
discussed above. Yellow ware faceted shards were
possibly made in imitation of silverware (see
Figures 27 and 28), and could have been
used as chalices or for more mundane
household purposes such as a cup
salt. Some had the stem decorated
with a contrasting white frill,
as shown in Figure 29.

Figure 27 – Lids from site 6
including faceted yellow ware

Figure 28 – Bases for cups
or chalices from site 6

Figure 29 – Decorated
stems from site 6

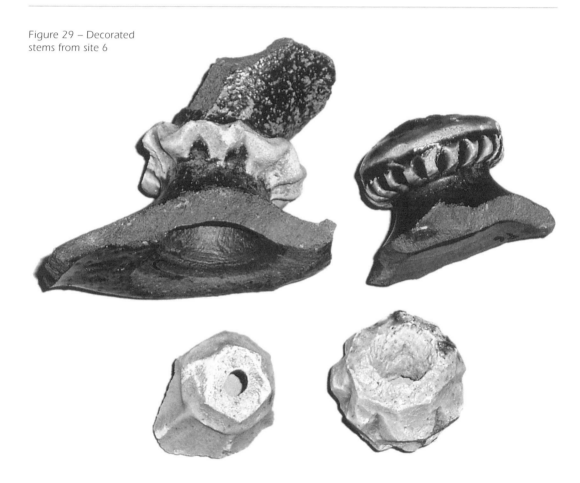

There were no examples of feathered wares, which suggests that the site had gone out of production before this became fashionable in the seventeenth century. Impressed decoration on Midland Purple ware from site 6 is shown in Figure 30. Other impressed decoration from sites 1 and 10 is shown in Figure 31.

Figure 30 – Midland Purple:
decorated rims from site 6

Figure 31 – Impressed
decoration from sites 1 and 10

The shards that match the finds from Austin Friars in Leicester are probably the bases or covers of cups or chalices. They are fired to red or dark brown, decorated with fine strips of white clay and glazed. The decoration is inventive and detailed — the clay has been laid on and then pricked into the body with a fine point at very close intervals. It is meticulous and painstaking work, and we suggest that these designs were based on lace patterns (see Figures 32–4).

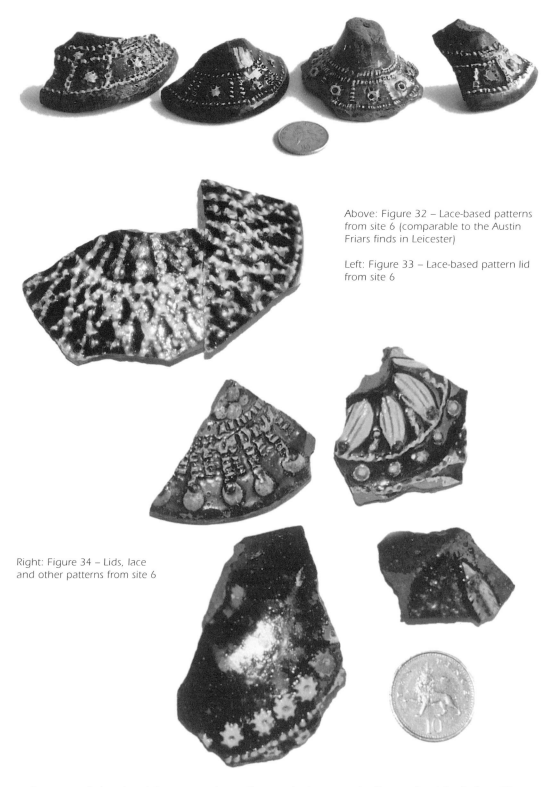

Above: Figure 32 – Lace-based patterns from site 6 (comparable to the Austin Friars finds in Leicester)

Left: Figure 33 – Lace-based pattern lid from site 6

Right: Figure 34 – Lids, lace and other patterns from site 6

A group of the site 6 fragments have flower designs, set in lines of pricked clay (Figures 35–6). One fragment has a crescent on it and another has a feather-like pattern.

Above: Figure 35 – Flower and other designs from site 6

Right: Figure 36 – Impressed plant pattern from site 6

Three small shards (Figure 37) show parts of a pattern of fishes — herring or mackerel type — around a base, possibly a chalice because of the Christian symbolism of the fish, or possibly a heraldic device. An identical example was found in the Newark excavations in 1972.[12]

Figure 37 – Lid, fish design from site 6

Figure 38 – Animal decoration from site 6

While it is easy to postulate a reason for the choice of fish as a decorative motif, there seems to be no reason for the choice of a dog other than the decorator's preference. Three fragments show a realistically observed portrait of a type of lapdog fashionable from the earlier 1500s (Figure 38). The animal is lively, lifelike and accurate, and the modelling is executed with skill. The edges have not split, and the modeller has been able to show detail down to the claws. It is the ancestor of today's King Charles and Cavalier King Charles spaniel; the breed had a longer nose then and the tail was not docked. Both these features can be seen on the shards. This breed was established in Europe before being brought to England, hence contemporary references to them as French or Maltese spaniels (though they do not bear resemblance to the modern breeds of these names). A spaniel is included in a composite painting of Henry VII, Elizabeth of York, Henry VIII and Jane Seymour, sitting on Jane's skirts;[13] the original was painted in 1537. Two dogs are shown in a portrait of Mary I and Philip of Spain from 1554.[14] In an unfinished 1575 portrait sketch of Elizabeth I, one of these dogs is sitting on a pillar beside her; in another finished portrait, she is shown with the dog at her feet.[15] When Mary Queen of Scots returned from France in 1561 after the death of her husband, she brought several dogs with her, including some of this type, and it is likely that this is how they became known as French. One was found hiding under her skirts after her execution in 1587. Harrison, however, called them Maltese spaniels in 1587, describing them as 'the spaniel gentle, or comforter'. He said they were brought from Malta, and were 'little and pretty, proper and fine, and sought out far and near to satisfy the nice delicacy of dainty dames and wanton women's wills, instruments of folly to play and dally withal in trifling away the treasure of time'. He gave a scathing description of women who made a pet of their dogs, condemning them outright for their behaviour; he did not approve of it at all.[16]

Two shards have similar incomplete animal motifs: one is possibly a bull, the hindquarters with obvious masculine attributes and tiny cloven hooves, and the other is perhaps a pig (Figure 38). The quality of the modelling is superb.

Although site 6 made decorated wares in small quantities by comparison with its total output, the quality is outstanding. The site has also produced many shards of finely potted black Cistercian ware bodies. An archaeological assessment of the site might produce more evidence about this significant pottery.

There are four little pottery heads at Calke Abbey collected, along with other items, by Miss Matilda Lovell of Calke Abbey from an unknown Ticknall site, said to be two miles long, during the mid-nineteenth century; most probably site 11. Miss Lovell did not write a report on her finds. Some were given to the Jermyn Street museum, then passed to the Victoria and Albert Museum in 1936 where they are kept in store. She also gave a tyg, a jug and a bottle to the Victoria and Albert in 1901.[17] Most of her collection was bought by her nephew, Sir Vauncey Harpur Crewe, in about 1896 and has remained at Calke Abbey since then, along with other items he bought locally. It is now in the care of the National Trust. Jewitt described finds made 'in the course of draining operations on the site of the old works', and he illustrated the little heads along with other pots.[18] Miss Lovell's finds probably came from the same site. A few others are in the possession of local people, one of which came from the Potworks Farm site.[19] Our fieldwalking has since turned up a further thirty-three examples comprising heads and ruffs from five sites: 1, 9, 11, 17 and 24.

They seem to follow a decorative tradition for heads and faces already established, for example, on Kingston and Coarse Border wares in the Surrey area, which are found from the mid-thirteenth century to the sixteenth. Some can be dated by fashion in a similar way to those from Ticknall when they show the barbette and fillet headdresses worn in the thirteenth and fourteenth centuries.[20]

These little heads have representations of faces which were obviously made without much care for reality (Figures 39–42). They were made in the Ticknall white fabric which turns yellow under a lead glaze, and their eyes were generally added in a brown or red slip. Noses were generally added in the body clay, or they could be indicated simply by impressed holes. The mouth is usually just a short slit — some heads do not have one. They generally have headdresses and collars with details picked out in the same slips. The heads appear to have been made separately from the collars, and some have broken at the join, so that there are examples of heads without collars, and collars without heads, as well as complete heads and collars. Some of them were very crudely modelled. They were made as supports for chafing dishes, or thumbstops for handles on mugs or jugs; the example from site 24 still has part of the mug body and the top of the handle attached.

Figure 39 – Tudor heads from site 11

Figure 40 – Tudor
heads from site 17

Figure 41 – Tudor
ruffs from site 11

Figure 42 – Tudor ruffs from site 17

It became clear as we studied these heads and collars that, however crude they were, they changed in tune with changes in fashions. Ticknall is far from the centre of fashion in London, but local people would be able to keep up with such changes because of the proximity of Ashby Castle, Tutbury Castle and the many gentry houses in the area. When in residence, grand families would bring the latest trends with them. A study of the reserve collection in the National Portrait Gallery enabled us to trace the changes. Although it is not possible to date the heads precisely because of the longevity of some fashions, it is possible to say that they were not made before the date of the fashion they show.

Necklines, collars, ruffs and headdresses provide the information, together with indications of decoration and jewellery. The Medici collar, giving an open V-neck with standing sides, was introduced in the 1530s and remained popular until about the 1560s. The collar was usually lined with a paler colour. It could be worn with a chemise, which had a high neck and a stand-up collar, often embroidered and frilled; this could be worn closed by tying its strings or left looser. From about 1545 to the 1580s a low, square neckline on a tight-fitting bodice was popular. This neckline could be used to display jewellery, or it might be filled with a gathered, high-necked chemise with a standing collar and the frill left open at the throat. After 1560 the chemise frill was generally closed or replaced by a ruff with sides meeting under the chin. The closed cartwheel ruff appeared from about 1570, but it really gained popularity after 1600. The square neck, originally plain, could later have a stiff, flyaway lawn and lace collar rising from the sides. The ruffs or collars could be jewelled, lace-trimmed or embroidered.

A French hood was worn with the Medici collar from about 1530 to 1580, with a specifically English variety worn from 1525 to 1558. The latter has become associated particularly with Mary Tudor (1553–8). It continued in use until about 1630 in less fashionable circles. Both types were worn well back on the head, and fitted closely round it. The original French hood had a stiff, wired foundation and curved to the front to cover the ears. The front border could be decorated with jewels or edged with tightly pleated lace. The crown was raised at the back into a projecting horseshoe shape. This could also be decorated, and it was generally finished with a tail or curtain of pleated or plain fabric which dropped down to the shoulders. The English variety preferred a straight front border with the top of the crown flattened across the head. It was wider at the temples, and turned at a sharper angle to cover the ears. The crown and curtain were as before. The edges and the crown were often decorated with lace or jewels, particularly pearls, and a single large jewel could be positioned in the centre front. The hair was concealed except for that over the temples and in front of the hood. During the later years of Elizabeth's reign, court ladies might wear elaborate jewels in their hair, especially at the centre front, instead of a headdress.[21]

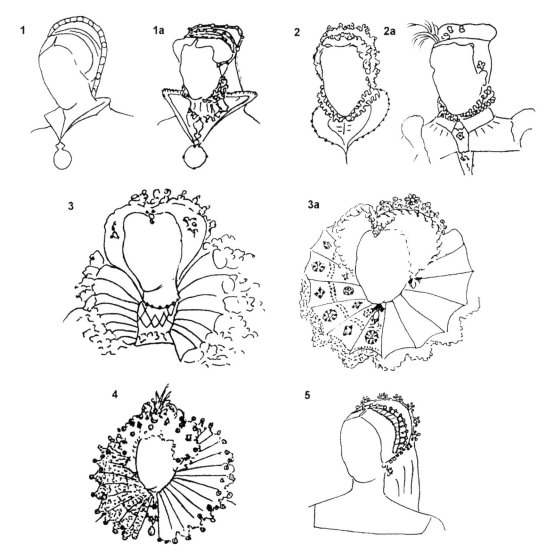

Figure 43 – Changing fashions

One of the collars in the Calke Abbey collection is based on the Medici neckline and appears to be worn without a chemise, as in the portrait formerly thought to be of Catherine Howard, who died in 1542, in the National Portrait Gallery . It was a style also favoured by the young Mary Tudor in the 1540s (Figure 43, 1 and 1a). The majority of the collars are from the next fashion, with a ruffled chemise frill which meets in the middle. The frill gradually expanded, standing out further from the neck, and eventually became the ruff (Figure 43, 2 and 2a). Three National Portrait Gallery  portraits show this type: Eleanor

Benlowes in 1565, an unknown lady in 1567 and a 1569 portrait of a girl aged 21. One of the heads from the Calke Abbey collection, and the one found at site 9, both have this type of wide frill meeting in the centre. One collar shows a decorated ruff, where dark slip is used around the edge of the ruff to indicate a lace trim. This style seems to come in during the late 1580s and persists for ten years or more (Figure 43, 3 and 3a). Portraits of Lady Kennedy and Lady Chandos of 1589 illustrate this type of decoration. One of our collars, and one which was found in 1976 at Napton-on-the-Hill, Warwickshire,[22] both show elaborate jewelled and lace-edged ruffs of the type seen in portraits of Queen Elizabeth I around the 1590s (Figure 43, 4). These two are likely to be from the same source, the placing of the decoration on the collar is so similar. There is some indication that one or two may have been full cartwheels from the 1590s, but damage makes it difficult to be certain.

The heads show classic French hoods though there may be an indication of the English variety. It is difficult to be sure since the modelling is so crude. Most have parallel markings on the head which could be hair drawn back or the tightly pleated lace frill on the front edge of the hood. Where the impressed marks run into the hood, it is likely that they are intended as the lace edge (Figure 45). The National Portrait Gallery reference gives dates in the 1530s and 1540s for this style: Anne Boleyn 1533–6, Mary I in 1544 and an unknown lady of about 1540 (Figure 43, 5). Most of the heads show the projection at the back of the hood which supported the fabric tail or curtain. The site 9 head is a particularly good example. In the Ticknall heads, we interpret the drop of dark slip in the centre front of the headdress as a jewel; two of the Calke Abbey headdresses and five or six of ours have central jewels (Figure 46). A Ticknall head of this type has been found in the dig at Bagot's Park glassmaking site in Staffordshire (SK09622751); it has a dip in the centre front

Figure 44 – Tudor head found at Napton-on-the-Hill (compare with Figure 42)

of the hood for the large jewel there.[23] Assuming that the lines of slip decoration shown on the headdresses are intended to be the supporting hoops for the hood, which were decorated with embroidery or jewels, they would fit the period from 1530 to the 1560s. The example from Napton-on-the-Hill (Figure 44) is a composite of the late jewelled collar, with a French hood which has three large jewels in the crown.

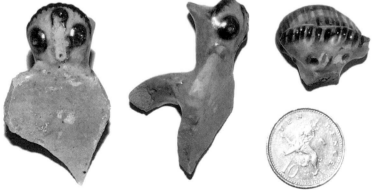

Figure 45 – Front and profile of Tudor head from site 24, and another from site 1

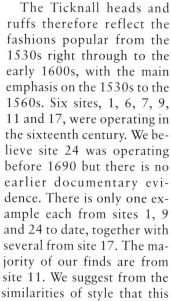

Figure 46 – Profile and top view of Tudor head from site 11

The Ticknall heads and ruffs therefore reflect the fashions popular from the 1530s right through to the early 1600s, with the main emphasis on the 1530s to the 1560s. Six sites, 1, 6, 7, 9, 11 and 17, were operating in the sixteenth century. We believe site 24 was operating before 1690 but there is no earlier documentary evidence. There is only one example each from sites 1, 9 and 24 to date, together with several from site 17. The majority of our finds are from site 11. We suggest from the similarities of style that this is probably the source of the heads in the Calke collection, found when the field drains were laid in the nineteenth century. Some heads may reflect the provincial persistence of the fashion for French hoods. None of the Ticknall heads appears to have come from vessels like that illustrated by Brears in his type-series.[24]

Some of the wares used a pale clay which fired to yellow under a lead glaze, often referred to as 'white' Ticknall in the inventories. In Leicestershire, five white Ticknall references occur between 1674 and 1718.[25] The first is to a 'parcell' of white Ticknall at an inn; next was a 'salt of white Ticknall' in 1678; then there were eleven pieces in a Leicester kitchen in 1679, and unspecified white Ticknall ware in 1706. All these are given group values with other items. Finally there was 'A White Ticknall plate 4d' in a house in Leicester. Elsewhere, white Ticknall is recorded six times, between 1670 and 1718.[26] The first two are to 'some whitt Ticknies' and 'White Ticknalls', while the third is more specific: 'six white Ticknall dishes 2s', again giving a price of 4d each. The other three references are to 'White ticknell ware', 'some White Tickney ware' and 'white ware & other Ticknall pots', all with group values. The close correlation of both sets of dates does suggest that the white Ticknall may not have been produced in quantity much before 1670, though it may simply be under-recorded. It seems more likely, however, that it was a new product, priced accordingly, and appraisers noted the novelty. The friable, flaky quality of the white body suggests that potters did not adapt their firing techniques to this clay very successfully.

References to painted Ticknall ware occur in Leicestershire from 1637 to 1692.[27] This was the type of Continental-influenced slipware that was made in England in Somerset (Nether Stowey and Donyatt), north Devon (Barnstaple and Bideford), Kent (Wrotham) and Essex (Loughton and Harlow) by 1620, and in Staffordshire by the 1640s. Its manufacture had spread to Potterspury in Northamptonshire, Wrenthorpe in West Yorkshire and Buckley in North Wales by the 1650s.[28] The inventory dates for painted Ticknall suggest that this area used the new technique at least as early as the Stoke-on-Trent area. The Leicestershire painted Ticknall ware descriptions are '5 Ticknell painted dishes' and '7 pent$^d$ dishes ... a pent$^d$ chamber pott' both in 1637, ten 'peeces of painted Ticknall dishes' (1649), and four 'Ticknall painted plaites' in 1691. They were all given group values which prevents the estimation of individual values, though it is worth noting that the ten painted dishes from

1649 were listed with other high-value and high-status goods including a Venice glass and a looking glass. We have not yet found any references to painted plates in other counties, though Margery Clowes's 'two faire Tickne dishes' which she left to her sister-in-law in her will in 1642 could have been slipwares.[29] Robert Adey of Rugeley had 'Two Ticknall dishes' in the 'house' in 1695, suggesting they were on display and may also have been slipwares.[30]

Ticknall platters were made for show as much as for use. They were larger pieces, listed in Leicestershire between 1606 and 1711.[31] They tend to be found in the better rooms of the houses. Platters in other counties are mentioned between 1616 and 1736.[32] Non-Leicestershire references to platters correlate closely to the dates for Leicestershire. Like the slipwares, they were probably one-off pieces made to order. Most references give the number of platters involved, but where the reference is just to 'platters', they have been counted as '2+', on the grounds that there must have been two, but may have been more (Figure 47).

| Decade | 1600 | 1610 | 1620 | 1630 | 1640 | 1660 | 1670 | 1680 | 1690 | 1700 | 1710 | 1730 |
|---|---|---|---|---|---|---|---|---|---|---|---|---|
| **Leics** | 1 | - | 7, 2+ | 25, 4+ | 8 | 7 | 15 | 2 | 1 | 1 | 3, 2+ | - |
| **Non-Leics** | - | 2 | - | 4, 2+ | - | 4 | 2, 4+ | 2 | 4+ | 2+ | - | 2, 2+ |

Figure 47 – Ticknall platters

In both areas, the peak decades for platters were the 1630s and the 1670s. References to them tail off more sharply in Leicestershire than in other counties, though the pattern suggests that Ticknall production may have been at its best during the mid-seventeenth century.

There is some evidence for prices of Ticknall platters. Inventory entries occasionally refer to Ticknall ware without grouping it with other items, so it is possible to estimate prices. Richard Burrow, for example, had 'Two tickne platters valued at 0-0-3d' in 1673. There are problems, however — it may not be accurate to divide the value given by the number of pottery items in the entry, as there were variations in size, quality and age which all affected the value given. Nevertheless, such a method is the only one available to us to estimate the price. Using this method, we obtained a value of 2d for a platter in 1635 and 1675, two valuations of 1½d each in 1673, and values of 1d and ¾d each in 1633.

The way that so many inventories group Ticknall ware with other items in the dairies makes it difficult to value the pottery, as illustrated by William Foxe of Claxton who had 'a Chourne & ix Ticknall Cannes' worth 4s in 1616. The cans seem to be worth 2d each, leaving at least 2s 6d for the churn. Some inventory entries do list only dairy items however. Thomas Venables of Loughborough died in 1625, and his inventory listed '7 butter pottes 7 Ticknall panchens' at 3s.[33] Between 1614 and 1682, Leicestershire pancheons varied in price between ½d and 2d each, giving a maximum value of 1s 2d here.

Joseph Hyde supplied Sir Henry Harpur with pots, and his bill of 1805–6 survives (Figure 48). These prices are for new ware, whereas inventory prices are for second-hand ware and depend on the appraisers' accuracy. It included six 'Milk Pans' with two porringers at 1s 8d, 'one Large Pan' at 1s 4d, and '3 Large Pans' with six pots for birdseed at 4s 6d. The individual prices seem to be 3d each for the milk pans and 1d each for the porringers, 1s 4d for the large pans or pancheons, and 1d each for the birdseed pots. There were also 'Nine Pots for Fowls 3s' in the dairy bill, at 4d each; these were the chicken feeders made in the form of dishes in concentric rings so that the seed was not wasted. It has not been possible to estimate individual prices for butter pots for most of the period, but Hyde's bill included '3 Large Butter Pots' at 2s, giving a price of 8d each. Venables' inventory and another from Youlgrave do suggest that the butter pots were more expensive items. Richard Bird had '1

**S$^r$ Henry Harpur Bart to Joseph Hyde**

|  |  | £ | s | d |
|---|---|---|---|---|
| 1805 | Pots for the House | | | |
| Jany 25th | a Dozn & half Porrigers & a Bason | 0 | 2 | 0 |
| Feby 6th | half Dozn. Veninson Pots Do. Pans | 0 | 3 | 0 |
| | to a strike of Peas | 0 | 10 | 0 |
| Ap 19 | 3 Large dishes & a gug | 0 | 2 | 11 |
| May 14th | to Dozn of Poringers half Dozn veninson | 0 | 2 | 6 |
| Novr 18th | to half a Dozn. Chimney Pipes 2 Mug Pots | 1 | 1 | 8 |
| 20th | half Dozn. Pans to 14 veninson Pots | 0 | 3 | 9 |
| | to Eight Mug Pots & a Bason | 0 | 2 | 3 |
| Decr. 10th | 1 Dozn. & half of Pots for supe | 0 | 1 | 6 |
| | gug & Chamber Pot | 0 | 0 | 6 |
| 23th | to half a Dozn Chimney Pipes | 1 | 1 | 0 |
| 31st | 2 Large Pans 4 Dishes | 0 | 2 | 6 |
| | | | | |
| | Dairey House | | | |
| Feby. 11th | to half Doz Milk Pans 2 Poringers | 0 | 1 | 8 |
| | one Large Pan | 0 | 1 | 4 |
| Apr. 11th | Nine Pots for Fowls | 0 | 3 | 0 |
| May 16th | 3 Large Pans half Dozn Bird Pots | 0 | 4 | 6 |
| Augst 22th | 2 Chamber Pots & 2 gugs | 0 | 1 | 2 |
| Novr 18th | 3 Large Butter Pots | 0 | 2 | 0 |
| | | | | |
| | Stables & Kenels | | | |
| Feb 19th | half a Dozn. Pots for Dogs | 0 | 3 | 0 |
| | 4      Do.   Do. | 0 | 1 | 0 |
| July 16th | 2 Chamber Pots & a gug | 0 | 1 | 0 |
| Augst 22th | 7 Pots for Fowls 4 Chamber Pots | 0 | 2 | 10 |
| Decr. 10th | half a Dozn. Pots for Dogs | 0 | 1 | 0 |
| | | 4 | 16 | 1 |

pd. April 15 1806

Figure 48 – Joseph Hyde's bill for pots 1806[34]

steyne 3 butter potts with other lytle tickna pottes' worth 14s 6d';[35] this is a high value for Ticknall ware though we do not know how many pots were included in the last phrase. Richard Gamble's dairy only contained the pottery: '3 milke boles 6 panchins wth other Ticknell ware' worth 6s 8d.[36] Assuming the pancheons were worth 1s at 2d each, that leaves 5s 8d for the three milk bowls and what must have been quite a large quantity of Ticknall ware. Even allowing 2d each for the milk bowls as it is impossible to guess their size, the money would buy another thirty-one pots at 2d each. This might not be excessive — Margery Knyveton had twenty 'peeces of ticknall ware, potts and panpottes' in her dairy.[37] A more informative set of values is George Mather's 'seaven Ticknall pots towe panssions and foure mylke boules' worth 2s.[38] On known values this could give 7d or 8d for the pots and 2d or 3d each for the pancheons and bowls. In 1639 Thomas Sadler had six milk pans and four butter pots worth 1s 6d in his inventory, suggesting values of either 2d for the pancheons and 1$^1$/$_2$d for the butter pots,[39] or 1d and 3d. John Dakin's four milk pans and one cream pot were valued at 1s in 1681.[40] In the next year John Marples had seven Ticknall pancheons valued at 2s 4d, which works out at 4d each.[41] They may have been new or large ones, as this value is double the Leicestershire value for a pancheon. Sarah Middleton's '3 ticknall milkpans' were only worth 3d in 1698.[42]

The account books kept by the Burdett family at Foremark Hall covering the period from 1757 to 1789 have regular entries of purchases of Ticknall pottery for the house and the garden. They paid 1s 2d for '6 milch panchans & creampott' in 1783,[43] suggesting 2d for each item. The house had recently been built and the 1757 entry relating to pots seems to be for quality ware for the house, probably from Staffordshire and bought through a Derby dealer. It reads, 'Pd Mr Haslam for Earthen Ware £4 5s 0d'; Haslam was not a Ticknall shopkeeper. This would buy very large quantities of Ticknall ware.

The garden was fashionably laid out with a terrace, lake, views and a kitchen garden with hothouses where exotic fruits were grown. Two purchases of '5 doz of sasors [saucers] & for 1 flower pots' and '2 doz of large sasors for flowr pots' were made on 18 August and 4 September 1764; each cost 3s. Individual prices could be $^{1}/_{2}$d each for the small saucers and 6d for the flower pot, and $1^{1}/_{2}$d each for the large saucers. On 8 November 1765 2s was paid 'for the caridg of the pots and sasors from ticknel'; this was clearly another similar purchase. Carriage was expensive at a third of the value of the goods. Between 1767 and 1771 Sam Long, a Ticknall potter, made large pots for the hothouses. Three purchases were for 'pots for the pins' ('pins' were pineapples), and they cost 12s 6d (22 October 1767), £2 2s $1^{1}/_{2}$d (21 September 1769) and £1 7s 6d (16 September 1771). None of these entries specified numbers or sizes of pots. But Sam Long supplied '6 pots for saving trees 12s' on 23 April 1768, giving a price of 2s each. On 6 October 1769 he was paid 7s for a dozen and a half pots, so they cost about $4^{1}/_{2}$d each.

Isaac Hill, another Ticknall potter, was supplying Foremark by 1774. That year, he was paid £2 3s on 23 February 'for pots and sawsers', and 10s on 14 March for '6 dozen of Eardes pots' (eared pots had two lugs for lifting them up) at about $1^{1}/_{2}$d each again. Joseph Hyde, whose bill to Calke Abbey has been discussed, was paid 14s on 6 October 1781 for 'pots for the garden'. On 20 August 1785 an unknown potter supplied '2 doz of saucers for flower potts' at 2s 6d or $1^{1}/_{4}$d each. '2 doz of small garden pots' cost 2s, or 1d each, on 27 March 1786. More 'Garden Potts' cost £1 16s 8d on 10 April 1787, and James Onions from Hartshorne was paid for them; he must have delivered them as he was not a potter. On 7 March 1788 Joseph Hyde was paid £1 9s 3d for yet more 'Garden Pots', and both these orders must have been for large numbers of pots. On 5 June a 'Water plate and Covers and flowr pot pans' were delivered by John Wayte for 16s 6d; Wayte was not a potter. The Burdetts bought '3 doz of Garden potts & a mug pot' on April 23$^{rd}$ 1789 for 3s 1d, suggesting that each item cost 1d.

The outdoor offices at Foremark were also served by Ticknall potters. On 14 March 1778 '2 hand bowls for the use of the Kennell' were bought for 2s. At 1s each, these were more expensive, and presumably larger, than the 'Pots for Dogs' supplied by Joseph Hyde to Calke Abbey. Elizabeth Wane brought 'six pots for the use of chickins' on 14 August 1778 and was paid 4d for them; at perhaps $^{1}/_{2}$d and 1d each they were much cheaper than Hyde's for Calke. The pots bought for the diary have been discussed above, but the 'pot to put Walnuts in' at 6d may have been for pickling walnuts which would probably have been done in the outside offices.

Building work was still going on in 1788. On 11 January '4 chimney potts at 18d' were bought for 6s, and another six at the same price on 21 February for 9s. Joseph Hyde was paid £1 16s for 'chimney pipes' on 21 October 1788. This would buy eighteen chimney pots at 2s each. In his bill for Calke, Hyde charged 3s 6d for 'Chimney Pipes' and he may have used the term 'pipes' for the larger items. John Cope, who ran a lime yard and the brick works in Ticknall, supplied '6 Ridg tiles' for £1 on 27 December 1788.[44]

Staunton Harold house and park were being developed at much the same time, and local potters supplied them too. George Richards made pots for the garden there in 1771–3.[45]

| Value | <6d | 7d-11d | 1s-1/6 | 1/7-2s | 2/1-2/6 | 2/7-2/11 | 3s | 3/1-3/6 | 4s-4/6 | 5s | 6s-6/8 | 8s | 10s | 12s | 15s | 16s | £1 |
|---|---|---|---|---|---|---|---|---|---|---|---|---|---|---|---|---|---|
| Leics | 9 | 30 | 51 | 13 | 18 | 1 | 3 | 6 | 3 | 3 | 1 | 1 | 1 | 0 | 0 | 1 | 0 |
| Non-Leics | 21 | 3 | 53 | 17 | 7 | 0 | 0 | 8 | 2 | 5 | 4 | 0 | 1 | 1 | 1 | 0 | 2 |
| Total Refs | 30 | 33 | 104 | 30 | 25 | 1 | 3 | 14 | 5 | 8 | 5 | 1 | 2 | 1 | 1 | 1 | 2 |

Figure 49 – Frequency of values for Ticknall pots 1585–1741

The values of Ticknall ware in the inventories (other than values already analysed) have been totalled to give an understanding of the likely amount to be found in a household, and the number of times each value occurs is shown in Figure 49. This shows a concentration around the lower values, raising questions about the higher value households. The Ticknall ware forms a very small proportion of the inventory total.

In the Leicestershire series, there are ninety-two references to Ticknall products described variously as 'ware', 'pots', 'vessels', 'stuff' or 'brass'. They do not give details of the items valued. These references are not grouped with other items so the values only apply to the Ticknall pottery in the household. The earliest is from 1585 and the last from 1711. Six inventories have Ticknall ware worth up to 6d, three from before 1600 and three from after 1660. This corresponds with the periods of growth and decline in the industry. The commonest value for Ticknall ware over the entire inventory series is between 1s and 1s 6d. Three values of 3s 1d to 3s 6d were in the period of growth (1607, 1633 and 1635) and one in Ticknall's decline (1699). Six inventories valued at more than 3s 6d indicated Ticknall ware in larger quantities, four (1597, 1626, 1631 and 1634) during the industry's growth period, and two (1658 and 1667) as it began to decline. These figures demonstrate Ticknall's hold on its markets, even into the period of decline. One household had Ticknall ware worth the exceptional sum of 16s in 1612; one had 8s worth in 1631; another had pots worth 10s, again an exceptional sum, in 1634. It is clear that the most valuable, and the most frequent, Leicestershire listings were all made in the period of Ticknall's greatest prosperity. A further forty-four of the Leicestershire inventories specified the types of Ticknall pots in entries which only listed Ticknall ware and the figures are included in Figure 51 (p.112).

Outside Leicestershire there were 137 of these unspecified, Ticknall-only references between 1605 and 1741, and the details are shown in Figure 49. The lowest value was 2d with two early references (1630 and 1633) and three late (1684, 1694 and 1741). The 1633 reference implied that there were several pots: 'Other tittnell ware there 2d'.[46] The pancheons and pots had been valued as the previous item. The commonest value again was 1s to 1s 6d, with fifty-three references between 1629 and 1699. Most of these were 1s. Most of the values of 1s 7d to 2s between 1625 and 1732 were for 2s. It is noticeable that the non-Leicestershire references cover a longer period than the Leicestershire references, with more in the high-value categories. The 5s values were all late, between 1664 and 1725. The 6s values occurred in 1628, 1648 and 1727, and there was one for 6s 8d in 1680. In 1721 there was a value of 10s; in 1615, 12s. One inventory had pots worth 15s in 1699 and two had pots worth £1 in 1626 and 1665. Both areas record their first value of 4s in the 1630s. Leicestershire had one early value of 5s (1626) in the industry's growth period, whereas elsewhere they started in 1664. The 1628 value of 6s is non-Leicestershire but it was 1680 before this area had a value of 6s 8d. Leicestershire had that in 1597, plus 8s in 1631 and 10s in 1634. 10s did not appear in the non-Leicestershire area until 1721, though it had had 12s in 1615, close to the date of 1612 in Leicestershire for a value of 16s.

In the account books relating to Wollaton Hall, Nottingham, was an entry which gave the value of Ticknall ware and the cost of taking it from Ticknall to Wollaton:[47]

*Dec 1573 To John Bennet that he paid for Tycknall potes*        ij$^s$ iij$^d$
*And for the carridge of the same pottes*        xj$^d$

It is the only reference we have which gives the cost of carrying pots at this date; it seems expensive in proportion to the value of the pots.

| Occupation | Number in in Leics | Year From | Year To | Number not in Leics | Year From | Year To |
|---|---|---|---|---|---|---|
| Gentleman | 4 | 1633 | 1663 | 4* | 1633 | 1683 |
| Clerk | 2 | 1635 | 1681 | – | – | – |
| Mercer | 1 | 1687 | – | – | – | – |
| Fellmonger | 1 | 1627 | – | – | – | – |
| Tanner | – | – | – | 2 | 1637 | 1684 |
| Carrier | 1 | 1667 | – | 1 | 1639 | – |
| Chapman | – | – | – | 1 | 1676 | – |
| Farmer | – | – | – | 1 | 1645 | – |
| Yeoman | 20 | 1606 | 1690 | 25 | 1615 | 1730 |
| Husbandman | 13 | 1623 | 1690 | 21 | 1612 | 1725 |
| Labourer | 7 | 1612 | 1711 | 3 | 1617 | 1669 |
| Shepherd | 3 | 1658 | 1682 | – | – | – |
| Miller | 2 | 1666 | 1673 | – | – | – |
| Blacksmith | 1 | 1635 | – | 3 | 1630 | 1677 |
| Coppersmith | – | – | – | 1 | 1665 | – |
| Scuttle maker | – | – | – | 1 | 1639 | – |
| Sawyer | – | – | – | 1 | 1688 | – |
| Carpenter | 2 | 1632 | 1635 | – | – | – |
| Joiner | – | – | – | 2 | 1633 | 1638 |
| Wheelwright | – | – | – | 1 | 1638 | – |
| Mat maker | 1 | 1663 | – | – | – | – |
| Weaver | 4 | 1626 | 1661 | 2 | 1636 | 1637 |
| Spinster | 2 | 1663 | 1683 | 2 | 1661 | – |
| Tailor | 3 | 1634 | 1678 | 1 | 1631 | – |
| Shoe maker | 2 | 1667 | 1691 | 2 | 1677 | 1681 |
| Glover | – | – | – | 1 | 1635 | – |
| Tow dresser | – | – | – | 1 | 1683 | – |
| Baker | 1 | 1635 | – | – | – | – |
| Butcher | – | – | – | 3 | 1637 | 1638 |
| Milk seller | – | – | – | 1 | 1741 | – |
| Brewer | 1 | 1667 | – | – | – | – |
| Inn or tavern keeper | – | – | – | 2* | 1625 | 1627 |
| Lead miner | – | – | – | 3 | 1681 | 1694 |
| Collier | – | – | – | 1 | 1684 | – |

* Includes one widow

Figure 50 – Occupations of sample owners of Ticknall ware

Analysis of the occupations of the deceased for this set of 136 Leicestershire inventories shows that Ticknall ware was bought by a wide social range (Figure 50). Fifty-four inventories did not record occupation, and it is not possible to obtain an occupation for most widows, so the unknowns among the men, and the eleven widows, have been ignored. In one case, information has been added from other sources. The most frequent purchasers of Ticknall ware were yeomen, husbandmen and labourers — the medium and small farmers and the labourers who might keep a cow to supplement their income. This reflects the importance of Ticknall's products for the dairy and buttery as well as for basic kitchen use.

The occupations of the non-Leicestershire owners were not given for thirty-nine out of the 137 inventories. There were eight widows where the family occupation was not given, and two whose occupations have been counted in with others in the same occupation. Ninety individuals can be placed socially, in twenty-six different occupations, a much wider range than for Leicestershire. As before, the most frequent purchasers were yeomen and husbandmen, but the wide range of craftsmen reminds us of how self-sufficient most people had to be in the past. Some of the owners may have combined farming with a specialist skill, as the Derbyshire lead miners did.

When Ticknall built its workhouse under the Old Poor Law, the pots required were bought from the local potters. Ten of the named bills — the majority — were paid to Joseph Hyde between 1 May 1784 and 25 May 1793. One was paid to Isaac Hill (April 1792). Seven do not specify the potter. The first undated purchase in 1784 was for 'half a dozen dish pots 3d', or $^1$/$_2$d each. On 20 May 1784 the overseers bought 'more pots and a jug 6d'; these are the only two references which do not simply say 'pots' with no further detail. Four purchases ranged from 3d to 6d; one was for 10d; three were for 1s. Five were between 1s 5d and 1s 11d. There was one at 2s 1d and another at 2s 8d. The remaining three were for higher values, 4s, 5s 2d and 5s 6d, which would have bought considerable quantities of pots.[48]

The surveyors of the highways bought broken pots from the dumps to spread on the roads in the eighteenth century. For example, in October 1790 they spent 6s when they 'p[ai]d Isaac Hill for 18 loads of pot bits at 4d'.[49] When Severn Trent Water were renewing the pipes in 1995 a layer of crushed pot shards could still be seen about 9in below the current road levels, and it was widely used in field gateways throughout the parish.

The inventories list a great variety of pots made in Ticknall, but they are mostly grouped with other items and it is not possible to estimate values. However, they do show the range of goods produced in the area. From the Leicestershire inventories which specified the types of pottery it has been possible to estimate comparative values (Figure 51, p112).

While the non-Leicestershire inventories duplicate some detail, they do add more information, though in each of these instances the pottery is described only as ware, pots, brass, stuff, vessels or parcels. In 1624, four 'peeces of Tycknell brasse iiii$^d$' were worth 1d each. In 1633, 1635 and 1639, six pieces of Ticknall cost 1s, or 2d each. Another inventory in 1639 listed four pots for 1s so they would have been 3d each. In 1661 there were a dozen pieces of Ticknall for 2s, again giving an individual price of 2d. Thirteen pieces occurred in 1630, at 2s 2d, or 2d each.[50] In 1681 a dozen pots were valued at 1s 6d or 1$^1$/$_2$d each.[51] Three of this set suggest that pots were sold at thirteen for the price of twelve — a 'baker's dozen'. Wetherill states that the 'potter's dozen varied according to the size of the piece', which supports the suggestion.[52] In 1617 'thirteen pieces of ticknellware' were valued at 3s.[53] At twelve to the dozen, they would have cost 3d each; at thirteen, the cost would be an impossible fraction. Another thirteen pots were listed at 1s 6d in 1636; for twelve this would give prices of 1$^1$/$_2$d each but thirteen would present problems.[54] In 1681 an entry had thirteen pots at 2s, suggesting 2d each for twelve.[55] Some purchasers bought in bulk direct from the potters — when John Hall delivered '18 Ticknall bottles' to Melbourne Hall in 1670, they cost 1s 1$^1$/$_2$d, or $^3$/$_4$d each.[56]

| Date | Pancheon | Pot | Platter | Jug | Can | Mug | Dripping pan | Chafing dish | Bowl or dish | Possett pot | Chamber pot | Stean | Plate | Ware |
|---|---|---|---|---|---|---|---|---|---|---|---|---|---|---|
| 1597 | | | | | | | | | | | | | | 2d |
| 1614 | 1d & 2d | 2d & 4d | | | | | | | | | | | | |
| 1612 | | | | | | | | | | | | | | 1s 4d |
| 1616 | 2d | | | | | | | | | | | | | |
| 1620 | 2d | 6d | | | | | | | | | | | | |
| 1621 | | | | | 2d | | 2d | | | | | | | |
| 1623 | 2d | 5½d | | | 2d | | | | | | | | | |
| 1626 | 2d | 2d | | | | | | | | | | | | |
| 1629 | ½d or ¾d | | | | | | | 2d or 3d | | | | | | |
| 1632 | 1d & 2d | 1½d | | | | | | | | | | | | |
| 1633 | | | ¾d & 1d | | | 1d | | | | | | | | |
| 1635 | 1d | 1d | 2d | | 2d | | | | | | | | | |
| 1637 | 2d | 2d & 4d | | 2d | | | | | | | | | | |
| 1641 | 2d | 1s | | | | | | | 2d | | | | | |
| 1663 | | 1s | | | | | | | | | | | | |
| 1667 | | | | | | | | | 2d & 1d | | | | | |
| 1670 | 2d | 1d | | | | | | | | | | | | |
| 1673 | 2d | | 1½d | 1¾d | | | | | | | | | | |
| 1675 | | 1d | 2d | | | | | | | 1½d | | | | |
| 1682 | 1d | 1d | | 1d | | 1d | | | | | | 2d | 1d | |
| 1684 | | | | | | 1d | | | | | | | | |
| 1691 | | | | | | | | | | | | | 2d | |

Figure 51 – Estimated values for Ticknall ware in Leicestershire

Shopkeepers had Ticknall in larger quantities, like Mrs Gover who had '8 Dozen of Ticknall pottes at 3d', worth 2s. This was 3d per dozen, so they were small pots which sold at ¼d each.[57] It is not possible to estimate individual prices for the 175 pieces of Ticknall valued at 10s 6d in a shop stock in 1736; they must have been in mixed sizes[58] and it suggests that 10s bought about 170 pots. Taking this as a likely approximation gives some interesting insights into the larger sums for the Ticknall ware found in probate inventories. The numbers of pots that could be bought for a larger sum are estimated in Figure 52.

| Value | £1 | 15s | 12s | 10s | 6s 8d | 6s | 5s | 4s | 2s | 1s |
|---|---|---|---|---|---|---|---|---|---|---|
| Quantity | 340 | 255 | 204 | 170 | 117 | 102 | 85 | 68 | 96 | 17 |

Figure 52 – Estimated minimum quantity of pots for given values

As 1s is the commonest value listed, it suggests that there could be quite large numbers of Ticknall pots in the dairies and butteries, and that the named items costing 2d, 3d or more each were notable because of their relative expense. The values over 4s are the most interesting since they suggest that the owners either had very large households, were trading the pots or were keeping an inn. Below that value, it is likely that the pots were for normal household and dairy use. William Knight of Oakley, Staffordshire, had Ticknall ware worth 5s and also had three mares, a two-year-old colt, a saddle and a packalant. He was described as a yeoman but this strongly suggests that he was selling pots using packhorses.[59] Local hawkers of Ticknall pots, and their stock, are discussed later.

Only five of the Ticknall potters' inventories itemised pots with a value. John Standley died in 1667 and in his inventory all the tools of his trade were listed in the 'potting house', with 'pots fired & unfired', all together worth £5 14s 6d. This suggests that he was making pots for the next firing before he had sold all the pots from the last one, but it does not allow an estimate of the numbers of pots.[60] Henry Tetley's inventory was taken in 1684, and when he died he left 'Raw potts' worth £1 in his workhouse, at least 370 unfired pots.[61] Samuel Potter's inventory is especially helpful as it gives the value of a kiln full of fired pots: 'Potts that was mad & unsould an ovenfull £3'.[62] This would be at least 1,020 pots and could be more if smaller pots were fired inside larger ones. Elnor Gover's prices would suggest 2,800. In Edward Long's workhouse there were all the tools of the trade, clay 'of all sorts', and 'fired pots ready for sale 10s', suggesting at least 170 pots.[63] The last of the group, Richard Cox, had the tools and 'Potts burnt & unburnt 5s', probably about eighty-five pots.[64] These figures can only be rough estimates as they would depend on the size of the pots.

J. C. Wedgwood, the pottery historian, stated that as late as 1710–15 the output of a Staffordshire potter never exceeded £6 per week, and the average output of the forty potteries then working was £3 10s per week. His estimate for the output of all forty in one week was only £139 10s. The potter made 10s per week profit plus 6s for his work as the master potter. Wedgwood stated that there were never more than six employees at a pottery, mainly family members.[65] Comparing these figures with Samuel Potter's ovenfull suggests that Ticknall potters were producing at much the same rate and for much the same price as those at Stoke-on-Trent.

Hyde's bill gives some late individual prices and is directly comparable with Wedgwood's figures on date. The basins and porringers work out at 1½d and 1¼d respectively. The first and second sets of venison pots were 2½d each, but those in the third set of fourteen were probably 1½d each. The six pans supplied in February 1805 cost 3½d each; those supplied in November were 4d each. It is more difficult to estimate the price of the two large pans supplied in December — they were less than the single one priced at 1s 4d, perhaps 1s. This would leave 1½d each for the dishes. The six pans in November seemed to be 4d each. The three large dishes in February appeared to be 11d each and the jug 2d. The six chimney pots in December gave a firm price of 3s 6d each. Applying the same price to the November order left 4d each for the mugs. They must have been larger or better-quality mugs than those ordered later in the month, which seem to have cost 1½d each with the basin at 1s 3d. The eighteen soup dishes cost 1d each. The jug and chamber pot supplied with them probably cost 2d and 4d respectively. Two jugs were supplied with two chamber pots in August, and the prices seemed to be 8d each for the chamber pots and 3d each for the jugs. The two chamber pots bought in July 1806 seemed to have cost 4d each, with a jug also at 4d. If the four chamber pots bought in August 1806 were also 4d, the seven 'Pots for Fowls' may have ranged between 4d and 2d each. The first set of dog bowls were 6d each, the second set were 3d each and the last set were 2d.[66]

The prices for Ticknall ware given in the shop lists, workhouse purchases, bills for the grand houses and the values of kiln contents probably give the best idea of retail prices. It must be remembered that the inventories record second-hand values.

There is evidence from shards of mottled ware and unglazed creamware found on four sites that there was a very belated attempt in the later eighteenth century to catch up with the smart new products of the Stoke-on-Trent district. Wetherill notes that salt glaze, tor-toiseshell, mottled and creamware all utilised ball clay from Devon,[67] so at least some Ticknall potters had access to it. The evidence is entirely based on fieldwalking finds at kiln sites, and there is no documentary evidence to support it — by the time it was being made, the inventory system only summarised testators' possessions. These finds show that some Ticknall potters were aware of new developments and tried to keep up with new fashions, if only for a short time.

At site 11, brown mottled ware was found in the dump. There was no creamware — the other shards were from ordinary white, red and black wares. Two white salt-glazed fragments were found. One is part of a jug lip; the other is part of the rim of an octagonal plate with a milled edge. There is one fragment of creamware from a plate, but not from the rim. These might be dismissed as domestic ware bought from Stoke-on-Trent and discarded when broken, except for the fact that there is also a shard of unglazed body which could have been intended for either salt or lead glazing. Shards of marbled ware, with red and yellow clay rolled together, were found. A shard of brown salt-glazed ware found here has impressed patterns typical of Nottingham and this one is likely to be a domestic discard at this date. The body is too grey for the Ticknall clays. This site finished in the 1750s and we believe the last potters here were the Hansons.

Site 24, which is one of the most important sites in the Ticknall production area in terms of material found there, is near Calke Mill; both are on the Melbourne side of the boundary. They are unfortunately now under Staunton Harold reservoir. Site 24 should not to be confused with site 25, at Furnace Farm, Melbourne (see Figure 5, p.00).

It is ironic that the two sites which probably produced creamware, 24 and 25, both occupied opposite ends of the valley which was flooded, thus precluding further archaeological investigation. Shards from the pottery dump at site 24 were used to grade the sides of Staunton Harold reservoir and can often be found when the reservoir is low. The evidence discussed here came from the dry summers of 1994 and 1995. There were plenty of the usual Ticknall products in black, yellow and red wares, and some greenish shards too. Good examples of feathered wares were found, all suggesting production in the seventeenth and early eighteenth centuries. Without doubt, the most interesting early example found here was the little figurine, unfortunately without her head, of a woman in the fashions of about 1625. Her dress has an embroidered skirt with a girdle and a deep V-neckline. She wears a wide neckerchief called a whisk with a deep, falling lace trim and her cuffs are of lace. She carries a muff under her right arm. The figure is clearly ornamental and was not intended to be used, for example, as a salt cellar. It is an early, representative figure (Figure 53).

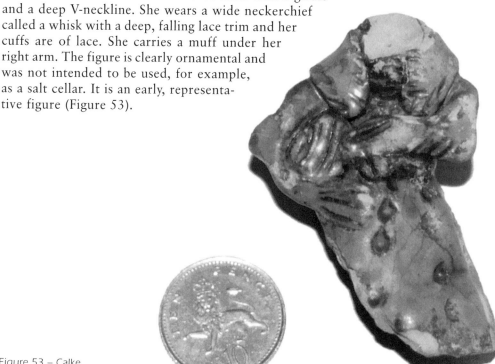

Figure 53 – Calke figurine from site 24

Significant numbers of white salt-glazed fragments were found, and some of these had extremely fine bodies and cleanly turned feet underneath the base. Some had incised lines round the pots. There were several good examples of the dot-diaper-and-basket pattern, and a larger number of the barley pattern. There were a few bead-and-reel pieces. One piece combined barley and basket. Two different patterns were a diamond-leaf-and-dot rim, and a repeating pattern of wavy lines of varying prominence parallel to the edge. A few fragments of a much coarser salt-glazed ware in a bluish-grey colour used a different type of clay and may have been domestic discards. Sites 24 and 11 were the only ones in the Ticknall complex which might have produced white salt glaze.

Site 24 turned up samples of creamware including a broken unglazed creamware knob from a sugar bowl and five unglazed, plain fragments from plates. A conical unglazed knob from a teapot had a steam hole, and is similar to one described among the site 25 finds.[68] There was one shard of unglazed plate rim, which appears to be a variant on the royal pattern, with four lines of fluting emphasising the shape. There are similar examples from the disputed Melbourne creamware pottery (site 25) at Derby Museum and at the Victoria and Albert Museum. The glazed fragments included a twisted handle and a broken knop. There were plates with several designs. The popular feather-edge design had eight barbs on the feathers like those from Melbourne, and there was an unglazed example. Barley pattern, dot-diaper-and-basket pattern, and bead-and-reel pattern were all well-known patterns represented on the plate rims. In addition, there was the royal pattern with fluting which Towner called a reeded border. There was one fragment of the loop-moulded edge called cock's-tail by Towner in his account of the Melbourne finds, which he dates to around and after 1785.[69] One pattern however was different from the popular Staffordshire patterns or the Melbourne ones. It was a shape like the bead-and-reel plate but with a fine line of beading inside the rim accentuated by tiny fleurs-de-lys, with a leaf between them. Another fragment has the fleurs-de-lys but not the line of beading (Figure 54). Several dozen shards from creamware pieces without patterning were found, showing fine, well-potted work (Figure 55).

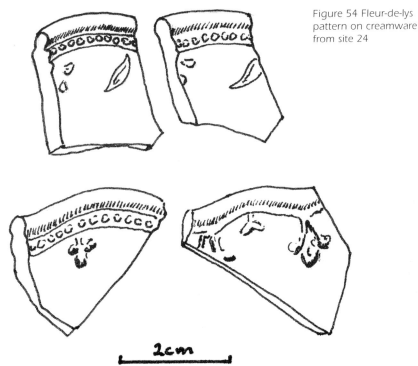

Figure 54 Fleur-de-lys pattern on creamware from site 24

2cm

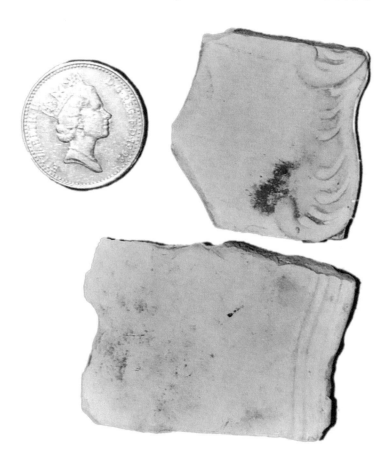

Figure 55 Unglazed
creamware from site 24

Fine pieces of tortoiseshell ware turned up. Three appear to be tea bowls with delicate foot rims. The smallest is only ³/₄in outside diameter to the foot rim, the next about 1¹/₄in and the third would have been about 2¹/₄in. The other three are body pieces. Mottled wares were also made on site 24.

There were examples of brown salt glaze with banded or overall decoration as at Melbourne, and mottled ware body shards. The latter appears to be made from local clay but the brown salt-glaze ware is not — it is too grey.

The shard evidence suggests that this site was operating originally to make the usual Ticknall products, and may have done so for many years. Then in the 1770s and 1780s the potter here may have begun to branch out into more fashionable wares, even though white salt glaze was going out of fashion by then. It is of course possible that all the shards found from the dump here were domestic discards, but the presence of unglazed samples very strongly suggests that white salt glaze and creamware were both produced here for a short time. The tortoiseshell wares may or may not have been made here but the skills were available.

The ex-Melbourne furnace site (25) appears to be the only one producing brown salt-glazed wares in the Ticknall area. While the finds of 'true wasters in the shape of vessels collapsed in the kiln'⁷⁰ indicate that Melbourne was making brown salt glaze and it was not imported Nottingham or Chesterfield wares for domestic use, we have not found any wasters at Calke Mill (24) to date because of the difficulties of getting access to the site.

John Cox had been the potter at site 24. He was buried on 9 August 1762 and it seems likely that by the time he died Thomas Hyde was working at the pottery, as discussed in Chapter 3. From the shard evidence the pottery continued, with Thomas Hyde attempting to break into Staffordshire's markets. Towner's date of 1780–5 for the cock's-tail design suggests that the site was working at least until then.

Brown mottled ware shards were found at site 20, where the Tetley family had been potting since at least 1670; their kiln is shown on the 1735 map of the Huntingdon estates.[71] We do not know when the Tetleys started to make this new pottery, or how long they continued to make it. No creamware or salt-glazed ware has been found on this site so far.

Another Calke site was producing brown mottled ware but not creamware in buildings rented by George Vernon from the Calke Estate (site 22). Vernon was not a potter himself. He was a carpenter and joiner, and we have no evidence for whether he was sub-letting the building himself, or whether it was an arrangement with the landlord. David Hyde was potting there until 1787 when Vernon died. All the shard evidence points to the late eighteenth century. The buildings were pulled down soon after Vernon's death as part of the estate's policy of taking land in hand in the fifty years from 1761. This made several farms redundant and seven Calke farmhouses were demolished. Vernon's land was re-let, with the barn and orchard; neither survived long.[72]

This is the same George Vernon who, with George Roberts, a Derby plasterer, was behind the Furnace Farm pottery at Melbourne (25). We do not wish to join the debate over attribution of pottery to this site — the arguments for this can be followed in Towner's work.[73] Instead we offer a little more evidence and some fresh interpretations, based on the extensive research for the Ticknall potteries. R. B. Brown succinctly outlined the history of the site, which had been leased to the Lloyds as an iron furnace, noting that Vernon and Roberts took over the lease for it on Lady Day 1774.[74] It was no longer a furnace, and could not have been a pottery before that date. Two years later came the famous advertisement: 'Wanted, A Journeyman Potter (at Melbourne Derbyshire) that can throw and turn Cream-colour'd ware. A sober man may have constant Employ and Good Wages'.[75] All the literature on Melbourne notes the difficulty of accepting it as a pottery (never mind as a creamware site) because of lack of documentary evidence of anyone working there. It may be that no documentary evidence survives because the potters were employed on verbal agreements. It is worth noting that we have no written contracts for any potters at any site in Ticknall.

We suggest that Vernon and Roberts acted as entrepreneurs to set up the pottery and then employed some Ticknall potters to work there, in the same way that Vernon had a potter working in the outbuildings at his home in Calke. Further, we strongly suggest that the Melbourne pottery should be viewed in the context of the Ticknall industry rather than in relation to the Derby works. Ticknall and Calke are much closer than Derby; site 24 is only three-quarters of a mile away. The area had 300 years of experience behind it. It could supply skilled potters well known to Vernon and there is the evidence discussed above that other potteries in Ticknall and Calke may have been trying to make pottery of better quality than the usual coarse wares. In this context, Melbourne should not be seen simply as 'a small country pottery'[76] with no resources of tradition, skill or technical competence to support it, though we would not argue that it was 'one of the most important eighteenth century creamware factories in this country'.[77] After the creamware was abandoned, the site provides evidence that the ware made there was consistent with the general Ticknall products, such as the pancheons, chamber pots and brown and yellow flecked wares in the possession of Ann Lardeur.[78] Barrett described the finds as 'grey and red lead-glazed earthenware such as was produced by many a country pottery'.[79] He also noted that brown salt-glazed stoneware was made at Melbourne, like that produced in Nottingham and north Derbyshire.

However, some evidence does survive, which may provide proof that there was indeed a pottery at Melbourne. The settlement examination of William Blore was taken on 4 November 1774, some six months after Vernon and Roberts took over the Melbourne lease.

Blore was described as a 'labourer', but that is somewhat misleading. The examination records that he was

> born at Ticknall, place of settlement of father, bred a potter under his father at Ticknall, never bound apprentice, nor hired for a year in any service, hired by the week to work at a pot kiln att Melbourne for about 7 weeks, married a poure [poor] woman in Melbourne whose mother possessed a cottage in Melbourne and with whom they lived, said mother left him with his wife in possession of said cottage.[80]

The wording of the examination implies that this pottery is the ex-furnace site, close to the village of Melbourne, not that near to Calke Mill. William had been employed there for about seven weeks prior to this examination. This suggests that he probably continued to work at the pottery. He had married Mary Dimock at Melbourne in 1773. They had two children baptised at Melbourne in 1774 and 1776. Blore would have worked as part of a team of six — his employer, presumably the master potter, and five other men including himself as the labourer. The contracts to get clay on Derby Hills which were made between a group of Ticknall potters and the Melbourne Estate during the 1760s indicate that this was the usual way of working: '... if any person employs more than Five Workmen in the Pot work, which are called a Set ...' they were to pay more clay rent.[81]

The dates here suggest that the advertisement may have been placed when Blore took his family back to Ticknall; perhaps other potters left around the same time. It may be that by then Vernon and Roberts really were trying to poach a creamware potter from Derby. The Cockpit Hill works did not close until 1779. The thin deposit of creamware at Melbourne could be the result of a very limited production run of less than four years, followed by a longer life for the coarseware pottery.

Jewitt did not mention a pottery at Melbourne, but he did write at some length about Ticknall. If the Melbourne pottery was seen as part of the Ticknall complex when he was writing, this may account for his silence. Similarly, if the output of Melbourne was seen as 'Ticknall' locally, as the potteries in Calke parish were, it could perhaps account for the lack of purchases of creamware by name. We do have evidence of purchases of Ticknall ware for Calke Abbey, Foremark Hall and Melbourne Hall at different dates, though, if any were purchases of creamware, it does seem surprising that it was not described in some way that reflected its quality. Brown stated that Mr Bailey 'did not find a pottery; he found shards of unglazed creamware, and a few glazed pieces, and also brown glazed earthenware, but not one single whole piece was found'.[82] We do not accept this as conclusive evidence against the pottery. We have only found one small whole piece, a little square salt cellar, on any of the twenty or more sites we have investigated during fifteen years of research. Brown also notes that there is no mention in any of the 'traditional sources' of the Melbourne pottery, and again we would draw a comparison with Ticknall. Here, the last pottery at Potworks Farm is often referred to as 'the Ticknall pottery' as if there had only been one.[83] Given the evidence we present here about the scope of Ticknall's market distribution, the number of working sites and potters, and the long spans of production dates, it is even more surprising that so little about Ticknall pottery appears in the same traditional sources. The fact that the Melbourne site was unknown until 1957 would account for the absence of recognised Melbourne pottery in major collections prior to that date.

Given that some key creamware plate patterns at the site near Calke Mill are identical to those of Melbourne, we wonder whether some of the moulds, and perhaps some of the equipment like lathes, may have been sold to the pottery near Calke Mill. Clearly, from the archaeological evidence, many of the Melbourne moulds were thrown on the tip, but some may have survived to go elsewhere. It is possible that Thomas Hyde, having acquired the skill to make creamware and tortoiseshell wares, bought some of them. Creamware manufacture required skills in throwing, turning, making handles and spouts and firing the kilns, and there would also be some general labouring required. There must have been a team of potters at both sites.

# References

1 Usher, H. (1989), p20

2 Reeves, D. (1947), pp153–4

3 Northampton Central Museum, Manfield Collection, Item No.1920 Fdl-40

4 Manchester City Art Gallery, Greg Collection, Item No. 41

5 Fitzwilliam Museum, Cambridge, Glaisher Collection, items 48, 49, 50, 51

6 Leicester Museum, ref. 46.1870

7 Hyde, J. (1974)

8 pers. comm. D. Barker

9 Alvey, R. C. (1974), p45

10 Coppack, G. (1975), pp44–76; Woodland, R. (1981), pp81–125

11 Irving, A. L. (forthcoming)

12 Alvey, R. C. (1974), p45

13 Plumb, J. H. and Weldon, H. (1977), pp48, 62. The portrait is by Remigius van Leemput

14 Cavalier King Charles Spaniel Club website

15 Strong, R. (1987), pp86, 114. The sketch is by Federico Zuccaro and we are grateful to Mrs Lesley Smith of Tutbury Castle for this reference. The portrait is attributed to Marcus Gheeraerts the Elder

16 Edelen, G. (1994), p342

17 Usher, H. (1989), p2

18 Jewitt, L. (1878), pp151–3

19 In private hands

20 Pearce, J. and Vince, A. (1988), pp40–2, 61, 131, 164

21 Cunnington, C. W. and Cunnington, P. (1954); Cunnington, P. (1964); Nesfield Cookson, Mrs (1934); Wilcox, R. T. (1958)

22 In the possession of the Ticknall Preservation and Historical Society

23 Information from Dr C. Welch, Staffordshire County Council Development Services, site reference 'Pottery BP98 Site 11'

24 Brears, P. C. D. (1971), pp20, 23

25 Eleanor Lander 6 November 1674; Thomas Goddard 25 May 1678; Elizabeth Biddulph 22 March 1679; Samuell Bailey 12 August 1706; Benjamin Burstall 26 November 1718; all ROLLR.

26 John Cooper the elder 25 January 1669/70; Elizabeth Harding 15 March 1670/71; Thomas Beckett, 10 March 1676/77; all from Cockroft, J. (1999); Dorothy Bates 19 May 1680 LJRO; William Pratchett 16 September 1685, Cockroft op. cit; Samuel Hews day and month unknown 1718, pers. comm.

27 William Yard 11 October 1636; William Burslem 24 April 1637; Edward Wades 25 November 1649; Esther Watson 23 February 1691; all ROLLR

28 Barker, D. (1993), pp11–12

29 Margery Clowes 18 October 1642, in Cockroft, J. (1999)

30 Robert Adey probate 1703/4 LJRO

31 Thomas Watts the eldest n.d. 1606; John Dalby 31 January 1621; John Coop 29 January 1627; Richard Hopkin 5 April 1628; John Winsor 11 January 1629; Ann Pynder 3 December 1633; Ralfe Bowman 7 October 1635; William Scotten 2 April 1636; William Burrows 30 May 1637; Peeter Bunney 4 January 1638; Humphrey Atterton 20 February 1643; John Massie 23 January 1649; Margarett Breay 30 October 1660; Thomas Manby 21 December 1668; William Roberts 8 September 1669; Elizabeth Oswyn 31 October 1671; John Tue 16 September 1673; Richard Burrow 27 June 1673; William Henson 3 August 1675; John Alderman 26 January 1675; Thomas Field 10 July 1675; Robert Groves 21 November 1675; Walter Oxford 5 December 1675; Thomas Palmer 11 March 1687; Richard Bray 24 October 1699; Thomas Boasworth 17 June 1709; Nathaniel Callice 13 March 1710; Thomas Roberts junior 15 May 1711; all ROLLR

32 William Johnson 3 December 1616; Thomas Smithe 22 July 1633; both LJRO; unknown widow n.d., 1634, pers. comm.; Ann Stafford 25 October 1636 LJRO; Ann Trubshaw 24 July 1665, pers. comm.; Ric Chamberlane 5 June 1671; John French 6 March 1679; Samuel Stanley 20 January 1680; Robert Reeve 24 September 1680; Daniel Hammant 20 August 1680; all LJRO; Burdett Accounts, December 1697 and 17 January 1699, D5054/13/5/1 DRO; Edward Wallis n.d., 1700, pers. comm.; Phoebe Pimm n.d., 1716, pers. comm.; Thomas Bailey n.d., 1734, pers. comm.; John Doncaster n.d., 1736, pers. comm.

33 Thomas Venables 29 June 1625 ROLLR

34 D2375m/119/3 No. 67 DRO

35 Richard Bird 6 April 1637 LJRO

36 Richard Gamble 14 January 1639 ROLLR

37 Margery Knyveton 19 April 1624 LJRO

38 George Mather 22 August 1632 LJRO

39 Thomas Sadler 27 June 1639 LJRO

40 John Dakin 18 October 1681 LJRO

41 John Marples 30 August 1682 LJRO

42 Sarah Middleton 29 September 1698 LJRO

43 D5054/13/5/2 DRO

44 ibid.

45 25D53/2226 ROLLR

46 William Larke 23 September 1633 LJRO

47 HMC, *Report on the Manuscripts of Lord Middleton* (1911), p440

48 Ticknall Overseers of the Poor Accounts, 1784–93, in private hands

49 D1396A/PS 1/1 DRO

50 Felicia Ward 27 July 1630 LJRO

51 John Byssell 27 May 1630; William Milburne 6 December 1633; Francis Ellton 20 November 1635; John Morris 2 April 1639; Maurice Abellis 17 September 1639; Ralph Turner 18 November 1661; all LJRO

52 Wetherill, L. M. (1983), p18

53 Unkown inventory, Bedworth, n.d., 1617, pers. comm.

54 William Roe 27 September 1636 LJRO

55 John North 27 February 1681 LJRO

56 Account Books 23 December 1670 MH

57 Mrs Elnor Gover 26 September 1634 LJRO

58 Admon. 1736/121 LA

59 William Knight 15 November 1680 LJRO

60 John Standlye 20 January 1667 LJRO

61 Henry Tetley 23 September 1684 ROLLR

62 Samuel Potter 24 April 1688 LJRO

63 Edward Long 14 June 1718 LJRO

64 Richard Cox 14 November 1732 LJRO

65 Thomas, J. (1971), pp5–6

66 D2375m/119/3 No. 67 DRO

67 Wetherill, L. (1971), p14

68 Barrett, F. (1961), pp150–1, Plate 147 (6)

69 Towner, D. (1978), p106; Towner, D., 'The Melbourne Pottery', paper read at the Victoria and Albert Museum, 17 January 1970, pp20–1

70 Barrett, F. (1961), p151

71 DG 30/Ma/9/4 ROLLR

72 Manpower Services Commission (1988), pp43, 52

73 Towner, D. (1978), pp105–18

74 Brown, R. B. (1978–9), pp96–7

75 Derby Mercury, 1 March 1776, p4 column 2 DLSL

76 Thorpe, A. (1961), p148

77 Lockett, T. (1985), p76

78 pers. comm. A. Lardeur

79 Barrett, F. (1961), p149

80 D655 A/PO389 DRO

81 52/8/9 MH

82 Brown, R. B. (1978–9), p96

83 See for example Thorpe, A. (1961), p147

# 7. Ticknall's Markets

Kinder stated that Ticknall's markets were confined to the eastern side of England but he did not suggest how far north or south the markets reached. In our research we have looked for evidence of where the pottery went, so that the market area could be quantified.

Some groups of probate inventories are statistically valid in that all the extant inventories for the area or period have been searched. Other groups have only been sampled, or drawn from material sent by family or local historians who have noted Ticknall ware during the course of their research. Published volumes of inventories have been used as well. The coverage of the midland counties is far from complete. As mentioned in the introduction, we have read every inventory in Leicestershire, all those for the 1630s and for 1680–4 in the Lichfield diocese, and all the Cheshire inventories for 1631.

On the documentary evidence, the Ticknall potteries were working from the 1530s to the 1880s (Figure 56). Archaeological evidence shows that the actual start date must be earlier, however.

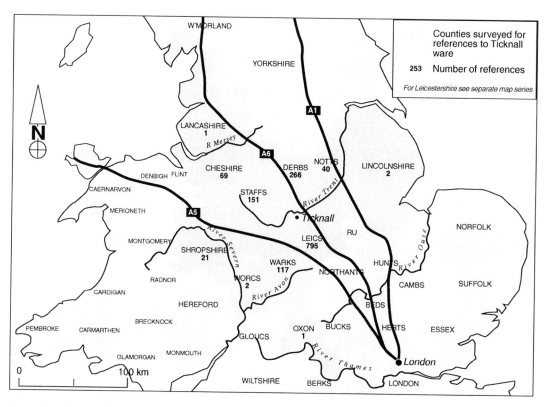

Figure 56 – Known distribution of Ticknall ware 1537–1809

The results of the research were mapped to show the overall number of references per county.[1] The map shows that Kinder was only partly correct in his description of the Ticknall pottery trade. The wares were distributed across the whole of the midlands, not just the east, and reached into Lancashire in the north and Oxfordshire in the south (Figure 57). The poor evidence from Northamptonshire may be explained by the limited survival of the county's early inventories.

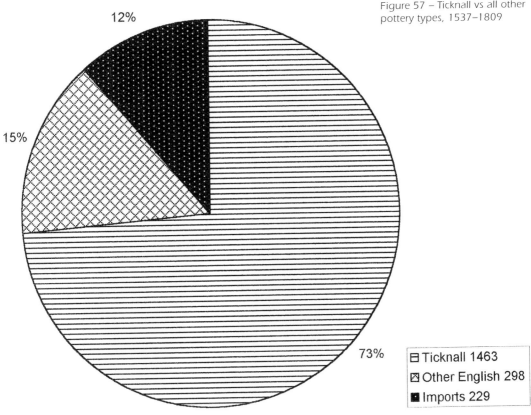

Figure 57 – Ticknall vs all other pottery types, 1537–1809

12%

15%

73%

| Legend |
| --- |
| ⊟ Ticknall 1463 |
| ⊠ Other English 298 |
| ▣ Imports 229 |

Almost three-quarters of the named pottery references in the inventories were to Ticknall ware (1,463 references). The dominant recognition of Ticknall ware is summarised in Figure 58. This gives some indication of the quantity of pottery produced, as well as its market penetration, though it does not reflect the relative quality of each source.

A breakdown of the summary figures to compare Ticknall with its closest domestic competitors was made. It is surprising that Burslem does not figure more strongly, even in Staffordshire. There are, however, at least as many references in the probate inventories to unspecified 'earthenware' as there are to all the named types, and much of this ware probably came from Staffordshire. It may have been so common that it was taken for granted that its source was known. It may be that the appraisers only referred to pottery by name when it came from somewhere other than Staffordshire and so was thought worthy of comment. If this was the case, then Staffordshire products would form the largest proportion of the pottery noted in the inventories.

| Source | No. of Refs |
| --- | --- |
| Ticknall | 1463 |
| White | 164 |
| Black | 53 |
| Boston | 27 |
| Burslem | 23 |
| Wednesbury | 12 |
| Yellow | 8 |
| Nottingham | 3 |
| Yorkshire | 2 |

Figure 58 – Ticknall vs all other named English pottery 1537–1809

There are some problems with identification of the generic wares, and they change over the period. When the early references to Ticknall white wares were made, they probably referred to the cream-coloured body with a lead glaze, which gave a yellow finish, that is often found on the kiln sites. Ticknall white wares are not to be compared with the true white wares made in the Stoke-on-Trent area from the 1720s. Ticknall's potters used the local coal measure clays and not Devon or Cornish clays. They were probably called white because they were the nearest that could be produced from the local clays, and they were 'white' by comparison with the wares produced from the red clays. The Ticknall potteries were not the only ones to have made white wares — most inventory mentions did not give a source. The majority of them have dates before 1720. We only have twelve references after this date which were likely to be true white wares. The white wares could be the same as the yellow wares; references to the latter span the period 1596 to 1637.

Six pottery types are only mentioned once: Bolingbroke in Lincolnshire, Ely, King's Lynn, Preston, London and Crich. There is one mention of pottery from 'Boultean', which we have not been able to identify.

Ticknall distribution has been analysed by county to try to identify the peak periods as well as the pattern of distribution over time. The data covered the period 1537–1809, and the results are shown in Figure 59.

| Decade | Leics | Derbys | Staffs | Warks | Ches | Notts | Salop | Lincs | Oxon | Lancs |
|---|---|---|---|---|---|---|---|---|---|---|
| 1537-53 | 1 | - | - | - | - | - | - | - | - | - |
| 1550-9 | - | - | - | - | - | - | - | - | - | - |
| 1560-9 | 1 | 1 | - | - | - | - | - | - | - | - |
| 1570-9 | 1 | - | - | - | - | 1 | - | - | - | - |
| 1580-9 | 3 | 1 | - | - | - | - | - | - | - | - |
| 1590-9 | 18 | 3 | - | - | - | - | - | - | - | - |
| 1600-9 | 19 | 5 | - | - | ? | - | - | - | - | - |
| 1610-9 | 45 | 15 | - | 4 | 3 | - | - | - | - | - |
| 1620-9 | 78 | 19 | 4 | 3 | 6 | - | - | - | 1 | - |
| 1630-9 | 169 | 96 | 37 | 45 | 16 | - | 7 | - | - | - |
| 1640-9 | 56 | 10 | 4 | 1 | 4 | - | - | - | - | - |
| 1650-9 | 24 | - | 3 | - | 1 | 1 | - | - | - | - |
| 1660-9 | 91 | 7 | 14 | 1 | 12 | 1 | - | - | - | - |
| 1670-9 | 106 | 16 | 20 | 4 | 12 | - | 1 | - | - | 1 |
| 1680-9 | 107 | 43 | 45 | 50 | 11 | 5 | 6 | - | - | - |
| 1690-9 | 44 | 23 | 8 | 9 | 2 | 5 | 1 | - | - | - |
| 1700-9 | 19 | 5 | 2 | - | - | 9 | - | - | - | - |
| 1710-9 | 9 | 3 | 3 | - | - | 9 | 2 | - | - | - |
| 1720-9 | 2 | - | 8 | - | - | 3 | 1 | - | - | - |
| 1730-9 | 1 | - | - | - | 1 | 6 | 3 | 2 | - | - |
| 1740-9 | - | 1 | 3 | - | - | - | - | - | - | - |
| 1750-9 | 1 | 1 | - | - | · | - | - | - | - | - |
| 1760-9 | - | 5 | - | - | - | - | - | - | - | - |
| 1770-9 | - | 3 | - | - | 1 | - | - | - | - | - |
| 1780-9 | - | 8 | - | - | - | - | - | - | - | - |
| 1790-9 | - | - | - | - | - | - | - | - | - | - |
| 1800-9 | - | 1 | - | - | - | - | - | - | - | - |

Figure 59 – Ticknall distribution by county 1537–1809

The period from 1537 to 1699 shows the widest range, with ten counties having references to Ticknall ware. Leicestershire has the most references, because all the Leicestershire inventories have been read rather than because more Ticknall pottery was sold in this county. In the 1630s the figures are higher for Derbyshire, Staffordshire, Warwickshire and Shropshire because all the Lichfield diocese inventories for this decade have been read, and for Cheshire because all the inventories for 1631 have been read. The Lichfield diocese inventories for 1680 to 1684 have also been read as a sample, so that the figures here are higher than for the adjoining decades. In the 1620s and 1630s the potteries were thriving, with good recognition and a good reputation. They seem to have been successful, strong rivals to the Staffordshire area. During the 1640s and 1650s, the period of the Civil War and Commonwealth, the system of probate was disrupted and wills were proved centrally. Far fewer inventories survive. In the 1660s in Leicestershire there is a noticeable increase in the numbers of wills and inventories proved, some of which appear to have been held over from the 1650s. By the 1680s the Ticknall potters were losing out to Staffordshire. There were larger numbers of potters working in Staffordshire and there are no widely recognised potters from Ticknall like the Toft, Simpson, Glass or Meir families from Stoke-on-Trent.

It can be seen that from 1700 there is an overall decline in both numbers of references to Ticknall ware and in their distribution by county. There is no further evidence for three counties, and whereas the peak figure in the 1630s was 169 references in Leicestershire, the highest figure after 1700 is nineteen, also in Leicestershire. Nowhere else has more than nine references. After 1720 even Leicestershire's numbers show a marked decline. After 1750 the pattern shown in the inventories has shrunk to Derbyshire, with the exception of a Cheshire reference in the 1770s. Even in its home county, the market area appears to be very close to Ticknall itself. From 1700 onwards there is a noticeable trend for the inventories to value the goods in a room, including the pottery, as a single item. Pots were still being made in quantity and distributed throughout this period, from a number of sites, but the evidence declines because of this.

A full, statistically valid comparison was made for 1631, with all available information from Leicestershire, the Lichfield diocese and Cheshire. Leicestershire had the largest number of inventories with 184, and is the only county for which references to generic 'earthenware' have been counted; there were six of these as well as the twelve Ticknall references. There were no other named pottery types in Derbyshire or Shropshire. Figure 60 shows all the Ticknall ware, and Figure 61 shows all other named pottery types, both English and imported.

Right: Figure 60 – Ticknall distribution, 1631

Below: Figure 61 – All other named pottery distribution, 1631

| County | No. of Refs |
|---|---|
| Leicestershire | 12 |
| Derbyshire | 10 |
| Staffordshire | 6 |
| Warwickshire | 2 |
| Cheshire | 7 |
| Shropshire | 2 |

| County | Black | Burslem | Wednesbury | Yorkshire | China | Stone | Delft |
|---|---|---|---|---|---|---|---|
| Leicestershire | 1 | - | - | - | 1 | - | - |
| Derbyshire | - | - | - | - | - | - | - |
| Staffordshire | - | 1 | - | - | - | - | - |
| Warwickshire | 1 | - | 2 | - | - | 2 | - |
| Cheshire | 1 | 2 | - | 1 | 2 | - | 1 |
| Shropshire | - | - | - | - | - | - | - |

A comparison of all named pottery types was made for the Lichfield diocese for 1680, when out of 645 inventories, sixty-four mentioned pottery (Figure 62). It is noticeable that there were far more generic 'earthenware' references, but only one to Burslem ware. It is likely that most of these came from the Staffordshire pottery areas, particularly since they were in the diocese. There is an equal number of references to Ticknall ware, which shows its widespread recognition. The white ware could be from either Staffordshire or Ticknall. Wednesbury was just inside the diocese, and also in Staffordshire, though its products should not be classed with the main potting area around Burslem; they were distinct, as their recognition shows. The painted dish was likely to be from the Burslem area, though such items were also produced in Ticknall. At this period, Staffordshire was making a name for its painted and jewelled wares. The Boston pottery was recorded in Whitwell, north Derbyshire. The only imported ware was the very fashionable china.

| Pottery Type | No. of Refs |
|---|---|
| Earthenware | 27 |
| Ticknall | 27 |
| White | 5 |
| Boston | 1 |
| Burslem | 1 |
| Wednesbury | 1 |
| Painted dish | 1 |
| China | 1 |

Figure 62 – All pottery references, Lichfield diocese, 1680

The Ticknall potters of course had to sell their wares by whatever means worked best within the limitations of the period. The probate inventories in particular are helpful in telling us the final destinations of the pottery, and when these had been mapped patterns of sale began to emerge. In general, the most important sales method was the regular network of local fairs and markets. Richardson has observed that, 'until the concentration of population into towns and the advent of good transport services, fairs and markets were the most important means of trading'.[2] They were established all over the country, often in the Middle Ages, and were strictly regulated both as to frequency and place. Fairs were held annually on specified dates, and markets were held on a particular day or days of the week, so that a potter needing to sell his wares knew which towns to attend and when. Tolls had to be paid in order to sell in the market or fair.

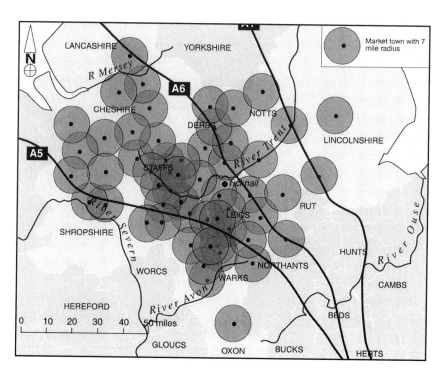

Figure 63 – Market distribution patterns for Ticknall ware, 1560–1806

In the late Middle Ages, Bracton, a writer on legal matters, 'defined a new market as harmful at law if it was held within two days of an existing market and within six and two-thirds miles of it'.[3] Thus the generally accepted market radius was about seven miles. Figure 63 shows all the market centres used for the distribution of Ticknall wares, taking a 7-mile radius for each market centre. In each case, mentions of Ticknall ware have been found within the market radius. Some markets also provided a service for areas beyond this radius, where the outlying area was not served by another market, and the outlying references have been mapped with the closest market area on individual maps. It shows that, on our evidence, the greatest concentration of markets lay in the central midlands, from central Leicestershire through north Warwickshire and into central Staffordshire. The market frequencies thinned out in east Leicestershire, and we only have evidence for two in Lincolnshire. Clearly, this may simply be the result of the fact that we have not been able to search the Lincolnshire inventories with the thoroughness used in Leicestershire. In the west, the market areas covered most of Cheshire, but without the intensity of the central areas. Northern Shropshire was covered but so far we have no evidence for the rest of the county. The one Lancashire market, Bolton, adjoined Stockport in Cheshire. A fairly close pattern of markets served Derbyshire and Nottinghamshire. Our evidence to date provided a solitary market in Oxfordshire. The trader would have had to cross Northamptonshire in order to reach Oxfordshire, suggesting that Ticknall pottery may have been sold there in spite of the lack of evidence to date. The pattern of markets shown here suggests that sales of Ticknall pottery may have spread gradually from market to market. Many customers had access to more than one market and local people attended different markets on different days, to sell farm and other produce. The overlapping market areas shown here may record the business history of Ticknall's expansion.

The non-Leicestershire Ticknall references were mapped for each market area to see what information could be gained about distribution routes or return trades, and examples only are included. The maps cover varying time spans because all the references for each area were included, however widely spaced. The maps shown give an indication of the period when Ticknall ware was reaching each area. Though we recognise that the data cannot be complete, the maps give some idea of the trade's development over time. In some cases it is possible to trace likely routes by combining market areas. In others, the destination suggests a likely return trade. A full list of the markets is given in Figure 64.

| Staffs | Warks | Leics | Derbys | Cheshire | Salop | Notts | Lincs | Lancs | Oxon |
|--------|-------|-------|--------|----------|-------|-------|-------|-------|------|
| Abbots Bromley | Birmingham | Ashby-de-la Zouch | Alfreton | Chester | Ellesmere | Newark on Trent | Grantham | Bolton | Banbury |
| Cannock | Coleshill | Hinckley | Ashbourne | Congleton | Market Drayton | Nottingham | Lincoln | | |
| Cheadle | Coventry | Leicester | Bakewell | Macclesfield | Shrewsbury | Worksop | | | |
| Leek | Henley in Arden | Loughborough | Chesterfield | Malpas | Wellington | | | | |
| Lichfield | Kenilworth | Lutterworth | Derby | Nantwich | | | | | |
| Newcastle-u-Lyme | Nuneaton | Market Bosworth | Tideswell | Northwich | | | | | |
| Rugeley | Rugby | Market Harborough | Wirksworth | Stockport | | | | | |
| Stafford | Solihull | Melton Mowbray | | | | | | | |
| Stone | Southam | | | | | | | | |
| Tamworth | Stratford-on-Avon | | | | | | | | |
| Tutbury | Sutton Coldfield | | | | | | | | |
| Uttoxeter | | | | | | | | | |
| Walsall | | | | | | | | | |
| Wolverhampton | | | | | | | | | |

Figure 64 – Markets by county used for the distribution of Ticknall ware

It is clear that the markets selling Ticknall ware were not all in major centres of population. There is a spread of developing industrial towns and cities such as Birmingham, Coventry, Newcastle-under-Lyme, Leicester and Nottingham. Smaller places were becoming industrialised: Walsall and Wolverhampton, Rugby, Chesterfield, Worksop and Bolton. Other markets were in towns which were still mainly rural such as Abbots Bromley, Tutbury, Uttoxeter, Henley-in-Arden, Market Bosworth, Tideswell, Malpas, Ellesmere and Banbury.

In the series of tables that follows, the data have been analysed to show market concentrations and the supply period. References which fall outside the 7-mile radius of any market have been included with the nearest market town. The tables also show market overlaps, and the number of references which fall into the overlapping area; these pots could have been purchased at either market. The overlapping areas give a clue as to how the distributors of Ticknall pottery developed their market penetration.

| Market | Dates | No. of Refs | Number beyond 7 miles | Overlaps with | Number in Overlap |
|--------|-------|-------------|----------------------|---------------|-------------------|
| Bakewell | 1630-1719 | 11 | 0 | Wirksworth | 1 |
| | | | | Chesterfield | 0 |
| Chesterfield | 1630-1689 | 13 | 4 | Bakewell | 0 |
| | | | | Wirksworth | 0 |
| Derby | 1560-1799 | 112 | 26 | Ashbourne | 2 |
| | | | | Wirksworth | 1 |
| Wirksworth | 1630-1719 | 29 | 0 | Derby | 1 |
| | | | | Bakewell | 1 |
| | | | | Chesterfield | 0 |

Figure 65 – Selected 7-mile radius market area details: Derbyshire

Ticknall lies just beyond the market radius for Derby, and it is probable that the river Trent formed a natural boundary to the south for Derby market. The area south of the Trent was served directly from Ticknall. Chesterfield had long had important trading links. Bakewell and Wirksworth both had links with the lead trade. Figure 65 shows the distribution of Ticknall pottery from Derby.

There is a good coverage of the area, with the main concentration north of the Trent in Derby itself (Figure 66). The thirty-six references at Foremark, a high number, derive from good estate accounts. Although the river Derwent was navigable up to Derby it does not seem to have been a trade route for the pottery. The map shows a typical scatter of distribution for a county town, and a long history of supply from the sixteenth century to the end of the eighteenth. Derby was well known for its cheese market, and it also had a large market for pottery, like Uttoxeter and Nottingham. The Honourable John Byng, later 5th Viscount Torrington, recorded a conversation when travelling from London to the midlands by coach in 1790. A fellow traveller, Miss H, 'brag'd of the Derby market, as abundant of meat, and what not, and likewise garden stuff; at which the Islingtons were much surprised; she also said that the quantity of pots sold was astonishing; to which I remark'd "That was a very necessary article".'.[4] The Islingtons were passengers from London.

Ticknall itself did not have a market, but it clearly acted as its own local distribution centre along with the pot hawkers based nearby. So far we have nine references at Repton and a single reference at Milton. At Foremark, the Burdett family regularly bought Ticknall pottery for the kitchen and the garden in the late eighteenth century; the pots were delivered directly by Ticknall people. Two were at Ingleby, where there was a local wharf on the river. Stanton-by-Bridge with two references and Swarkestone with three face each other over the river Trent and are linked by the medieval causeway of Swarkestone Bridge. Melbourne had sixteen, and King's Newton had two. In the late seventeenth century the owners

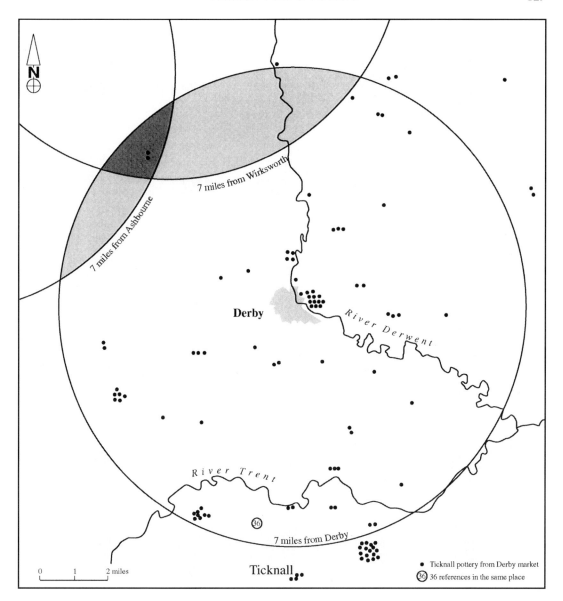

Figure 66 – Distribution of Ticknall pottery from Derby market, 1560–1799

of Melbourne Hall were buying Ticknall pots for the kitchen. For example, on 23 December 1670 John Hall was paid 1s 1¹/₂d for eighteen Ticknall bottles which he had delivered.⁵ The Harpur Crewes at Calke Abbey also bought items directly from the potters. There are several references from Hartshorne, Swadlincote, Church Gresley, Castle Gresley, Linton and Smisby. Pots were sold at Ashby de la Zouch and reached Measham, Oakthorpe and Donisthorpe, all mining villages.

Wirksworth was the centre of the lead mining trade; the Barmoot Court which controlled the industry was (and is) held there. Lead had been mined in this area at least since Roman times, and there was an early wind-driven smelter on Bole Hill between Wirksworth and Cromford. There were many rich mines within the market area, which because of the geography might appear to have been concentrated into a smaller radius than usual. However, Defoe describes it as *a large well-frequented market town, and market towns being very thin placed in this part of the county, they have the better trade, the people generally coming twelve or fifteen miles to a market, and sometimes much more; though there is no very great trade to this town but what relates to the lead works ... This town of Wirksworth is a kind of market for lead; the like not known any where else that I know of, except it be at the custom-house keys in London.*[6]

In his summary of the trade on the river Trent, Defoe notes that the barges carry 'lead, coal, wood, corn [and] cheese in great quantities' down the river.[7]

The Wirksworth to Derby road did not run along the river valley but took the better-drained high ground even in the later part of the eighteenth century when the turnpike network was created. The road then was part of the 1756 Derby to Chesterfield stagecoach route; it ran over the line of older packhorse tracks. All but one of the Ticknall references in this market area are found in lead mining communities, suggesting a return trade like that to Nantwich for salt. Though further north, a find in one of the mines supports this: 'At Hill Top Mine, one of the Great Hucklow mines, which was worked at least from the start of the seventeenth century, in the nineteenth century a find down the mine produced coins from 1605–80, tools, tygs, and tokens dated 1667'.[8] Tygs were a common Ticknall product at this date.

The Derby to Chesterfield corridor was an important trade and industrial route. It served the coal mines and the iron and copper works which were directly on the road or had easy access to it. Some places such as Alfreton, Belper and Denby were involved in both coal and metal production throughout this period. Others were coal mining villages: North Wingfield, South Normanton, Snelston, Heanor, Kilburn and Smalley. The lead working village of Crich was also within reach of this route. Ticknall ware was recorded in all these villages. It is likely that it made its way along this route via Derby market to the homes of the industrial workforce which looked for a cheap and practical product.

| Market | Dates | No. of Refs | Number beyond 7 miles | Overlaps with | Number in Overlap |
|--------|-------|-------------|----------------------|---------------|-------------------|
| Leek | 1600-1699 | 14 | 1 | Newcastle under Lyme | 3 |
| | | | | Ashbourne | 0 |
| Lichfield | 1600-1689 | 46 | 9 | Tamworth | 14 |
| Newcastle under Lyme | 1630-1749 | 15 | 2 | Nantwich | 2 |
| | | | | Market Drayton | 0 |
| | | | | Leek | 3 |
| Stafford | 1630-1749 | 11 | 3 | Uttoxeter | 1 |
| Tamworth | 1600-1749 | 29 | 0 | Lichfield | 14 |
| | | | | Coleshill | 4 |
| | | | | Nuneaton | 0 |
| Uttoxeter | 1628-39 | 15 | 4 | Stafford | 1 |
| | 1680-89 | 7 | | Ashbourne | 1 |
| Walsall | 1639 & 1682 | 3 | 0 | Wolverhampton | 0 |
| Wolverhampton | 1725 | 1 | 0 | Walsall | 0 |

Figure 67 – Selected 7-mile radius market area details: Staffordshire

Even in Newcastle-under-Lyme, next to The Potteries, there was a recognised market for Ticknall ware (Figure 67). The market at Leek may have been used to buy dairy ware as the surrounding Staffordshire Moorlands was a dairying area. Lichfield was a cathedral city and an important coaching centre, and the high number of references here may reflect the need to cater for travellers. Uttoxeter, as has already been discussed, was a dairying centre. It is rather surprising that Walsall and Wolverhampton did not obtain all their pottery supplies from Stoke-on-Trent and Wednesbury, but Ticknall was clearly a recognised product here. We do not have any references to Staffordshire before the seventeenth century but they continue well into the heyday of Staffordshire's eighteenth-century production.

The most significant place in each county is shown here. Nottingham featured early in the supply of Ticknall ware, and both Nottingham and Wellington continued to record it until the mid-eighteenth century (Figure 68).

| Market | Dates | No. of Refs | Number beyond 7 miles | Overlaps with | Number in Overlap |
|--------|-------|-------------|------------------------|---------------|-------------------|
| Nottingham | 1569-1749 | 30 | 4 | - | 0 |
| Wellington | 1690-1749 | 7 | 0 | - | 0 |

Figure 68 – Selected 7-mile radius market area details: Nottinghamshire and Shropshire

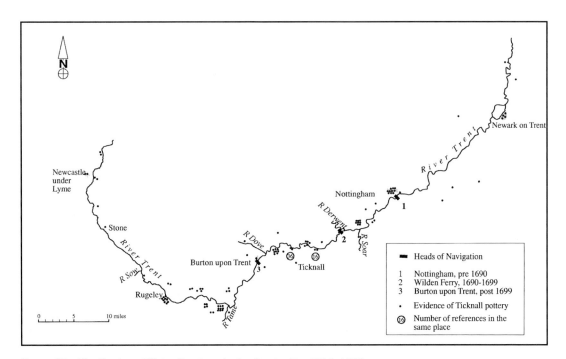

Figure 69 – Distribution of Ticknall pottery in the Trent valley 1560–1799

The river Trent was a very important trade route, taking goods from the centre of the country in river barges to Gainsborough where it was trans-shipped to seagoing vessels for Hull. From Hull the ships sailed along the coast, north to Newcastle and south to London. Some went further. The Trent was made navigable in stages. Nottingham was the head of the river until 1690 when it was extended to Wilden Ferry (where the A6 crosses the Trent just downstream from Shardlow). In 1699 it was extended again to Burton-upon-Trent and, though it was not extended further, trade continued along the river valley via packhorse routes. Figure 69 shows the significance of the river for the distribution of Ticknall pottery over an exceptionally long period. Archaeological evidence of Ticknall pottery found at Newark Castle and at Nottingham supports the documentary evidence.

All our references for Warwickshire fell into the seventeenth century, the period of Ticknall's greatest prosperity (Figure 70). The area served from Coventry market was concentrated to the north of the city, with a major overlap of market area with Nuneaton. This suggests that the trade was still spreading south, albeit slowly. There was a cluster of fourteen references north-east of Coventry, apparently indicating somewhere more important than the city of Coventry. These are to the small agricultural village of Bulkington, where all the probate inventories have been checked,[9] enabling us to understand how extensively Ticknall penetrated even tiny places. It shows how much more information is probably still undiscovered.

| Market | Dates | No. of Refs | Number beyond 7 miles | Overlaps with | Number in Overlap |
|--------|-------|-------------|----------------------|---------------|-------------------|
| Coventry | 1600-1699 | 38 | 0 | Nuneaton | 22 |
| | | | | Rugby | 3 |
| | | | | Tamworth | 0 |
| Nuneaton* | 1600-1699 | 45 | 6 | Coventry | 22 |
| | | | | Rugby | 0 |
| Rugby | 1630-39 & 1680-89 | 8 | 0 | Coventry | 3 |
| | | | | Nuneaton | 0 |

Figure 70 – Selected 7-mile radius market area details: Warwickshire. N.B. This is only the half of Nuneaton's 7-mile radius which is in Warwickshire. The Leicestershire half is included with the series of maps for the county.

If the market radii are superimposed on the routes from Tamworth to Solihull, they show how the trade in Ticknall pots may have gradually spread from market to market, moving further away from the production base. Examples of Ticknall ware have been found at the Temple Balsall dig site, which is within the market radius for Solihull. Eighteen references are directly on the roads and a further eleven are within the market areas.

Stockport had barely begun to expand by the date of the last of the Ticknall references, and our most significant market town in Cheshire for Ticknall ware was Nantwich (Figure 71). Supply here was mainly in the seventeenth century but as in Staffordshire it continued for a surprisingly long time into the mid-eighteenth century. Nantwich had an ancient salt industry coupled with excellent dairying on the Cheshire plain. The presence of Ticknall pottery in the town, with a scatter in its market area, suggests that there may have been an exchange trade between Nantwich and the east midlands. Salt was being sent east, and pottery west, to the mutual benefit of both communities.

| Market | Dates | No. of Refs | Number beyond 7 miles | Overlaps with | Number in Overlap |
|--------|-------|-------------|-----------------------|---------------|-------------------|
| Market Drayton | 1630-1679 | 12 | 0 | Nantwich | 1 |
| Nantwich | 1624-1688 | 46 | 2 | Market Drayton | 1 |
| Stockport | 1600-1749 | 13 | 2 | - | 0 |

Figure 71 Selected 7-mile radius market area details: Cheshire

All the Ticknall ware references from the Leicestershire inventories have been mapped (Appendix 1, Ticknall Pottery in Leicestershire). Eight of the main market towns in the county are shown on each map, together with significant roads and the rivers Trent (on the northern boundary), Soar (rising in the south and flowing through Leicester and Loughborough to join the Trent) and Wreake (the tributary of the Soar which flows from Melton Mowbray). The canal system to Market Harborough and the south is also shown. Ticknall lies just over the county's north-western boundary.

The Leicestershire inventories are bound in volumes by year. All the early references are in the north and north-west of the county except for the possible one in Leicester. By the 1590s Ticknall pottery distribution was becoming more frequent, spreading particularly to the south almost to the county boundary between Hinckley and Lutterworth. Later maps show that the mentions of Ticknall ware were spread more evenly over the county, and that it had reached the rich dairying areas in the east. By 1610–19 the map indicates a growing use of Ticknall ware along the line of the Wreake valley and around Melton Mowbray. Then the emphasis shifted to the western half of the county. There was a clear concentration from the north-west corner, along the valley of the Soar, in Leicester and then to the south-west of the county. Another group suggested a trade route along the line of the A444, which passed east of Market Bosworth to Hinckley. By 1629, the numbers of references to Ticknall ware had grown fairly steadily.

The decade 1630–9 was significant for the Ticknall potters, and it shows in the growth of their sales in Leicestershire. There were dense accumulations in Loughborough, Leicester and Long Clawson (north of Melton Mowbray; there is still a noted dairy producing Stilton cheese there), and there were lesser concentrations along the Wreake and around Market Harborough. The numbers of inventories recorded during the 1640s and 1650s fell because of the Civil War and Commonwealth changes imposed on the system. Even in the 1640s, however, Ticknall ware sold in larger quantities in the west and centre of the county than in the east. Our information for the 1650s comes mainly from a much reduced number of wills and inventories which were held over for probate until after the Restoration, which is the reason for an apparently much reduced distribution pattern for the 1650s. After the Restoration, with the re-instatement of the old probate system, the numbers of references rose again, suggesting that there was probably much the same trade during the two previous decades as in the 1630s and 1660s; it was the evidence that had suffered rather than the trade. Now the concentrations suggested trade routes along the Soar valley to Leicester, and along the A444. The entire southern sector of the county had Ticknall references and the villages in the western half could be served from Leicester, Hinckley, Lutterworth or Market Harborough. There was much less in the extreme east and north-east of the county. At the junction of the Soar and the Wreake, the villages of Syston, Sileby and Barkby were developing their dairy trade, and showed a marked concentration of references. This intensified in the 1670s when there was interesting evidence for Ticknall ware regularly reaching the dairies along the Wreake and following a lesser trail into the cheese-making villages beyond Melton Mowbray. The 1680s again emphasised the importance of the dairy trade along the Wreake valley.

After 1680 the number of references to Ticknall ware in Leicestershire declined sharply. But even with reduced numbers the patterns of distribution were familiar. The Wreake concentration still dominated, and the Soar valley, the A447 and the Hinckley to Market Harborough sector in the south still showed a Ticknall presence. Moving into the eighteenth century, references steadily declined. This apparent collapse of the Ticknall pottery industry was due much more to the decline of the system of making inventories than to the decline of the potteries, though they had begun to lose market share slowly in the 1670s and 1680s. They did not keep up with the new developments in Staffordshire, and this signalled the start of a slow decline. In terms of numbers of potteries working, and numbers of potters employed, however, the decline did not hit home for another generation.

An overview of the maps suggests that the main trade routes were the river valleys and the market towns. The other significant route was the line of the modern A447, and the villages in this area would have been served directly by hawkers following regular routes around the villages. We suggest this because so many of these villages appear in each decade, where other villages in the east of the county only appear occasionally. The same seems to be true of the southern sector where the same villages appear regularly. There was a clear link between the developing dairying and cheese making villages and the presence of Ticknall ware; we discuss the frequency of Ticknall ware mentioned in dairies elsewhere. In the towns, Ticknall ware was mainly found in the kitchen and the buttery, or in the occasional dairy. Some references were in the hall, parlour or chamber but these were references to better pieces such as platters.

The map series shows the distribution of Ticknall ware as it was recorded through the probate inventories. In spite of the limitations of the probate system, it provides the best evidence we have for the widespread and common use of Ticknall pottery. It also shows that Ticknall ware was a recognised type over the period.

The importance of the rivers, and later of the canals, as general distribution routes in Leicestershire is clear from the map series. While no documentary evidence for early use of the Trent by potters from Ticknall has survived, there is evidence from other trades for its use from the Humber to Nottingham since the early Middle Ages, and as far as Shardlow and King's Mills (Castle Donington) when there was enough water to pass the shallows. However, there is evidence for the probable transport of Ticknall pottery by water in the references to ware packed in vats or casks. The head of navigation for the large sailing barges on the river had been Nottingham until 1690, then Wilden Ferry near Shardlow until 1699, and Burton-upon-Trent after that. There were small wharves at different dates along the Trent within easy reach of the village where pottery could be delivered for collection and onward transmission, such as Ingleby, Swarkestone and King's Mills. After the Trent was made navigable to Burton-upon-Trent, warehouses were established on its banks at Willington and Weston-on-Trent. Tracks to these places, and the wharves and warehouses, are marked on a map which seems to have been drawn as part of the proposals for the Trent and Mersey Navigation. The Act was passed in 1766 and the map may date from a year or two before that.[10] The wharf at Ingleby is two miles from Ticknall, Swarkestone is just under four miles and Willington is five miles, via Twyford ferry. Though further away, King's Mills, Weston-on-Trent and Wilden Ferry are all west of the Soar confluence and could have been used for the pottery trade; Nottingham lies to the east of the Soar. The distribution of pottery references along the river valleys does suggest that the small craft trading along the rivers before they were opened up to the large sailing barges may have carried some Ticknall pottery.

The earliest relevant records found so far for the river trade are the Trent Navigation Boat Tables, starting from the 1780s. In four volumes, these record the numbers of boats licensed to trade on the river, the owners, where they were based and which regular trade route each boat was licensed for. They record the primary commodities carried by the boats and indicate whether they carry other commodities, though often the others were not specified. Volume 4 dates from 1815 and records 138 boats trading on the Trent. Some of them followed regular routes to the Wreake valley area where so many Ticknall pots have been recorded in the inventories, and may indicate that the pottery had been traded this way before the records begin. They could provide an explanation for the concentrations in these villages. Boat 546 was owned by Joseph Johnson of Derby and sailed by William Johnson, carrying coal to Derby; its previous owner had been Mr Hutchinson of Ticknall. 'This boat was built by Mr John Leland, at Shardlow, in the year 1797, for Mr Hutchinson of Ticknall, who sold her to Mr John Etches of Derby, in 1799, of whom the present Owner purchased her, in 1807'.[11] Gilbert Hutchinson and Thomas Cope had lime yards in Ticknall and traded extensively. Although he sold Boat 546, Hutchinson did own others, and was using them, for example,[12] to deliver large quantities of plaster and other cargoes to Wedgwood's works. He would have been well placed to deliver Ticknall pottery along with his other cargoes, though it is not recorded. Two potteries were still working in 1815.

# References

1 Since the maps were prepared, more information has been found and the updated figures have been used throughout in the graphs and the text
2 Richardson, J. (1986), p229
3 Harding, A. (1993), p108
4 Bruyn Andrews, C. (ed.) (1935), p155
5 Estate accounts 1662–1673 MH. We are grateful to Philip Heath for drawing our attention to this source
6 Defoe, D. (1983), pp31–2
7 ibid., p16
8 Kirkham, N. (1978), p638
9 Information collected by Mr E. A. Veasey and supplied by Mr D. Barker
10 Map entitled 'Plan of River Trent from Willington to Cavendish Bridge', surveyed by Robert Wyatt DLSL
11 DE4420/1 ROLLR
12 Items 4055-22; 4055-23 and 4055A-22; 4055B-22; all WMM

# 8. Ticknall's Competitors

The known distribution of wares from other potteries in our sources was analysed for comparison with distribution from Ticknall. To some extent, descriptions of the ware give a picture of what was produced, but items were not always described in detail. Some indication of the productive years of the potteries can be seen from the dates of the first and last references, though the figures are not comprehensive. It may be that searches in areas local to these potteries would produce further information. Our sources may be on the fringes of their market areas, thus suggesting limited production. The analyses do, however, give accurate comparisons with Ticknall ware references, as they are all drawn from the same sources.

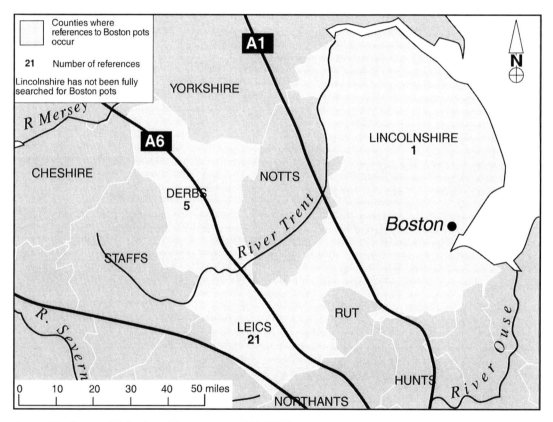

Figure 72 – Known distribution of Boston pots, 1586–1696

Boston was Ticknall's earliest recorded competitor, covering the period from 1586 to 1696 (Figure 72). The first twelve references were all in Leicestershire, six between 1586 and 1595, and six between 1602 and 1614. The ware was described as pots, jugs or bottles, mainly pots; in this group of references, there were no bottles, and only three jugs (two in 1589 at Wymeswold; in 1608 a probable reference in Leicester; and in 1612 probably at Market Harborough). Each of these was listed as part of a longer inventory item and not valued separately. There were nine other references to Boston pots, of which three were to single pots. In 1606 a single pot was valued at 4d,[1] while two were valued at 10d in 1612.[2]

The next two were in Derbyshire, at Twyford in the south for a jug in 1623[3] and Chesterfield in 1624. Chesterfield was a well-established market town and some of its tradesmen were well off. This reference was to '2 boston Jugges with pewter covers' worth 1s 4d,[4] belonging to Hugh Galley, a baker. It was a style copied from imported German stoneware, which had covers and feet added after the ware was imported. Sometimes, as here, they were in pewter, the cheapest metal, but they could be in silver or silver gilt too. There are two fine examples with silver covers and feet in Exeter Museum, with the silverwork done by local craftsmen. It was a well-established fashion. Our earliest reference was to 'A cover cup & ii other erthe pottes x[d]' in the 1558 inventory of Arthur Cooke, a Southampton trader.[5] It was in any case a statement of wealth and status, and the next two references reinforce it. George Kelton of Thringstone, Leicestershire, had 'the plate two silver booles one gaylt salt with a Cover five silver spoones one bosterne Judg with a silver Cover', together worth £10 in 1634.[6] Surprisingly, these were all in the dairy house and the dairy, usually rooms where cheaper, basic items were found. Robert Wood, a Derby ironmonger, had 'one Little Boston Jugg with a silver and gylte cover and foote' worth 10s in the same year, but he kept it in 'the best Chamber'.[7] It must have been much more elaborate than the 'One Earthen Mugg lipt with Silver' worth 2s, which belonged to George Tilley of Lutterworth in 1695.[8]

Three more references to Boston pots occur in Leicestershire (1634 Leicester; 1638 Redmile; 1662 Thorpe Acre): 'twoe boston Potts', a 'bosten Jugg' and '3 bosterne jugges' which were with all the dairy equipment in the milkhouse.[9]

Ralph Clarke of Grantham in Lincolnshire was a mercer in 1630. Among other things for sale in his shop he had Boston jugs, though the inventory does not specify how many nor their separate values.[10] Vincent Scudamore of Ashby de la Zouch in Leicestershire was also a mercer and his shop goods included a range of pots such as '15 old bosters judges & others' at 1s 3d.[11] It is impossible to tell where the other pots came from. They included ten 'spout potts' at 1s 8d, thirteen 'large gallon potts' at 2s 2d and '2 doz. & halfe of small gallon potts' at 2s 6d. The 'gallon potts' are probably galley pots, for items like ointments.

In 1670 Peter Chaveney of Quorndon, Leicestershire, gentleman, had six Boston bottles in the buttery but a separate value was not given.[12] Six Boston jugs in Whitwell belonged to a smith in 1680; they were listed with two earthen pots and together they were worth 1s 6d.[13] Three more Boston bottles appear in the inventory of Raph Rolin of Castleton in Derbyshire in 1683.[14] More useful detail is recorded in the inventories of two other shop-keepers. In 1688 John Warberton was an ironmonger in Leicester but sold other things too. Listed in his shop goods were 'Bosling potts 4 dozen' at 6s 9d and '4 dozen of Bosling potts' at 2s 8d.[15] Daniel Ogden kept two shops, at Lutterworth and at Dunton Bassett, in 1695. At Lutterworth he had '4 bostern Juggs' at 2s and at Dunton Bassett he had '4 boston Juggs of 2 qts' at 1s. This shop also had '4 Juggs' at 4d but the inventory does not specify where they are from.[16] It is worth noting for the shop inventories that the appraisers could recognise different types of pottery, and presumably so could the customers too. We must assume where pottery types are named and for sale that there was a demand from customers for it. The last reference occurs in January 1696 for John Smith of Pickwell, Leicestershire, who had two Boston bottles.

A. J. White's study, *Post-Medieval Pottery in Lincolnshire 1450–1850*, attempted to estimate the market radius of the Lincolnshire potteries. For Boston, he suggested a radius encompassing local villages, Lincoln and Boston itself.[17] This gives a market radius of about 12½ miles,[18] which is a common market area for a small pottery, but our evidence shows that it went further afield than that. The range is at least 66 miles. Our evidence produced one reference in Lincolnshire, five in Derbyshire and twenty-one in Leicestershire; the latter have been separately mapped in Figure 73, p138.

In Lincolnshire, White gives a radius of about 15 miles for the Bolingbroke and Harefield potteries; Bourne and a scatter through south Lincolnshire for the Bourne pottery; and Louth and its local villages for the nineteenth-century pottery at Louth. Nothing is known

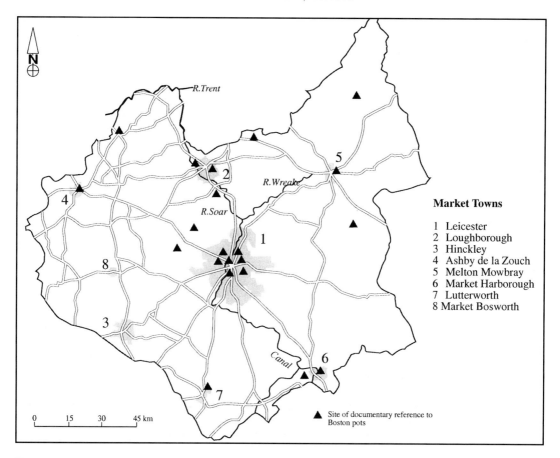

Figure 73 – Documentary evidence of Boston pots in Leicestershire, 1586–1696

about the distribution patterns for the early potteries at Coningsby, East Keal and Kirkstead, or for the late eighteenth-century pottery at Spalding. The medieval potteries at Toynton All Saints and Toynton St Peter however had a radius of about 32 miles, reaching to Lincoln and even as far as Norway. Their heyday was before either Ticknall's or Boston's but their range was extensive. In the post-medieval period they suffered from competition from the new site at Bolingbroke and by the seventeenth century they were out of business. White stated that the distribution of Bolingbroke pottery reached to Lincoln, and our only evidence is for a Lincoln candle maker in 1631 who had '20 doz Bolingbroke small potts £1'; presumably he was selling them in his shop.[19] If they were all the same size they would have been sold at 1d each. There are no references to Bolingbroke pots elsewhere in our sources.

The same candle maker sold pots from Ely, again in quantity. He had '51 Ely pots' valued at £1 14s, but there is no individual description of them.[20] Ely's market range was therefore about 65 miles overland, but 105 miles by sea. The Hull port books record Hull's coastal trade. The entire inbound port book for 1654–5 has been searched as a sample for glass and pottery entries, and there is only one where the source of pottery goods is named. This is a reference to the arrival of 5,000 'Ely tyles' on the *Amitie* of Stockwith;[21] her master, William Lumber, was trading in them himself. She had picked them up at King's Lynn. White notes a reference to 'Lynn plates' which were imported to Boston via London in 1710, and which illustrates the complexity of the trading patterns.

Fifteen other ships arrived with pots packed in barrels, baskets, hampers or chests, and only one gives a description of the contents: the *Elizabeth* of Hull brought '22 barrells single white plates', along with one barrel of unspecified 'potts'.[22] The white plates were probably tin-glazed wares and could have been imported from Holland or made in London. John Cutler of London owned this cargo. The coastal outwards port book for 1654–5 has two references to the pottery trade, one to the *Supply* of York carrying '4 baggs of Apothecary potts' for John Rogers in November and one to the *Providence* of Hull carrying 'two tonnes of butter in CC potts and two firkins'[23] in December. The book does not state the source for the pots but we know that butter was sold at Uttoxeter market for the London trade, using pots made in Ticknall, and traded down the Trent via Gainsborough and Hull. The 200 butter pots are the only reference to butter packed this way; more commonly it is packed in firkins. The *Elizabeth* of Hull also carried 6,000 bricks weighing one ton, along with groceries in casks in 1655.[24] There were no other references to clay items. The first reference to pottery other than butter pots going down the river did not occur until 1672, when there was '1 cask off Earth ware'. In 1676, 'xi baskets of earthen ware' were shipped out with no source mentioned for either consignment.[25]

Only one reference to Preston pots occurs in our sources; in 1617 a Lincoln inventory listed '2 preston earthen pots' valued at 1s.[26]

Wednesbury is a good example of a local pottery which served a defined hinterland generally with a limited range. The name was usually given as variants on 'Wedgebury'. The town is close to the county boundary between Staffordshire and Warwickshire, and sold its wares into both counties. The Staffordshire sales were in West Bromwich, Chebsey, Perry Barr and Kingswinford. In Warwickshire, single references were in Sutton Coldfield, Birmingham and Barkeswell. Five were in Aston near Birmingham: one in Aston itself, three in Erdington and one in Bordesley. This gives a market range of about 22 miles to Chebsey, but all the others are within a 10-mile range. Our references occurred between 1631 and 1683, and the pottery was working in 1686 when Dr Plot wrote, 'They make divers sorts of Vessels at Wednesbury, which they paint with Slip, made of a reddish sort of Earth gotten at Tipton'.[27] Wetherill noted that coarse earthenware and slipware were in fact made in Wednesbury from the fifteenth century in potteries similar to those in Ticknall. From the inventories (1660–1710), they were smaller than the Burslem works with fewer tools and one workhouse.[28] She listed six Wednesbury potters' inventories — two in the 1670s, three in the 1690s and one in 1705. For Ticknall in the same period she listed five potters' inventories — 1674, 1681, 1695 and two in the 1700s.[29] The inventories do not necessarily reflect the number of potters working in a given decade. Evidence shows that there were at least twenty-four working potters in Ticknall in the 1670s, nineteen in the 1680s and 1690s, twenty-five in the 1700s, twenty-three in the 1710s, thirty in the 1720s and twenty-four in the 1730s. Some were family members, some employees, but it shows how easily underestimates of potters and therefore production can be made.

Eight of our twelve Wednesbury references were to undifferentiated 'ware', with one just to 'pottes'. Only the three quoted below were detailed enough to give individual values for the pots. Richard Deely of Bordesley, Aston, had 'Certayne small parcels of Wedgbouri platters and pottes' worth 2s 6d in 1631.[30] Mainly the pottery seems to have been similar household and dairy wares to those produced in Ticknall and Staffordshire. Elizabeth Bell of Barkeswell had 'vii shelves iiii creampottes v milke panc[heo]ns & othr Wedgbery ware' worth 4s 6d in her buttery in 1634.[31] William Dickens of Birmingham had 'Wedgebury vessels' worth 4d in 1635 in the backhouse.[32] Robert Allen of Aston had Wednesbury ware in the dairy in 1683 but it was valued with the 'White earthen ware' that he also had.[33] We do not know whether white ware was made there or whether it came from elsewhere — it could be tin glaze at that date.

Only one reference to pottery made in London appeared in our sources, which we found surprising given the extent of trade from the capital into the provinces. William Mathfield of Leek, Staffordshire, kept a shop and when he died in 1680 he had 'Whyte and paynted London ware of earth' worth 10s 6d in his shop inventory.[34] This would be London-made Delft and stoneware from potteries such as that at Fulham, with products such as those listed in the Pickleherring pottery inventory of 1699.[35]

We had also expected to find frequent references to Burslem wares and other Staffordshire pottery in quantity. Although we found only twenty-two Burslem references, plus one to Staffordshire ware, we nonetheless think that it was around in quantities greater than any other named pottery types, as explained above in relationship to Figure 58. The references spanned the period 1625–1742, with sixteen references in Staffordshire, four in Cheshire, one in Leicestershire and one in Derbyshire, plus another possible Derbyshire reference. The Leicestershire reference was clearly to better-quality ware. John Vincent of Kegworth had 'Boslom ware' in the closet in his parlour in 1682, usually a place where valuable items were kept.[36] Two Cheshire references were for Nantwich in 1681 and 1685, both just described as ware and grouped with other items. In 1631 Edward Reddish of Gawsworth had 'Borselam ware' worth 12d.[37] John Skelhorne of Withington provided interesting evidence for the fact that both Burslem and Ticknall competed in the same markets; his inventory listed 'Burslam pots & Ticknall ware' worth 1s[38] in 1631. Supporting evidence is found in two more inventories, from 1676 in Rugeley and 1680 in Wolstanton. Peter Smith had 'Ticknall & Burslem ware' worth 5s, and John Burslem had 'Burslem & Ticknall ware' worth 2s. The descriptions show that the appraisers could recognise the difference.[39] It was not so clear to the appraisers of William Montfort's inventory in Ashbourne in 1683, however. He had 'a small parcel of old Ticknall or Burslome ware' worth 6d.[40] In 1742 William Saywell put an advertisement for his pot shop in Derby in the *Derby Mercury* and among the types of pottery he sold he listed both Ticknall ware and 'Staffordshire' ware.[41]

The references in Staffordshire are all to 'ware' apart from one each to 'Burslem brasse' worth 1s and 'potts' worth 2s.[42] Several inventories give a value just for the Burslem ware but do not specify how much pottery the value covered or what exactly it was. In 1639, one lot of ware was valued at 3s 4d and another at 5s; in 1682 a value was 1s and in 1683 it was 2s.[43] One inventory describes the ware but gives no value: 'In the Buttery milk vessels of Burslem ware'.[44] One lists Burslem wares with 'white potts' in 1664. These must be the poorer-quality yellow wares as discussed above since they are too early for Staffordshire's true white wares.[45] The remaining references are grouped with other items and not described or valued separately. A puzzling 1633 reference for Barleston included 'Boultean ware 3s 4d';[46] it seems unlikely that the source was Bolton. It may refer to a type or pattern of Staffordshire ware.

When discussing the market range for north Staffordshire pottery, Wetherill states that it was 'larger than the immediate vicinity' of the potteries. She differentiates between the 'country' and the 'fashionable' markets for the later period, but observes that the market for slip and other domestic wares cannot be defined easily at all, though seventeenth-century Staffordshire slipwares have been found on archaeological sites in Chester, Bristol, Worcester and Kidderminster. The country trade 'probably did not extend much beyond the county boundary to the north and west, and not as far as the county boundary in the south and east', and this trade was in 'butter pots, "coarse" ware for kitchen use, and various kinds of blackwares and slipwares'. The coarse wares were sold 'for most of the period before 1760'. She notes that butter pots were confined to a 15- to 20-mile radius from Burslem, and the chief market was Uttoxeter, about 20 miles away. Selling coarse domestic pottery outside Burslem's local region meant that the potters would come into direct competition with other local potters, and the record of a carrier of Burslem ware who was buried in Wednesbury in 1703 shows that Burslem ware was being sold within Wednesbury's area.[47] Sales of Ticknall ware in the heart of the north Staffordshire pottery district show another element of direct competition.

From the inventory descriptions it seems likely that only the Derby shop in 1742 would qualify as 'fashionable'. The 1682 Kegworth reference was clearly to good Burslem ware for the date, possibly slipware. The rest seem likely to be 'country' wares — four references are found in the buttery, one in the 'milkseller' and one in the 'houseplace'. Four more references were to the buttery, from the other items valued as a group with the pottery but where the room was not named. Derby is 31 miles from Burslem, fitting Wetherill's suggestion of a larger fashionable market, and Kegworth is 42 miles away. Apart from one unidentified place, all the rest fall within a 22-mile range, consistent with Wednesbury's range in our sources. The distances are tabulated in Figure 74. Nantwich, Gawsworth and Withington are in Cheshire and Ashbourne is in Derbyshire; Marchington is near to Uttoxeter. Apart from Ashbourne to the east, these country sales support Wetherill's analysis.

Nottingham pottery seems to have been first mentioned in John Dwight of Fulham's 1693 lawsuit, defending his patent rights to stoneware pottery. James Morley of Nottingham was one of the defendants; he made brown salt-glazed stoneware with shapes similar to those of Fulham but distinctively decorated with incised or stamped designs and often dated. Production finished around 1800.[48] It was noted by Daniel Defoe when he visited the city in 1724:

[In Nottingham] ... the chief manufacture carried on here is frame-work knitting for stockings, the same as at Leicester, and some glass, and earthen ware-houses; the latter much increased since the increase of tea-drinking; for the making of fine stone mugs, tea-pots, cups &c. The glass-houses, I think, are of late rather decayed ...[49]

This pottery must have been sold in Nottingham and the locality, though we have not so far found any references to it. It had a very wide market range, which must have reflected the quality of the ware as well as the improving transport system. Richard Hargrave of Stamford was a pot retailer who died in 1720. Among his shop inventory he had '8 Dozen halfe

| Place | No. of Refs | Distance |
|---|---|---|
| Kegworth (L) | 1 | 42 |
| Derby (D) | 1 | 31 |
| Rugeley | 1 | 22 |
| Wolaston | 1 | 20 |
| Marchington | 1 | 19 |
| Ashbourne (D) | 1 | 18 |
| Nantwich (C) | 2 | 15 |
| Withington (C) | 1 | 13 |
| Gawsworth (C) | 1 | 12 |
| Stone | 1 | 10 |
| Leek | 6 | 8 |
| Ubbeley | 1 | 3 |
| Seabridge | 1 | 3 |
| Newcastle | 1 | 2 |
| Norton in the Moors | 1 | 2 |
| Swinnerton Heath | 1 | ? |

C = Cheshire        D = Derbyshire
L = Leicestershire
All others in Staffordshire

Figure 74 – Burslem references: distances from Burslem

pint Nottingham Muggs' worth 9s 11d.[50] Fourteen years later Nottingham ware was recorded at Stratford-upon-Avon in the household of Nathaniel Mason, a wealthy gentleman. He had 'one Nottinghamshire Teapot' worth 1s on display 'on the cubbord in the little Parlour', so it was clearly regarded as good quality.[51] The pottery was mentioned in Deering's

*Historical Account of Nottingham* in 1751, and again in 1757 in Bailey's *Annals of Nottinghamshire*. The Morleys were still the owners, making 'a very considerable fortune' from their 'famous brown mugs for the use of public houses' which were 'of great celebrity throughout the whole of the Midland counties'.[52] It went further than that. Ann Shergold of Blandford Forum in Dorset was a dealer in ceramics with a wide range of stock. She died in 1759 and her shop inventory is most informative. It included four types of Nottingham wares: nine 'Quarts' at 6d each (4s 6d), fifty 'Pints' at 2d each (8s 2d), sixteen 'Half Pints' at 1d each (1s 4d) and three 'Beaking Dishes' at 2s 1d the three.[53] These were baking dishes which either sold at 8½d each or were in different sizes to account for the price. Draper noted that Ann Shergold only sold fine wares, including imported goods.

There was one reference to ware made in Crich in Derbyshire. William Saywell, the Derby shopkeeper mentioned above, included it in his 1742 advertisement. The pottery made brown stoneware similar to that of Nottingham. It seems to have started in 1666 when Thomas Morley, a potter, 'took over a plot of land from Lady Mary Dixie'. Another Thomas Morley was recorded as a potter at Morewood Moor, Crich, when he sold the pottery to Thomas Dodd in about 1727. Dodd went bankrupt in 1763 but by then the pottery, with two potworks, was being worked by Thomas Wheldon. George Bacon took over as the potter, and his son Edward converted it to a brickworks which was closed by 1810.[54]

Yorkshire pots were recorded in 1631 in a Cheshire inventory at Ashley; no occupation was given but the 'Yorkhen Pots' were worth 6s.[55] We were informed of another reference to Yorkshire pots in the Lincoln archives but the date was not passed on.[56]

| Decade | Leics | Staffs | Derbys | Warks | Notts | Ches | Salop | Lincs | Yorks | N'hton | Dorset |
|--------|-------|--------|--------|-------|-------|------|-------|-------|-------|--------|--------|
| 1630-9 | - | - | - | 1 | - | - | - | - | - | - | - |
| 1640-9 | 2 | - | - | - | - | 1 | - | - | - | - | - |
| 1650-9 | - | 2 | - | - | - | - | - | - | 1 | - | - |
| 1660-9 | 9 | 1 | - | - | - | 4 | - | 2 | 1 | 1 | - |
| 1670-9 | 12 | 3 | 2 | - | - | 4 | - | 3 | 3 | - | - |
| 1680-9 | 12 | 9 | 10 | 9 | 5 | 8 | 6 | 7 | - | - | - |
| 1690-9 | 16 | 2 | 1 | - | 3 | - | 2 | - | - | - | - |
| 1700-9 | 8 | - | - | - | - | - | 1 | 1 | - | - | - |
| 1710-9 | - | 1 | - | 2 | - | - | 1 | - | - | - | - |
| 1720-9 | 2 | 1 | - | - | 1 | - | - | 1 | - | - | - |
| 1730-9 | - | - | 1 | 1 | - | - | 1 | - | - | - | - |
| 1740-9 | - | - | - | - | - | - | 1 | - | - | - | - |
| 1750-9 | - | - | - | - | - | - | - | - | - | - | 2 |

Figure 75 – White wares by county 1630–1759

White wares without a place of origin dominated the generic wares in our sources, as can be seen in Figure 75. The early references are scattered. In 1554 John Ward, a Chesterfield shopkeeper, had 'halfe a dosyne wytte platt' worth 1s in his shop goods.[57] Raphe Hethcote, a Chesterfield brazier, had '3 whyte candlesticks' in 1577[58] (though these could be metal — it is a problem that both pottery and metal goods can be described in the same terms). A Chipping Norton widow, Elinor Simkins, had 'a white basen' with other goods in the hall in 1590.[59] There were no more references until the 1630s; then they occurred fairly regularly until the 1750s. After that date there were no references until 1800–9, when there were two for Leicestershire.

Some of it was good enough to be enriched with silver. Robert Newton of Ashby de la Zouch had 'a silver bole two silver salts six silver spoones and a white earthen pott ringed about the top with silver', together worth £8, in 1643.[60] John Glen of Lincoln had 'Two white earthen potts tiped with silver' worth 2s, along with several 'white earthen plates' at 4s, in 1662.[61] These good-quality items could be white tin-glazed stoneware from Holland, decorated in the German fashion.

It is difficult to differentiate the white ware references; they could be tin glazed, or the cheaper local pots made from yellow clays and lead glazed, as described above. Although items made from tin or silver can also be described as white, it is generally possible to distinguish between earthenware and metal goods from the context, and quite often the appraisers made the distinction clearly by listing metal goods separately. Although Ann Overing of Leicester had unspecified 'white ware', she had her 'Tinn ware in the Nook' and her pewter listed separately.[62] The problem arises when the earthenware is referred to as 'plate' for both singular and plural, following the terminology for silver, particularly when it is in the better parts of a house. For example, Mr Edward Wormwell of Melton Mowbray had 'a livery cubart with Whyte plate & glasses' in a chamber, worth 16s 8d in 1670.[63] From the position and the value, it could be mistaken for silver, but the appraisers specify the silver separately. Some of the white ware might be imported china. A 1684 reference lists 'one litell table with finne white ware upon it'.[64] This sounds like a tea table with its china ready for use. It was valued along with a couch, seven chairs and three stools at £2 and the context suggests a fashionable room. A similar example had 'one little Table parsill of White Earthen dishis' in the closet.[65]

Most of the white ware references were grouped with other items in the inventories, making it difficult to find prices for the wares. The earliest reliable value we have is from 1664 when Margaret Lampert, a Northamptonshire shopkeeper, had white basins at 6d each and five large white pots together worth 1s 1d. In 1673 John Sharpe of Lichfield had '4 little dishes, a bason and a chamber pot of white ware', together valued at 2s. If the basin cost 6d, the chamber pot could be 10d and the dishes 2d each. John Bayley of Sutton Cheyney in Leicestershire had 'Two white basons & a Sillibub pott' at 1s. John Orme's inventory from Drayton in Hales, Shropshire, was more informative, with four white dishes at 2s (6d each) and a white sugar dish at 4d. Mr Edward Phillips of Carlton in Lindrick, Nottingham-shire, had three white plates and a white bottle, together worth 3s 8d — possibly 1s each for the plates and 8d for the bottle. The inventory of a Lutterworth innkeeper, George Tilley, was equally informative, giving individual values of 3d each for three white salts. In 1697 the Burdetts at Foremark paid 10d for one white basin, perhaps larger than those priced at 6d.[66] The fact that there were many more inventories in the period 1670 to 1700 may have influenced the quantity recorded.

By the time there are specific prices in the next century, they may well refer to completely different types of white pottery. In 1734 Nathaniel Mason of Stratford-upon-Avon had '2 earthen white Tea pots' together worth 6d in one of his better rooms; by then they could have been white salt glaze, or some of Astbury's new pottery using north Devon pipe clay and flint. They could have been imported china. Mason also had '2 white pint mugs' at 4d each in a closet in the kitchen chamber. The following line reads '3 half pints 6d, 8 butter dishes 2s, 2 mustard pots 3d' which suggests they are also white ware but does not state the fact. The last two references were from the early nineteenth century and must relate to wares from the mass production of Stoke-on-Trent rather than to local pottery produc-tion.[67]

Shops are the most informative source for white ware prices, as noted with Margaret Lampert's inventory quoted above. William Dent was a Horncastle ironmonger and his 1679 inventory gives prices of $^1/_2$d each for white galley pots, $4^1/_4$d for large white candlesticks, 3d each for large white pots and for small white basins, and 9d each for white chamber pots. Small white pots were about $2^1/_4$d each or 2s $2^1/_2$d per dozen.[68] A Leicester shopkeeper, John Page, had '20 w[hi]tte chamber pots at 5d' each in his 1692 inventory, with other unspecified white pots which were not separately valued. Also in 1692, Thomas Morrison of Kegworth had five pottery entries listed in his shop inventory. One was '4 White pots 2s'; the others did not specify types of pottery.[69] Richard Hargrave of Stamford was described as a pot retailer in 1721 and in his stock he had 'Eight pieces of White Muggs and pieces' valued at 8d, 'Seven White Tea potts' at 2s 4d (presumably different sizes or qualities), and 'Seven White Muggs 8d four White Juggs 4d' together worth only 1s.[70] Ann Shergold's stock in 1759 included twenty-four descriptions of white wares, by this date certainly good-quality products from Stoke-on-Trent. She sold quart pots at 4d each, pints at 2d and half pints at 1d. Large chamber pots were $3^{1}/_{2}$d or 4d each and small ones were 3d. Large white hand basins cost 3d each, white saucers were about 4d per dozen and cups were about 2d per dozen. Tea pots varied in size and quality, ranging from about $^{1}/_{2}$d each to 1d and 2d, then 9d for large ones. A bowl was 1s 6d; spoon boats were between $^{1}/_{2}$d and 1d, as were butter dishes. Mustard pots were about $^{3}/_{4}$d, but English mustard pots were 8d each. Candlesticks were 3d each. There were basins at 6d and 9d and cream mugs at 3d. The coffee cups were the most expensive items of white ware, at between $5^{1}/_{4}$d and at 10d each.[71]

There were far fewer references to generic black wares than to white in our sources. They were found from 1556 to 1806. We have not yet found any references to black ware in Staffordshire and Nottinghamshire, though pottery of this type must have been used there. The early references were probably to the dark-glazed Cistercian wares, but the main period of our references could cover both Cistercian wares and other black wares. The likely sources for the early pots would be the Burslem area, Ticknall, Wakefield or Potterspury. There is plenty of fieldwalking evidence for the production of Cistercian wares at the earlier kiln sites in Ticknall.

Figure 76 shows the range of time and place for the black ware references. Leicestershire had twenty references, and Derbyshire had thirteen; none of the other counties had more

| Decade | Leics | Derbys | Warks | Ches | Salop | Oxon | Lincs | N'hton |
|--------|-------|--------|-------|------|-------|------|-------|--------|
| 1550-9 | - | 1 | - | - | - | - | - | - |
| 1560-9 | - | - | - | - | - | - | - | - |
| 1570-9 | - | - | - | - | - | - | - | - |
| 1580-9 | - | 1 | - | - | - | - | - | - |
| 1590-9 | 1 | 1 | - | - | - | - | - | - |
| 1600-9 | 2 | - | 1 | - | - | 2 | 1 | - |
| 1610-9 | 3 | 3 | - | - | - | 1 | 3 | - |
| 1620-9 | 4 | 2 | - | - | 1 | - | 1 | .. |
| 1630-9 | 4 | 2 | 3 | 1 | - | - | 2 | - |
| 1640-9 | - | - | - | - | - | - | - | - |
| 1650-9 | - | - | - | - | - | - | - | - |
| 1660-9 | 3 | - | - | - | - | - | - | 1 |
| 1670-9 | - | - | - | - | - | - | 1 | - |
| 1680-9 | - | 3 | - | - | - | - | - | - |
| 1690-9 | 2 | - | - | - | - | - | - | - |
| 1700-9 | 1 | - | - | - | - | - | - | - |

Figure 76 – Black wares by county 1556–1707

than eight. The first reference occurred in 1556 in Chesterfield in the inventory of John Aulte, a husbandman, who had 'thre beyre pottes and two black cuppes' worth 4d. Margaret Capper, also of Chesterfield, had '9 bear potes and 2 black potes' worth 1s 4d in 1588.[72] The most significant period for black ware was 1590 to 1669, when there were between two and five references per decade. From 1670 to 1707 there was only one per decade. Analysis of the descriptions of black ware shows that it was predominantly used for drinking, and was most commonly found in the buttery, in association with items used together: glasses, bottles, barrels, tundishes, blackjacks and jugs. The inventory of Edward Harwood alias Tomson of Banbury, a shoe maker, neatly reflects this. He had '4 black pottes to drinke in' listed in his buttery in 1606.[73] There were forty-one references to black pots, six to jugs, five to cups or drinking cups and two to beer pots. There was one reference each to a mugpot, a mug, a panpot and a basin. Many of the references were to black pots in surprisingly large quantities, whether for an individual household or for a shop. These pots registered the largest numbers of all the pottery types we recorded. They seem to have been in widespread use for drinking vessels by the seventeenth century, and they were cheap enough to be affordable even at the lower levels of society. Richard Mold of Leicester, for example, had twelve black pots in his buttery[74] and six was not an uncommon number. Two entries for black pots are interesting, one describing the pots as 'Indgoe blacke potts' and the other as 'blacke and red mugge pottes'.[75] There were two mentions of a 'band pott' with black pots, presumably a pot with a coloured band round it.[76]

Commercial stocks of black pots are again the most informative for prices and quantities. Thomas Cobbe of Sutton St James was a chapman in 1613 with seven dozen black pots for sale at 9d per dozen or $^{3}/_{4}$d each.[77] William Taylor of Harborough, described as a yeoman in 1625, had a shop with four dozen black pots at 6d per dozen or $^{1}/_{2}$d each.[78] James Smith of Stamford, a tallowchandler in 1630, had sixty black jugs valued at 10s (2d each) and one hundred dozen black pots (1,200) at £2 10s 3d (6d per dozen or $^{1}/_{2}$d each). This is an astonishing figure for pots of the same size and type. The figures discussed above for traders in Ticknall ware were for mixed wares. He also had an unspecified but obviously large number of 'blacke Potts & Juggs' valued at 13s 4d, perhaps around another hundred pots.[79] In 1631 a Market Harborough chandler, Edward Richardson, had seventeen black pots and a jug in his shop stock, valued with everything else.[80] Black pots were sold in Grantham in 1634 by Thomas Walton. He had some stored there and valued with other goods at 7s, and in his shop at Folkingham he had four dozen black pots as part of a valuation of £6 4s.[81] Margaret Lampert, the Northamptonshire shopkeeper discussed above, had '40 doz[en] small black pots at 3d doz' (worth 10s altogether or $^{1}/_{4}$d each) in 1664.[82] William Dent of Horncastle, also discussed above, had 'Eight dozen of Black potts att xi$^{d}$ y$^{e}$ dozen' in 1679.[83] Susanna Overing, who had a shop in Leicester in 1692, had '3 doz black pots 6$^{d}$ dozen' or $^{1}/_{2}$d each.[84] These figures suggest that the small black drinking pots were sold by the dozen or half-dozen rather than singly, and the domestic inventories would support this. Daniell Ogden of Lutterworth, who had a shop there and in Dunton Bassett, had '8 black potts' in the latter shop in 1695, selling at 2d each, which implies that they were larger pots than the common drinking vessels.

Generic yellow wares only occur in eight inventory references between 1596 and 1637, which is notably earlier than the production of Ticknall 'white' wares discussed above (1670 to 1718). There were six mentions of yellow pots, and one each of a yellow flower pot, a chamber pot and a pancheon. One inventory suggests by association that there was a yellow jug: '2 yellow potts and one Jugg' valued at 8d.[85] The yellow wares are found in the kitchen, the hall, the house and the dairy. There are no references to yellow wares in shop inventories. The best clue to the prices is in the earliest reference, for somewhere in Leicestershire in 1596. The deceased had 'five yellow potts & 2 yellow flower pots iiii$^{d}$', so that even if the pots were different sizes or qualities they were all probably worth 1d or less each.[86] Winifred

Tailer's two pots and a jug at 8d had higher values, perhaps 3d for the pots and 2d for the jug.[87] The remaining references were all grouped with other items, but the group values still suggest individual values of under 1d to 2d or 3d. The geographical distribution of the yellow wares in our sources is limited to Leicestershire, Derbyshire and Warwickshire (Figure 77), and must raise the possibility that it originated in Ticknall but was not recorded as such in the inventories. Fieldwalking evidence from our early sites suggests that Ticknall was making yellow ware from the mid-1500s onwards.

| Decade | Leics | Derbys | Warks |
|--------|-------|--------|-------|
| 1590-9 | 1 | - | - |
| 1600-9 | - | - | - |
| 1610-9 | - | 3 | - |
| 1620-9 | 1 | - | - |
| 1630-9 | 2 | - | 1 |

Figure 77 – Yellow wares by county, 1596–1637

Leather bottles and jacks provided more competition for Ticknall's output of jugs and mugs. There are references to them from 1572 to the early eighteenth century, mainly to bottles (forty-seven references in total), and jacks (thirteen references). There was one reference to a 'leather Costrell' in 1650, which was worth 8d.[88] Bottles and jacks clearly varied in size and age, occasionally being described as great, small or old. Two bottles were valued at 4d each in 1573, twice the value of the four wicker-covered bottles with them. In 1574, John Quick of Southampton had 'a lethren botell w[i]th a mouthe of tynn' worth 8d; this would have protected the leather from rotting and the pitch lining from chipping in use.[89] William Holland of Chesterfield had two leather bottles worth 1s in 1587, while William Newsam, a Chesterfield yeoman, had 'one lether bottel one wooden bottell and 3 litle lether Jackes 2s 4d'. Possibly the leather jacks and bottle were worth 6d each and the wooden one 4d.[90] In 1634 James Longsdowne of Shrewsbury had 'Three blacke Jackes and eight earthen Cupps 4s 4d', suggesting values of 8d for the jacks and 3$\frac{1}{2}$d for the cups. Three years later Nicholas Clarke of Chesterfield had an unspecified number of black jacks valued at 4s, which at 8d each would mean he had six jacks.[91] The fashion for lipping drinking vessels with silver was also applied to the black jacks, and there is a surviving example in the collection of the Leatherseller's Company in London. Nicholas Samon of Stoneleigh had 'one little black Jack with a silver brimme' worth 1s 6d in 1638; while tripling the value of the jack, the silver did not raise it as much as might be expected. We do not, of course, know the condition or extent of the silver decoration. A Market Harborough gentleman, Mr Thomas Meres, had '1 bason Jacks lipt with Silver £2' in 1688. It is possible that the basin was also lipped with silver, but although we do not know how many jacks there were, the value suggests something quite elaborate. Surprisingly, even treenware was treated this way — a 1633 reference has 'one wooden noggin tipt with silver' as part of a longer entry.[92] Apart from the silver mounted jacks, the values suggest that leather bottles, jacks and costrels were all more expensive than similar pottery items. Their geographical distribution was widespread in the evidence we have used and there is no reason to believe that they were not found all over the country (Figure 78).

In addition to the jacks, bottles and costrell noted separately, there were thirty-one leather bottles in mid-Essex in the seventeenth century and three in the eighteenth century.[93]

During the period of the study, information was collected and recorded on imported pottery for comparison, and while a full analysis is not appropriate here, a summary of the figures shows the extent of imported pottery in the sources. In general the imported wares were of a much higher quality than Ticknall's output, and were luxury goods. They did not compete directly with Ticknall ware though they can be found in the same households.

| Decade | Leics | Staffs | Derbys | Warks | Salop | Oxon | Lincs | Ches | Essex | Hants |
|--------|-------|--------|--------|-------|-------|------|-------|------|-------|-------|
| 1570-9 | - | - | - | - | - | - | - | - | - | 3 |
| 1580-9 | - | - | 1 | - | - | 1 | - | - | - | - |
| 1590-9 | - | - | - | - | - | 1 | - | - | - | - |
| 1600-9 | - | - | - | - | - | - | - | - | - | - |
| 1610-9 | - | 1 | 4 | - | - | 1 | - | - | - | - |
| 1620-9 | - | - | - | - | - | - | 1 | - | - | - |
| 1630-9 | - | - | 1 | 1 | 1 | - | - | - | - | - |
| 1640-9 | - | - | - | - | - | - | - | - | - | - |
| 1650-9 | - | - | - | - | - | - | - | 1 | - | - |
| 1660-9 | - | - | - | - | - | - | - | - | 1 | - |
| 1670-9 | - | - | - | - | - | - | - | - | 5 | - |
| 1680-9 | 1 | - | - | 1 | - | - | - | - | 1 | - |

Figure 78 – Leather jacks and bottles by county1572–1688

Usually the imported wares were in the better rooms in the house, while the Ticknall was generally found in the kitchen, buttery and dairy. Figure 79 details the date ranges in our sources for each type of imported ware.

The blue wares were German stonewares from the Westerwald region, often imported or re-imported via London through Boston for distribution in the midlands. The generic stonewares also came from Germany, from Westerwald and Lower Saxony, for example, and this group included bellarmines. White suggests that Boston had stopped importing it by about 1650.[94] The dates from our sources indicated a decline in the recording of stoneware after the 1630s, but it picked up again after 1680. It is possible that though imports had declined, the stoneware potteries in London, such as Pickleherring and Fulham, were supplying the domestic market with new goods by the 1680s. The dates for mentions of stoneware trimmed with various metals seem to support this theory. The popularity of this stoneware decorated with precious metals was

| Ware Type | Start Date | End Date |
|-----------|------------|----------|
| Blue | 1562 | 1692 |
| China | 1616 | 1809 |
| Delft | 1631 | 1809 |
| Holland | 1660 | 1715 |
| Stone | 1562 | 1809 |

Figure 79 – Imported wares 1562–1809

noticed by a foreign visitor: 'In 1558 Etienne Perlin noted in his *Description of England* that the English drank great quantities of beer not "out of glasses, but from earthen pots with silver handles and covers, and this even in houses of persons of middling fortune"'.[95]

The dates for all vessels trimmed with silver, silver-gilt, pewter or tin in our sources are laid out in Figure 80 (p148). They are mainly stone, plus leather, wood and china.

China first appeared in our sources in 1616. Though its mentions were erratic at first, they were well established by the middle of the century and thereafter appeared with increasing frequency and variety. The category included mentions of porcelain, and of Indian rather than China ware. It continued through to the end of our sources. Delft started to be recorded in 1631 and appeared until 1809, whereas Holland as a type was limited to the period 1660–1715. It may be that it became subsumed in the Delft category.

| Decade | Silver | Silver Gilt | Pewter | Tin | Not Specified |
|--------|--------|-------------|--------|-----|---------------|
| 1550-9 | - | - | - | - | 1 |
| 1560-9 | 1 | - | - | - | - |
| 1570-9 | 13 | 2 | - | 1 | 2 |
| 1580-9 | - | - | - | - | - |
| 1590-9 | 1 | - | 1 | - | - |
| 1600-9 | - | - | - | - | 1 |
| 1610-9 | - | 2 | - | - | - |
| 1620-9 | - | - | 1 | - | - |
| 1630-9 | 5 | 1 | - | - | - |
| 1640-9 | 1 | - | - | - | - |
| 1650-9 | - | - | - | - | - |
| 1660-9 | 2 | - | - | - | - |
| 1670-9 | - | - | - | - | - |
| 1680-9 | 3 | 2 | - | - | - |
| 1690-9 | 1 | - | - | - | - |
|        |   |   |   |   |   |
| 1750-9 | 1 | - | - | - | - |

Figure 80 – Vessels trimmed with metal 1558–1755

Sometimes the sources can give a misleading picture of pottery production. One statistically valid group is the wills and inventories for Chesterfield, which have all been published for 1521 to 1650. They make no mention of pots made in Chesterfield. However, Jewitt said that William Caskon, who died in 1517, was a potter. R. B. Brown noted that when Ralph Heathcote moved into a house in Chesterfield in 1501, he was described as a pot maker, brazier and bell founder. Brown assumed that he was a clay potter. Brown also noted a reference in 1641 to Francis Bretnor, pot maker, of Chesterfield.[96] If there had been a pottery in Chesterfield during this period it seems surprising that no mention was made of it in the inventories, but only generic earthenware is mentioned. Heathcote came from a wealthy Chesterfield family, heavily involved with the metal trades through several generations. The description 'pot maker' refers to casting metal pots rather than earthenware manufacture. The Caskon (Caskyne) family had similar interests and at one point ran a smelt mill. Bretnor was known to be involved in the metal industries. It is the terminology which has unfortunately misled both Jewitt and Brown. The Chesterfield potteries are well known in the late eighteenth century, when an advertisement for a journeyman potter was placed in the *Derby Mercury* by Jacob Ford of Chesterfield, 'proprietor at the above works' in 1776.[97] If the pottery was not started until later, it would explain why Chesterfield ware was not included in the stock list of the Derby pot seller, William Saywell, when he advertised in the *Derby Mercury* on 3 March 1742. A different problem occurs with the Crich pottery, where the only reference in our sources is from Saywell's advertisement, yet the pottery had been operating since 1666. We have not worked through a statistically valid group of sources for Crich, and its appearance or otherwise in the sets of inventories we have searched would be purely random. Even this may not be enough. No references to the potteries at Bolsover or Brampton appear in our sources though they fall within the period covered by them. The 'earliest mention of Brampton was in 1636, to the "Kiln Flats" on Brampton Moor (see Derbyshire Porcelain and Pottery, Matlock, 1965)', and its period of expansion was in the late eighteenth to early nineteenth centuries. Bolsover pottery was near the market place and was operated by Thomas and William Robinson, and Thomas Robinson junior, throughout the early eighteenth century. Brears notes that because of the complaints of a neighbour, Samuel Brailsford, about smoke pollution,

*four local tradesmen 'bound themselves under a sum of £20 payable to Brailsford to obtain the consent of the potters to stop the nuisance' (Downman, History of Bolsover, 1895). The potters agreed 'to remove or pull down the pot-work or pot-works, smoking house or smoking houses' on or before 24 June 1749, or to cease working them, under a sum of £40. Thus the pottery closed, and the Robinsons left to start a new pottery at Brampton, according to a local tradition.*

When the Bolsover site was redeveloped in the late nineteenth century, the pottery was found to be a 'highly glazed redware, with some incised slip decoration (now in the British, Nottingham and Derby Museums)'.[98]

Ticknall, Brampton, Crich and Bolsover had the only pottery industries in Derbyshire prior to about 1740, when the system of inventories was falling into disuse. It is likely that the Cockpit Hill works in Derby was started during the 1740s, though the exact date is unknown. The first record dates from 1751 when it was run by William Butts, a potter, Thomas Rivett, the Derby MP from 1747 to 1754, and John Heath, a local banker. Cockpit Hill made creamware, and possibly also brown and white salt glaze, tortoiseshell and other coloured glazed wares at this period.[99] Planché started the first china works in Derby at Nottingham Road in about 1748.[100] Of the four county pottery sites, Ticknall is known to have had between eleven and twelve potteries working throughout the sixteenth and seventeenth centuries, while only one is known for Crich and Bolsover at any date. Brampton may have had more than one in the early eighteenth century.

# References

1 Robert Whitehead 16 April 1606 ROLLR

2 Thomas Foster 1 April 1612 ROLLR

3 Simon Shallcrosse 25 December 1623 LJRO

4 Hugh Galley 1623/4 in Bestall, J. and Fowkes, D. (2001)

5 Arthur Cooke 3 May 1558 in Roberts, E. and Parker, K. (eds) (1992)

6 George Kelton 6 October 1634 ROLLR

7 Robert Wood 20 April 1634 LJRO

8 George Tilley 10 March 1694 ROLLR

9 Robert Jarvis n.d. 1634; Franncis Greene 26 March 1638; Bridget Smith 17 March 1662; all ROLLR

10 Ralph Clarke 1630 inv. no. 136/503 LA

11 Vincent Scudamore 1 January 1663 ROLLR

12 Peter Chaveney 18 May 1670 ROLLR

13 John Mee 22 September 1680 LJRO

14 Raph Rolin 15 August 1683 LJRO

15 John Warberton 12 April 1688 ROLLR

16 Daniell Ogden 6 August 1695 ROLLR

17 White, A. J. (unpublished thesis, 1989)

18 White's references are to kilometres, but we have consistently converted these to miles

19 Inv. no. 138/21 1631 LA

20 ibid.

21 TNA: PRO E190/319/4

22 ibid.

23 ibid.

24 ibid.

25 TNA: PRO E190/319/4, E190/312/6, E190/322/4

26 Inv. no. 121/113 1617 LA

27 Plot, R. (1686), p122

28 Wetherill, L. (1971), pp8, 141–2

29 Wetherill, L. (1983), pp45–6

30 Richard Deeley 13 June 1631 LJRO

31 Elizabeth Bell 7 April 1634 LJRO

32 William Dickens 26 September 1635 LJRO

33 Robert Allen 19 October 1683 LJRO

34 William Mathfield 30 September 1680 LJRO

35 Brittan, F. (1990), pp61–92

36 John Vincent 20 September 1682 ROLLR

37 Edward Reddish 16 May 1631 CRO

38 John Skelhorne 27 June 1631 CRO

39 Peter Smyth 19 April 1676; John Burslem 20 January 1679/80; both LJRO

40 William Montfort 29 August 1683 LJRO

41 *Derby Mercury* 3 March 1742, p4 DLSL

42 Thomas Gent 26 July 1631; Thomas Clowes 11 June 1683; both LJRO

43 William Taylor 5 July 1639; Frances Keelinge 31 August 1639; John Tunnycliff 7 January 1681; Margarett Lownes 28 September 1683; all LJRO

44 John Fenton 1683 (day and month unknown) LJRO

45 John Machin 19 September 1664 LJRO

46 John Eldershaw 11 April 1633 LJRO

47 Wetherill, L. (1971), pp76–80

48 Honey, W. B. (1945), pp57–9

49 Defoe, D. (1983), p16

50 White, A. J. (1979), pp290–1

51 Nathaniel Mason 28.2.1734 DR165/381 1734/5 SBT

52 Chaffers, W. (1903), pp789–90

53 Draper, J. (1982), pp85–91

54 Brown, R. B. (1994), p120

55 Randle Wright 16 July 1631 CRO

56 Inv. no. 161/24 LA

57 John Ward 3 April 1544 in Bestall, J. and Fowkes, D. (1977)

58 Raphe Hethcote 3 April 1577 in Bestall, J. and Fowkes, D. (1977)

59 Elinor Simkins 13 January 1590 in Havinden, M. (1965)

60 Robert Newton 7 January 1643 ROLLR

61 John Glen 28 May 1662 in Johnston, J. A. (1991)

62 Ann Overing 18 September 1682 ROLLR

63 Mr Edward Wormwell 2 May 1670 ROLLR

64 Ciccily Cooper 19 February 1684 ROLLR

65 Walter Chamberlain 9 March 1681 LJRO

66 Margaret Lampert 26 October 1664 NRO; John Sharpe 13 January 1673 LJRO; John Bayley 14 August 1674 ROLLR; John Orme 21 April 1681 LJRO; Mr Edward Phillips n.d. 1689 NA; George Tilley 10 March 1694 ROLLR; Burdett Account Books 6 April 1697 D5054/13/5/1 DRO

67 Nathaniel Mason 28 February 1734 DR165/381, SBT; Giles Turlington n.d. but after 1800; Mr Botterill 18 May 1809; both ROLLR

68 William Dent 1679 quoted in White, A. J. (unpublished thesis, 1989)

69 John Page 9 February 1692; Thomas Morrison 23 April 1692; both ROLLR

70 White, A. J. (1979), pp290–1

71 Draper, J. (1982), pp85–91

72 John Aulte 17 April 1556; Margaret Capper als Shearshawe 20 July 1588; both in Bestall, J. and Fowkes, D. (1977)

73 Edward Harwood alias Tomson 21 June 1606 NRO

74 Richard Mold 4 July 1614 ROLLR

75 Nicholas Taylor 30 November 1625 ROLLR; John Staine 6 June 1631 ref WS1631 CRO

76 William Abell 21 August 1635; Mary Lewes of Mancetter 19 October 1636; both LJRO

77 Thomas Cobbe n.d.1613 no. 113/13 LA

78 William Taylor 30 June 1625 ROLLR

79 James Smith 1630 quoted in White, A. J. (unpublished thesis, 1989)

80 Edward Richardson 27 July 1631 ROLLR

81 Thomas Walton 1634 quoted in White, A. J. (unpublished thesis, 1989)

82 Margaret Lampert 26 October 1664 NRO

83 William Dent 1679 quoted in White, A. J. (unpublished thesis, 1989)

84 Susanna Overing 23 September 1692 ROLLR

85 Winifred Tailer 26 April 1634 LJRO

86 Unknown inventory n.d. 1596 (in volume '1550 et diversis Annis') ROLLR

87 Winifred Tailer 26 April 1634 LJRO

88 Edward Harpur 24 September 1650 in Phillips, C. B. and Smith, J. H. (1992)

89 Richard Goddard the elder 1 February 1572/3; John Quick 28 June 1574 in Roberts, E. and Parker, K. (eds) (1992)

90 William Holland 1 November 1587; William Newsam 30 December 1617; both in Bestall, J. and Fowkes, D. (1997 and 2001)

91 James Longsdowne 12 May 1637 LJRO; Nicholas Clarke 30 August 1637 in Bestall, J. and Fowkes, D. (2001)

92 Nicholas Samon 21 August 1638 LJRO; Mr Thomas Meres 25 April 1688 ROLLR; Eleanor Sargenson 12 June 1634 LJRO

93 See Steer, F. W. (1969)

94 White, A. J. (unpublished thesis, 1989)

95 Poole, J. E., *English Pottery*, reviewed in *Ceramic Review* 167 (1997), p30

96 Brown, R. B. (1994), p97

97 *Derby Mercury*, 29 March 1776, quoted in Brown, R. B. (1994), p97–8

98 All references to Bolsover and Brampton from Brears, P. C. D. (1971), pp173–4

99 Rice, D. G. (1983), p21

100 Notes to the Derby Porcelain display in Derby Museum

# 9. 'All East England Through': the distribution network

Pottery by its very nature is a difficult product to transport any distance in quantity, as it is both heavy and fragile. We believe that when pots started to be made in Ticknall in the latter part of the fifteenth century, the potters must have taken their goods themselves, either on foot or by packhorse, selling as they went locally and at markets and fairs. At this period roads and tracks would have been rutted in summer, muddy and virtually impassable in winter. Transport by cart or wagon would have been impossible until much later when the roads began to be improved by turnpike trusts. However, if the earthenware produced in Ticknall was sent 'all East England through' and beyond, how did the potters manage to get their wares sent so far and who took them? This chapter looks at the people who were distributing the pots and the growth of that trade.

By the early seventeenth century those potters who were involved in pastoral farming may have had time and the animals to deliver their wares. Robert Fisher is an example of a potter who may have delivered goods with his four horses and packsaddles. However, potters delivering their own wares were probably not very significant in the distribution of the pottery from Ticknall. As the pottery trade grew, the selling of pots was taken on by specialist pot sellers or hawkers — they were working in the Halifax area by the second quarter of the seventeenth century.[1] In our area we have found evidence for specialised pot sellers or hawkers from as early as 1614, both in Ticknall and nearby in the Coleorton area.

The earliest known specialist seller was Edward Warden of Griffydam, a carpenter by trade. When his will was made in 1614[2] he listed a large number of debtors, many of whom can be identified as from Ticknall, including three, possibly four, potters. Humfrie Page owed 'xxiiij[tie] fatt of ware due at this time', John Holland and Thomas Cooke owed £5 worth of ware and 'Richard Holland of the Fortye' owed five separate debts for small sums lent. This latter reference suggests that Holland was living down near the Forty brook and perhaps working the site later worked by the Hanson family. These references imply that Warden had paid in advance for the ware from the potters and that it was packed into 'fatts' or casks for transport. These would have been unwieldy on a packhorse, but they could have gone down the river. There is another reference to a 'fatt'. Henry Blest owed John Pegge 'xxxvijs vd, and one fatt, and a hundred of ware' in 1621;[3] this had presumably been paid for in advance. It also suggests that both Warden and Pegge had a ready market. John Pegge may have been a Ticknall man, as a John Peg was buried in 1635. Alternatively, he may have been either the John Pegg of Coleorton who married in 1618 or the John Smith alias Pegg who married at Whitwick in 1626. Little is known about any of them.

The Warden family continued to be involved in selling pots after Edward's death. His son John, also of Griffydam, witnessed the will of the Ticknall pot maker Richard Gardener of Scaddows in 1614 and owed him a debt of 26s 8d in the inventory. By the time his own inventory was made in 1649 he had 'ware in the countrey' worth £1 12s 4d, a cottage in Ticknall worth £2 and he also owed £6 10s 4d for 'ware at Ticknall' with perhaps two kilns' worth of ware to sell. His inventory suggests that he had a considerable trade with the village. He had 'debts owinge which are desperate' worth £1 8s 8d and a large number of people to whom he owed money, a total of £42 1s 4d.[4] This suggests that by now the pot sellers were taking the pots to sell and returning later with the money.

By the 1620s two more pot sellers are known to have been involved. Henry Basford or Berrisford of Ticknall, described as a 'husbandman', had six horses at his death in 1626, as well as packsaddles and Ticknall pots worth £1.[5] This represents a considerable amount of stock — pots were priced between a farthing and two pence depending on size, with virtually no increase in price for several centuries.[6] Just how much stock he held may be suggested by the figures in Chapter 6, which suggest a possible 2,800 pots for a kilnful worth £3. These presumably were all of one size whereas Basford would have no doubt had a variety of types and sizes for sale. On this basis Basford's stock could have been a third of a kiln; it was certainly a considerable amount. Basford's inventory indicates debts owed to him but frustratingly there are just the bare amounts totalling £12 14s 4d and no names. His widow was responsible for the £8 18s 2d he owed in debts, but his creditors were not named. In 1626 William Wellands of Swannington had a 'little Ticknill ware' worth 5s as well as two horses and packsaddles in his inventory. He owed a long list of debts, including 20s 8d to 'Raph Holland', another Ticknall pot maker. Wellands also owed money to people in Newbold, Coleorton, Swannington, Osbaston, Derby and Leicester.[7]

Two others who were selling during this period and about whom little is known are John Mosendew, potter of 'Overton Sausey alias Colleoverton' whose will was proved in 1629, and John Price, potter, whose son was baptised in 1640 at Coleorton.[8] Here is another potential problem. They are described as potters, a term which today is associated with people who make pots. However it was also a term for those selling pots as well, synonymous with pot hawker.[9] There is also no indication in any wills, inventories or deeds in the Coleorton/Griffydam area of any potting tools, kilns or workhouses as there are in Ticknall. The lack of this equipment shows that the 'potters' of this area were involved in selling not making pots, particularly in the light of the development of the pot selling trade in this area in the late eighteenth and early nineteenth centuries which is described later. Documents often refer to a 'potter' or 'pot carrier', and it is only in the eighteenth century that the term pot hawker comes into use in this area. However, as a hawker most aptly describes what they were doing, it is the term that we will use. These early pot hawkers clearly represent an established trade in selling, and would all have been working earlier than the date we know which is their year of death.

In Ticknall the next reference to a known pot hawker comes in 1670 when William King died. His inventory shows he had one old horse and fifteen shillings' worth of Ticknall pots.[10] His debts 'oweinge by speciality & without' came to £23 10s. By the 1690s William Sanderson, who originated from Chipping in Lancashire, was selling pots. He had a child baptised at Stretton en le Field a few miles to the south-west of Ticknall in 1692, either on his way to or from Ticknall, and he finally decided to settle in 1701 when he brought his settlement certificate. Five more children were baptised at Ticknall.[11] Information on later pot hawkers based in Ticknall is harder to find than for the actual pot makers as they tended to be less well off. People from the village continued to sell the local pots, although references to them are sparse. There are indications that Ticknall men, and women, sold pots up until the 1890s, and there are no doubt others that are not known about.

In 1775 widow Mee was crossing the river Trent at Kegworth when her horse, with a load of pots on its back, fell off the bridge and 'both horse and load dashed to peices'. Her horse had been a good one, which had cost her ten guineas, and her fellow Baptists agreed to have a collection for her.[12] The parish officers, who gave so much help to the Blore family were also involved in the apprenticing of John Neville in 1808, described as a poor child of Ticknall and son of Francis Neville, pot carrier.[13]

There were shopkeepers in Ticknall from the seventeenth century and they may have sold pots as well. The earliest known was Francis Greenhough who had 'mercerie wares in the shoppe' worth £8 10s in 1636, as well as a packhorse and panniers.[14] Robert Shevyn, described as a mercer in his will of 1728, certainly sold pots as he had 'Earthernware, pattins, clogges and Broomes' worth 16s 6d in his shop; some of the earthenware must surely have been Ticknall.[15] His son Samuel was also a mercer and may have sold pots as well. John Cook had a pot shop in Ticknall by 1857; this was still in business in 1881. A map of 1857 shows it was towards the south end of the present Ingleby Lane; houses here were dcmolished in the 1960s when the lane was extended to Main Street.[16] Although we are aware of other, earlier, pot shops from the inventories in the midlands, there seems little evidence to suggest that shops were major distribution outlets for Ticknall pottery.

Nineteenth-century baptism registers and census records show that there continued to be specialist pot hawkers in Ticknall. The Dexter brothers, Thomas and John, were selling until their deaths in 1825 and 1832 respectively. John Dexter was helped on at least two occasions to buy pots with money from the parish officers in 1820 and 1821. William Brearley was given 12s by the vestry as late as 1824 to buy a basket of pots to sell. At least three generations of the Astle family were involved in selling, from Henry and John raising families in the 1820s through to their sons and possibly their grandsons. The same was true for the Beighton family. Descended from a long line of pot makers, many of the family had been involved in all aspects of the trade. By the 1800s brothers John and Samuel had sons and grandsons who followed them, selling pots until at least the 1880s. The Foster family was also travelling and selling pottery from around 1800 to the 1880s. In 1881 James Mumford was still selling pots assisted by his three sons. Other pot sellers in the village included John Jackson 1838–50, Charles Massey 1850–1 and Thomas Clarke in 1855.

However, the main group of pot sellers were concentrated just five miles to the east in the Griffydam/Coleorton area. This is where the earliest pot hawkers were found, particularly in the area centred on Coleorton Moor and Griffydam where the boundaries of Thringstone and Swannington (formerly in the parish of Whitwick) meet. Increasing numbers of pot hawkers have been found in this area from the seventeenth to the nineteenth centuries, as shown in Figure 81.

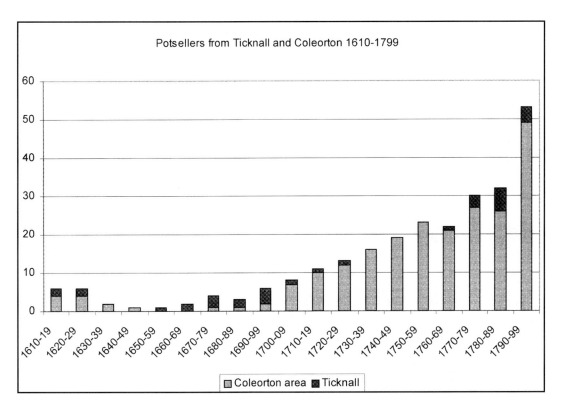

Figure 81 – Pot sellers from the Ticknall and Coleorton areas

During the latter part of the seventeenth century information for this area is sparse. William Woods of Breedon was described in his 1681 inventory as a labourer, but he also sold pots. He had a 'parcel of pots' worth £1 8s, together with five horses and mares, saddles and panniers.[17] By the 1690s the Knight family of Thringstone had started its long involvement with the pot selling trade; no fewer than eleven members of the family were involved over the next century. Jonas Knight's inventory of 1724 had '2 horses & their tackle' worth £5, and an old packsaddle as well as 'some valluable debts' of £5 10s. His wife had been buried at Calke in 1712.

From this time onwards there seems to be a steady rise in the number of pot hawkers. As well as the immediate Coleorton area some also came from Ashby de la Zouch and some of the nearby villages; some families also settled at Stapleton, on the way to Hinckley. The villages involved are shown on Figure 82.

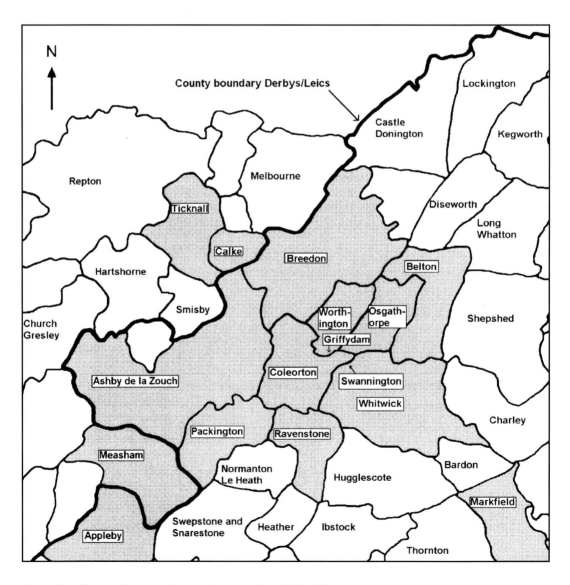

Figure 82 – Places with people involved in pot selling 1600–1851+

The sources give us little idea as to where these pot hawkers travelled and whether they really were responsible for the spread of Ticknall pots over a wide area. It is the eighteenth- and nineteenth-century references that give the clues. Richard Pemberton married in 1721 in Northamptonshire.[18] William Oakden of Breedon had contacts with Market Bosworth. His brother John, who also sold glass, appears to have moved to King's Lynn before 1760; both are known to have sold pots. William Palmer and his wife of 'Cole Orton Moor Leics., Dealers in Pot Ware and travellers' were at Rippingale in Lincolnshire in 1779 when they had a child baptised.

By the early 1800s pot hawkers from the Coleorton area were to be found all over the country. Joseph Bacon and Joseph Knight were 'gone a potting', John Field had 'gone a potting in Essex', and his neighbour Samuel Pemberton was 'out a potting and will not return for 7 weeks' when the solicitor's clerk called in 1803 at the cottages of some of the pot hawkers about the proposed enclosure of Peggs Green. Samuel Pemberton's entry gives some idea of the length of time that they spent on their away selling — he certainly was not delivering locally. It was not uncommon to take the family as did Andrew Sharpe whose son John was baptised in the parish of Charles in Plymouth in 1810; his father made sure this was recorded in Worthington parish register when he came back home. William Handford and his wife had a child baptised in Fareham in Surrey in 1813. George Else was obviously unwell when he made his will at Hitchin in Hertfordshire in November 1814. He died exactly one month later on 10 December, probably on the way home, as no burial record has been found locally. Probate was granted four months after he made his will.[19] Thomas Handford was unlucky enough to have some of his earthenware dishes, plates, jugs and basins stolen from him at Hertford in 1823.[20] John Bailey travelled to Edinburgh and two of his sons settled there. He was described as a 'china merchant of this city' when his daughter married there. In 1826 he mentioned a forthcoming trip there when he added a codicil to his will. He too was not buried locally, but his will was proved shortly afterwards, suggesting that he died whilst on his travels. William Field was in Liverpool by 1840 and was 'late of Liverpool Lancashire, glass and earthenware dealer now of Coleorton' when he made his will in 1856.

The number of pot hawkers concentrated in this area continued to rise, and they obtained their pots from further afield. More information becomes available from 1813 onwards when the baptism registers show occupations. The numbers peaked during the decade 1810–19.

By 1851, when there was only one working pottery in Ticknall, it is clearer where some of the pot hawkers travelled. The census transcriptions and indexes that have been completed for a number of counties have enabled more pot hawkers to be identified.[21] Quite a number are at home or living locally, such as Francis Ward and his family who were just a few miles away at Castle Donington. John Haywood and his wife were in Leicester and Joseph Willars had also settled there. Henry Cooper and family had settled in Northampton and Joseph Jones had settled in Warwick, where three of his children were born. William Smith was lodging in Halesowen; he had been born in Stapleton. Several were much further afield. William Litherland had a shop in Liverpool by 1851, Joseph Jakes and family were living with his parents-in-law at Batley in Yorkshire, whilst Thomas Hudson and his family were living in Gomersal in the same county. Michael Field and his family had settled in Great Yarmouth by 1835; by 1851 he had three shop assistants. John Scarborow from Thringstone had a shop in Brighton and Sarah Wileman was also selling there. Hannah Morton, born at Measham, was trading in china and glass at Hastings. Charles Price, from Coleorton, went first to Loughborough, and by 1835 his family was in Exeter. His brother Joseph was born at York, baptised at Coleorton, married in Hull and settled in Beverley selling pots. In 1851 he was visiting Exeter and stayed with his brother Charles. Simeon Griffin, from Thringstone, had been settled in Plymouth for twenty years and had children born there; he was described as a dealer in china. Members of the Bacon family from Whitwick were living in Hampshire and had branched into horse dealing as well as selling pots.

Hawkers from the Coleorton area still travelling to sell their pots included five adult members of the Tow family who spent census night at the Talbot Inn in Gloucester. At the opposite side of the country, James Gutteridge and his wife put up at the White Horse Inn at Wayland in Norfolk, whilst Joseph Gutteridge and his wife were at the George Inn in the market place at Guiltcross in the same county. William Hodges and Sophia his wife were there too, and the two couples may have been travelling together. Others had more basic accommodation — William Balls, his wife and three children, Joseph Baker and his wife, Joseph Smith, his wife and daughter, were all 'Dwelling in Tents' in Frogs Hall Road, Walsingham, Norfolk, and were described as 'Travelling in co. with Earthenware'. They were all born in Leicestershire, but that is all the information apart from their ages that they gave the enumerator — perhaps being disturbed on a chilly evening in late March did not go down too well. Nearby at the Bell Inn in the same lane was John Smith, also from Leicestershire. Although no birthplace is given for this latter group, there is sufficient information on pot selling families in the Coleorton area for us to be fairly confident that this is where those families were from. Not included in the above are a similar number of people from the Coleorton area who were described as either hawkers, travellers, commercial travellers or hawkers of hardware, smallwares or spar.

Not surprisingly, in view of the itinerant nature of their trading, the trade directories list just one earthenware dealer in the Coleorton area. John Webb was of Thringstone and was the only earthenware seller to appear in a trade directory.[22] The census shows he was born at Groton in Suffolk, but there is no trace of a baptism for him there. His parents could have been travellers from the Coleorton area. This illustrates another problem in tracing these pot hawkers — they may have been born on their parents' travels and only some of them were baptised in their home parish.

Hawkers had three traditional places for sales: door-to-door sales, markets and fairs. Pottery was sold in all three ways. Door-to-door sales were probably a steady source of income and would reach those who rarely went to markets. No doubt the pot sellers had regular routes in between markets and fairs, as did chapmen.[23] From the evidence of probate inventories we know that Ticknall pottery was spread over a wide area in the midlands (see Figure 53 in Chapter 7). The next part of this chapter looks at the evidence for all three types of sales.

Door-to-door pottery sales are often unrecorded. Even the better off bought goods from pedlars who called at their door. Parson Woodford living in Weston Longeville bought cloth from the pedlar who called at his door every ten weeks on a regular round. For his china, however, he went to Norwich where he had an account with a china merchant.[24] A rare description of a pot hawker calling at a house comes from Sir George Crewe. On a visit to Norfolk in 1816 he rode from Diss to Thetford and enquired his way at Bressingham. He recorded the following:

*A cart loaded with Earthenware was standing at the door. I asked the poor woman whether she was purchasing — she said Yes, if she could wish herself. I then asked her which Pot or Pan it was she had set her heart upon. The Salesman, lifting up a large red Pan, such I have seen used for milk in some of the dairies in Warwickshire, said 'She would fain have this, could she spare the money'. At which I gave her a shilling and 6 pence, being the price. The poor creature was as much astonished as delighted and was thankful in the extreme, and the Pot-man said 'Never could you have done charity where it was more truly deserved, for this woman has a very large family and is often hard set to get a morsel of bread'. I wished them good luck and trotted on ...[25]*

Fairs were held once or twice a year and were of prime importance in the Middle Ages. Towards the end of this period, however, fairs became more concerned with entertainment than with selling. Nevertheless, fairs drew the crowds so buying and selling still took place. Many towns had fair charters dating from the thirteenth century. Some had two, three or even four fairs a year, often combined with the annual hiring fair or 'statutes' for agricultural and domestic servants. The greatest fair of them all was Sturbridge fair held just outside Cambridge. Here stalls were set out in streets according to the goods sold. There was a pottery area where coarse pottery was separated from the fine china. This fair was described by Defoe in 1723:

*... the shops are placed in Rows like Streets ... and here ... are all sorts of Trades, who sell by Retale, and who come principally from London with their Goods; scarce any trades are omitted, Goldsmiths, Toy shops, Braziers, Turners, Milleners, Haberdashers, Hatters, Mercers, Drapers, Pewterers, China-Warehouses, Taverns, Brandy-shops, and Eating-Houses, innumerable, and all in Tents, and Booths ...*[26]

This fair was still going strong in 1827 when Horne's Year Book states 'in the meadow adjoining were the coal fair, pottery fair and Staffordshire dealers. The greater part of these articles were delivered from on board vessells which drew up close to the bank of the river'.[27]

However, it was the weekly market that was probably the main source of steady sales. Farming families travelled to the nearest market to sell their produce and to buy goods they needed; others came just to buy. Sometimes particular markets would be visited for different goods. Village carrier services were developing to transport people and their produce to the nearest market and ultimately they would link the county town with the towns and villages in its area.[28] Much business was done in the market and pot hawkers would have sold here, perhaps in the way William Litherland and his brother are reputed to have done.

*Both he and his brother Thomas began their careers selling china from baskets in the squares of market towns ... the two brothers Litherland would approach the square on a market day from opposite ends of the town, carrying baskets of ware on their backs, meet and start a quarrel about whose pitch was which; this drew a crowd, and when they judged it was big enough, the quarrel was settled and business could begin.*[29]

Pot hawkers also visited major towns and cities. A pot hawker from The Potteries was caught up in the Peterloo Massacre on his visit to Manchester to sell his wares.[30] Other hawkers placed advertisements for auction sales in the local newspaper, often selling what appeared to be good china. However good the china seemed, it would probably have been superseded by newer fashions and designs, thus enabling it to be sold more cheaply to people further down the social scale. L. Nathan, a licensed hawker from London, held such a sale in Leicester in 1825.[31]

Pot hawkers got their wares to market in a variety of ways. The progression of a hawker, pedlar or chapman from carrying a pack, to a barrow and then a packhorse, obtaining a cart and finally being successful enough to have a shop is a recognised one.[32] When Plot mentioned the distribution of pots from Burslem, he described the carriers as 'poor crate-men, who carry them at their backs all over the country'.[33] Plot was not the only one to observe them. Pamphleteers mention 'wandering glassmen, carrying glasses and earthenware, packed in straw on their backs'.[34] They would have either carried the pots in wicker baskets or used panniers if they had a horse available; both would be well packed with straw to protect the pots. Some perhaps carried their baskets like the 'potter' of Gainsborough, who, in the early nineteenth century, carried his wares into the country all day on his head; he probably obtained his stock via the river trade as Gainsborough was still a port at this time.[35] Any pot hawkers in the Coleorton area who started in this fashion perhaps either worked for or bought stock from an established pot hawker. They may also have carried pots in crates, either on their backs or on a packhorse. There was a pannier maker working in Whitwick in the 1750s — he no doubt supplied the pot sellers as well as the coal carriers of the area.[36] Wheelbarrows were another alternative. Three hawkers transported to Australia in 1789 with the First Fleet were said to have 'been hawkers, come out of Northumberland, pushing a barrow'.[37] Wheelbarrows were in use in the Coleorton district in the late 19th century when locally made 'spar bawbles' were hawked, either locally or a barrowload put on the railway to be hawked at the seaside resorts. This would have been a practical proposition for heavy and fragile goods.[38] It is quite likely that this is how some of the pot hawkers operated, though the four licenses so far found are all for hawkers on foot.[39]

Once a hawker had saved enough money he would buy either a packhorse or an ass. The packhorses would have been of the small and sturdy Fell and Dales type. The strong agricultural and mining base of the area meant that there were plenty of horses and carts or wagons available; horses were also bred in the area. By the eighteenth century there were recognised local coal and coke carriers who used packhorses, like Thomas Griffin whose will was proved in 1745.[40] John Bacon of Whitwick was described as a 'colecarrier' in his will, proved in 1801.[41] No evidence has yet been found for coal and pottery being carried by the same hawker, although the two trades could be found in the same family. The aforementioned John Bacon's wife was the sister of John Toon of Swannington, a 'pot carrier', who was one of Bacon's executors. It was no doubt due to his influence that some of the Bacon children hawked pots rather coal.

Asses were often used as they were cheaper to buy and keep than horses. Ticknall overseers are known to have helped pot hawkers buy animals and pots. The use of asses in both Derbyshire and Leicestershire was noted by the writers of agricultural reports. In Derbyshire, Farey notes that asses were used 'principally in the possession of the lower class of carriers of coals from the Pits in the vicinity of the Towns ... the carriers of Pottery wares, etc., and other things that are hawked around the country'.[42] Pitt noted that the ass could thrive on coarser food such as 'thistles, briars and hedge browsings', as well as being 'possessed of more hardiness, patience and perseverance than horses', which would have helped keep costs down for the pot hawker.[43] This thriftiness had been noted by John Morton in 1712 when writing about the pot hawkers from Derbyshire and Staffordshire, who sold in Northamptonshire and who were undercutting the local tradesmen: 'the potters of those two counties who bring hither their wares upon little horses or asses, usually begging their victuals do on that account afford their wares at such under-rates as our potters here cannot live so well upon the trade'.[44]

As the hawkers saved more money they could have afforded a cart, which would have enabled them to carry more stock. A single horse could pull a two-wheeled cart and thus one animal would be able to take the place of several packhorses. Perhaps some of them were like Robert Hill of Kidderminster who in 1851 had a 'travelling crockery warehouse'.[45]

The condition of the roads they travelled on was important — for pot hawkers to travel far afield with a horse and cart the roads had to improve. Coal had been mined since the thirteenth century in south Derbyshire and north-west Leicestershire. By the seventeenth century coal was delivered to Leicester, Loughborough and further afield. By 1727 deliveries were made from Swannington as far as Melton Mowbray, twenty-five miles away. However, it was in winter that coal was needed most, just when the roads were too bad to transport it. This meant that sales of coal had to take place in summer as Leicestershire roads were said to be 'totally impassable several months of the year'.[46] As an example, the main road from Ashby de la Zouch to Leicester was known as 'Sough Lane' because of its appalling state.[47]

Where it was the pottery manufacturers in Staffordshire prior to 1770 who were the driving force in improving the roads in The Potteries, in this area of Leicestershire it was the coal masters who pushed for turnpikes. Although the coal masters, keen to compete with the cheaper Nottinghamshire coal, pressed for what became the short-lived Charnwood Canal when it was proposed to extend the Soar navigation to Leicester, it was the roads that were most important in the transport system in this area until the railway age. Just how well the Coleorton area was placed for travel becomes apparent when the map showing the turnpiked roads is examined — good roads go in all directions. Ticknall pottery went through the Coleorton area. From Ashby de la Zouch one turnpike went to Rempstone and then on to Nottingham; one went to Loughborough, one to Leicester and another one to Stoke-on-Trent. This access in several directions is shown in Figure 83. The pot hawkers were well placed to distribute their wares to the eastern and southern counties of England.

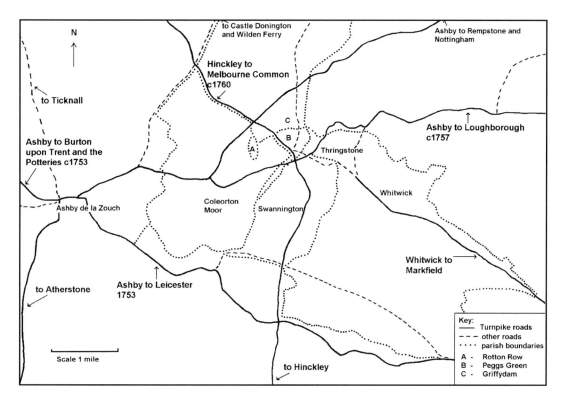

Figure 83 – Communications in the 1780s in the Coleorton area

Pot hawkers were becoming more numerous at the very time that the Ticknall potteries were in decline. Ticknall had provided the bulk of their stock throughout the seventeenth and early eighteenth centuries but by the mid-eighteenth century hawkers were getting stock from elsewhere. The rapid advances in the pottery industry meant that different and better-quality wares were available elsewhere, particularly from The Potteries in Staffordshire and nearby Derby. In 1780 the Derby banker John Heath went bankrupt; amongst his other business interests he owned the Derby Pot Works, also known as Cockpit Hill. The advertisement for the sale of the pots appeared in the *Derby Mercury* and mentioned this group of pot hawkers: 'This Earthen Ware will be Sold in different Lots, and is well worth the Notice of the Pot Carriers, in and about the Neighbourhood of Coleorton Moor. No less a Quantity than two Horse Loads will be sold to one person.' The earthenware itself was described as 'an Assortment of Enamell'd and Blue-and-White Useful CHINA; a large Quantity of Enamell'd Cream Ware, and plain Cream tentable Ware; a great Quantity of White Stone and Brown Ware.'[48]

William Duesbury who founded the Derby China Works bought much of the unsold stock, which continued to be decorated and sold slowly over the next forty years. The reference to the Coleorton Moor pot hawkers suggests that they were well known in the Derby area and probably already sold the wares.

There are also two pieces of evidence to show that some of the pot hawkers were making regular journeys to The Potteries to collect their wares; again both are from the 1780s. The first piece of evidence comes from the Wedgwood Archives. Three letters have survived from a Leicestershire pot hawker, Thomas Toon of Coleorton, for the period 1781–4.[49] His order is not easy to identify in terms of ware, but it was fairly basic. The other difficulty is that he wrote as he spoke, with a broad local accent. On 20 May 1781 he ordered '...Thos cups Sarses as I had at Three and sixpens a dosn and som pint mogs...', as well as 'all the seckend ware you hav as will be salab'. The dairy was not forgotten, with 'a fu botr bots'. As well as the cups and saucers, the fashion for drinking tea was catered for with '4 dos of tapots at eit shilens a dos.' He also wanted 'A fu gilded tapots'. Other items included 'lang plats and small ons the same as I had last'. His order was sent three weeks before he expected to come to The Potteries. This was not his first order, although it was the earliest to survive. Wedgwood certainly sold 'seconds' but he graded them right down to sevenths. He may have sold these to hawkers such as Thomas Toon.

Just six weeks later at the end of June Toon wrote with another order, again expecting to visit in three weeks' time, implying that he had sold the previous stock within that time.

*Juene 28 1781 Mr weegwood I shall be doun for This war a porpos in 20 days from this dat a doz of blu half pints 5dn of pint mogs 1 dn of pint cantrs 3 dn of quart cantrs 4 doz of 2 handl cups 6 to doz and pints and 24 3 dn of basons 24 and 30 1 dn of pints da 2 doz of tapots blu 24 1 doz of 18 do a fu cups sarces 3 or 4 doz 12 doz of plats larg and small This war most be redey a corden to Tim So nomor for yours Thos Toon.*

The final letter in the series, written in March 1784, suggests that his health was poor and in fact he was buried six weeks later at Whitwick.

*Clorton, March 2 1784, Sir I shall be down at your pot work if God givs mee my helth in a bout fortnight & I shall want 2 doz of Gilded Tapots & If you have ayne new fashorne as you Think will sell sav mee a few Things. from your Hu[m]b Sarvt Thos Toon.*

He would be unlikely to have gone for such a small order and probably called on a number of the manufacturers whilst there. It would have depended on just how much pottery he could transport, pay or get credit for, or hope to sell.

The second piece of evidence is the 1789 settlement examination of Joseph Burton, a labourer of Swannington, who in June 'went under his masters direction with Thomas Potter of Swannington's team to the pottery in Staffordshire to fetch potts ... sett off with the said team on Tuesday morning and returned on Saturday afternoon about six o'clock'.[50] That a team was sent suggests a considerable amount of pottery was collected. Thomas Potter was also a yeoman; his team was obviously not in use at this time of the year. However, it begs the question whether he took orders from the pot hawkers or whether he was buying the stock which others, perhaps employed by him, distributed. The evidence found so far does not say.

From 1790, however, there was another nearer source of pottery. In that year the fireclays of south Derbyshire in the Swadlincote, Church Gresley and Woodville area were recognised and began to be exploited. In 1816 finer wares started to be made in the area. By the 1830s there were around thirty potteries working and producing a variety of wares, not all for domestic use. The output was 'ten thousand dozens of pots per week' and an estimated '1500 dozens' had been sold 'To Hawkers, at the Works, sold in the midland counties'.[51] The pot hawkers from the Coleorton area were well placed and sufficiently numerous to market much of the pottery produced in the surrounding countryside and beyond. In addition they almost certainly took wares from Coleorton pottery from 1834 onwards.

'Spar' goods were another item that may have been sold initially by the pot hawkers. This was alabaster obtained from Chellaston, probably brought back to the Coleorton area as a return item from the coal trade to the wharves on the Trent.[52] The 'spar', as it was called, developed into a thriving business in turning and carving small items such as candlesticks, boxes and bowls, known locally as 'bawbles'.[53] Some of the pot hawkers are later shown as hawking spar and at least one became a manufacturer.

Some of the pottery they carried would still be Ticknall. At the beginning of the eighteenth century there were at least thirteen potteries working in and around the village; there were still twelve working in the 1750s, but only three by the end of the century. Ticknall pottery by this period was utilitarian, basic dairy ware in black and red glaze, pancheons, cooking pots, plates, mugs, jugs and butter pots. Some was produced in midlands yellow ware, and there were also slipware dishes. As there are no known marks for this pottery, little can be attributed with certainty, but the vast quantity of potshards on several sites known to be working in Ticknall makes it clear that the village was still a major producer of basic domestic pottery during the eighteenth century.

Other pottery available locally would have included the brown salt-glaze ware produced at Nottingham from the mid-eighteenth century. Little is known about how this was distributed, although it would have been within the range of the Coleorton pot carriers. The river Trent was navigable to Nottingham and pottery may have been distributed by river. Little work seems to have been done on the Nottingham potteries and the distribution of their wares so it is not possible to comment further on this at present. The hawkers may have gone as far as Brampton near Chesterfield where stoneware was also produced.

Little evidence of organisation of the trade has been found, although there are a few clues. An advertisement for a stolen horse in south Staffordshire in 1747 shows that it was with John Wilden, a potter employed by George Doane of King's Mills in Leicestershire, 'who travelled the country with earthenware on three asses and a horse'.[54] A partnership between potters Robert Pemberton and John Tugby was dissolved in 1803.[55] John Fields a farmer of fourteen acres employed four labourers in 1851.[56] This seems excessive. He was earlier recorded as a pot hawker and it would seem that he was employing the labourers for pot hawking rather than farming. The mention of a team going to The Potteries in 1789 suggests large quantities of pots being brought back and their distribution being organised by someone — perhaps Thomas Potter was behind this. Thomas Toon made reference to 'all that my Messuage or Tenement and the Warehouse Stables and other Buildings' in his will in 1791.[57] His estate was valued at under £1,000 and it is likely that this was the Thomas Toon known to have been a pot carrier in 1784 when he was mentioned in the will of his cousin, who was also confusingly called by the same name.[58] Having a base from which to collect pots in the local area would make sense and save many individuals going to Stoke in person. It would also help to account for the number of pot sellers found in this area.

As has been shown, several hawkers had progressed from travelling with their goods to having their own shops. As the nineteenth century pot hawkers travelled so far, they almost certainly built on the earlier trade routes from the sixteenth and seventeenth centuries, extending them as roads improved with the turnpikes. This would enable them to carry greater quantities in carts and with less likelihood of breakages. The cost of tolls would be offset by the larger market reached. Certainly it looks as if it was pot hawkers from the

Coleorton area who were responsible for spreading Ticknall pots so far.

It is noticeable, however, that the improvement in quality of pottery coincides with the decline of the Ticknall potteries, as does the increase in numbers of pot hawkers in the Coleorton area. Some of these men did well, putting their savings into small parcels of land and cottages where they lived; many married by licence and left wills. Their estates were valued at anything from £20 to £3,000. The Litherland brothers did best of all. Thomas had a shop in Ashby de la Zouch and his estate was valued at almost £16,000. His brother William ran a very successful china shop in Liverpool and was one of the re-founders of the present day Crown Derby China. In 1883 his estate was valued at a phenomenal £81,872 18s. All this contrasts sharply with the pot hawkers based in Ticknall. By the nineteenth century they tended to be amongst the less well-off villagers, sometimes receiving help from the parish and selling what had become a basic, rather old-fashioned ware.

# References

1 Brears, P. C. D. (1971), p40
2 Edward Warden 1611–15 ROLLR
3 Henry Blest 21 May 1621 LJRO
4 John Warden 1649/48 ROLLR
5 Henry Basford 5 August 1626 LJRO
6 White A. J. (unpublished thesis, 1989), p240
7 William Wellands 1626/91 ROLLR
8 John Mossendew 1628–9/348 ROLLR
9 White, A. J. (unpublished thesis, 1989), p58
10 William King, 5 May 1670 LJRO
11 D1396 A/PO 320 DRO
12 Melbourne Baptist Minute Book 25 Dec 1775; pers. comm. D. Bell
13 D1396 A/PO 650 DRO
14 Francis Greenhough 19 February 1635/6 LJRO
15 Robert Shevyn 9 April 1728 LJRO
16 D2375m/288/2 DRO
17 William Woods 1681/132 ROLLR
18 Marriage Bond 24 June 1721 NRO
19 George Else PR/T/1815/58 ROLLR
20 Hertford Quarter Sessions Michaelmas 1823 in *Leicestershire Strays* 4 (1985), p41
21 Brown, S. (unpublished dissertation, 1999), p86
22 White, W., *History, Gazetteer, and Directory of Leicester and Rutland* (1857) p525
23 Spufford, M. (1984), p70
24 Beresford, J. (ed.) (1935), pp183, 215
25 Kitching, C. (ed.) (1995), p21
26 Walford, C. (1883), p152
27 ibid.
28 Everitt, A. (1976), pp179–202

29 Letter from Litherland's descendant the late Mr Angus Bell to his cousin Mr John Yolland, Royal Crown Derby Archive and quoted in Gibson, H. (1993), p8

30 Wedgwood, H.A. (1970), p36

31 *Leicester Journal*, 4 November 1825, p3, column 2

32 Spufford, M. (1984), pp39–43; Barker, T. and Gerhold, D. (1993), p21

33 Plot, R. (1686), p124

34 Thirsk, J. and Cooper, J.P. (eds) (1972), p419

35 Miller, T. (1857), pp43–9

36 DE 40/39/41 ROLLR

37 Gillen, M. (1988), p346

38 Daniell, J. (1962–3), p36

39 DE 3486 1/2 and Misc 133 ROLLR

40 Thomas Griffin 1 May 1845 ROLLR

41 John Bacon 1801 (10) 1–2. ROLLR

42 Farey, J. (1817), p161

43 Pitt, W. (1809), pp293–4

44 Morton, J., *Natural History of Northamptonshire* (1712) quoted in Brears, P.C.D. (1971), pp41–2

45 TNA: PRO HO 107/2038 folio 275

46 Marshall W., *Rural Economy of Midland Counties* (1790), p37; quoted in Griffin, C.P. (unpublished thesis, 1969), p173

47 Hadfield C., *Charnwood Forest* (1956); quoted in Griffin, C.P. (unpublished thesis, 1969), p168

48 *Derby Mercury* 10 March 1780, p4, column 4

49 WMM 4891-6 to 4893-6

50 DE 432/3/218 ROLLR

51 Mammatt, E. (1834), p73

52 pers. comm. Denis Baker

53 Daniell, J. (1962–3), pp34–41

54 *Aris's Birmingham Gazette* 21 March 1747, pers. comm. David Brown

55 *Leicester Journal* 14 January 1803, p1, column 4; ROLLR

56 TNA: PRO HO 107/2084 fol. 824

57 Thomas Toon PR/T/1794/ 128 ROLLR

58 Thomas Toon PR/T/1784/ 202 ROLLR

# 10. The Decline of the Ticknall Potteries

Some of the reasons for the decline of potting in Ticknall have already been suggested indirectly, and others can be deduced from the history of the industry. A brief history of the use of pottery in this country during the period up to the seventeenth century has been outlined in the introduction. Changing fashions in tableware clearly affected the markets of all the local potteries; in some cases, new fashions introduced new types of competitors.

Ticknall had benefited from a swing to the use of pottery for drinking vessels in the sixteenth century when its decorated Cistercian wares held an important place in the market. By the 1620s Ticknall's industry was at least equal to Staffordshire's in size. In spite of its poor representation in the inventory sources, the north Staffordshire area provided the most devastating competition for Ticknall. Brears suggests that a significant factor in Staffordshire's ascendancy was the development of a better means of distribution for the pottery so that places were not limited to locally produced wares. This development took place there in the second quarter of the seventeenth century.[1] Pot sellers had appeared before that in Ticknall, however, acting as merchants for the trade — there are several examples in the first quarter of the century. Edward Warden was delivering Ticknall wares in 1610 and John Warden in 1614; Henry Basford was another early pot seller. The merchant system may, therefore, have developed in Ticknall rather than the Staffordshire area; if so, this may be one reason for the widespread early recognition of Ticknall ware. The growth and longevity of the Ticknall industry was probably due partly to its exploitation of the distribution system that had grown around the industry. Staffordshire expanded by catering to a more sophisticated market, especially from the 1630s, just at the time that the Stoke-on-Trent area expanded its pottery numbers beyond those at Ticknall. Its markets grew in major centres of population and taste. Both places used markets and shops in addition to pot hawkers.

After the Restoration in 1660 new fashions came into the country, setting a very high production standard: porcelain from China and Dutch tin-glazed wares, for example. Much effort was put into attempts to replicate these wares, at first without much success, until the Elers brothers made red teapots at Burslem to imitate the Chinese. Ticknall never attracted the Dutch potters, which meant that news of new techniques did not spread rapidly here as it did in Stoke-on-Trent. From the late seventeenth century Ticknall's potters were lagging behind Staffordshire's in terms of new designs, body composition, body shapes and glazing. Ticknall continued to compete in the late seventeenth century by supplying the basic market demands for cheap dairy and kitchen wares, and, on a smaller scale, copying Stoke-on-Trent's slipwares. It is interesting that Ticknall retained its brand recognition and market share until the first half of the eighteenth century, together with a track record of production. There were consistently high numbers of potters working from the 1640s, with the peak in the 1720s. Numbers then fell steadily until the 1780s, and after that more rapidly.

There were other elements which influenced people's choices as well, such as social status and growing purchasing power as the economy expanded. Ticknall's potters must have known about the new products from Staffordshire during the eighteenth century, particularly since the wares were carried overland to Willington on the river Trent for transmission downriver before the Trent and Mersey canal was built. This was a major wharf for the river trade, and close to Ticknall; news and ideas must have been exchanged there. But the potters apparently did not attempt to imitate the sophisticated new wares or take advantage of flints and clay coming up the Trent to the Derby china works and Stoke-on-Trent until thirty or forty years after they had been introduced, and by then the markets had moved on. Ticknall was not able to compete with Staffordshire for quantity or quality by the late eighteenth century. The potters had left it too late to penetrate the market.

Transport and distribution were clearly key elements in the success of the industry. In Stoke-on-Trent, Wedgwood was a major promoter of the Trent and Mersey canal, and several other potters invested in it too. Their intention was to provide a safer method of transport for goods to London. No Ticknall potter invested in the canal, either because they did not have the capital or did not see the need. The Ticknall tramway could have given them direct access to London and other markets after about 1802 when it was opened as part of the Ashby de la Zouch canal, but by then the industry was in terminal decline. The preamble to the Canal Act does not mention the carriage of pottery as an element of the proposed trade and the potters did not invest in it.[2]

Staffordshire's favourable geology, the development of new techniques and the concentration of new skills there meant that the county had become England's most successful producer of earthenware by the early eighteenth century. Once the county had gained this commercial advantage it never relinquished it. At first the potters used local clays; later they imported clays from the south-west and flints from the east coast. This shows that access to local clay was not necessarily the crucial factor. The price of local coal was more significant. By comparison, in Ticknall there was equally easy access to coal. Pilkington's claim that the loss of clay from the common at enclosure was the reason for the potteries' decline has been shown to be incorrect; other clay sources were available locally, and, if the potters had moved to the new wares the availability of local clay would have been irrelevant. Enclosure alone could not have been the reason for the general decline, as it took place in the 1760s and the numbers of potters continued at the same level until the 1690s. It may have been the trigger for the problems of individual families such as the Blores, who had no resources to fall back on as the industry contracted.

Several Staffordshire potters such as the Wedgwoods and Astburys were trying various recipes for making fine wares to meet the demand. Wedgwood spent much time in carefully controlled experiments with new bodies, glazes and firing methods,[3] and discussed his results with fellow members of the Lunar Society. There is no evidence for any Ticknall potter experimenting with bodies or glazes; they continued to make the same things in the same way. New techniques were introduced during the eighteenth century including press-moulding, slip-casting and Wedgwood's improved lathe for engine-turning. Then there was the development of transfer-printing, new glazing and firing techniques with the use of biscuit and glost kilns, and other decorative skills.[4] There is evidence that the Ticknall potteries which tried to break into the creamware markets in the late eighteenth century were aware of the new techniques and did use some — the Melbourne pottery advertised for a turner and there is other evidence for the use of lathes. However, no Ticknall potter invented any new techniques or machinery, nor did they patent anything. By comparison, in a random search between 1824 and 1865, fourteen patents from Staffordshire potters were reported in the *Staffordshire Advertiser.*[5]

Staffordshire's quality wares were expensive, however, and they catered for a wealthier market than Ticknall's during the eighteenth century. It may be that one factor that helped Ticknall to survive for as long as it did was the explosive growth of population in the developing industrial towns in the late eighteenth century — they still bought cheap essential coarsewares as they could afford little else. So did the rural poor — Stoke-on-Trent's best wares were beyond their pockets. The potteries also supplied 'seconds' (Wedgwood went as far as 'sevenths'), and much of this would be sold to pot carriers to distribute well down the social scale. A Nottingham author, observing his contemporaries' tea drinking habits in the mid-eighteenth century, wrote that 'not only the Gentry and Wealthy Traders drink it constantly, but almost every Seamer, Sizer and Winder will have her tea and will enjoy herself over it in a morning … even a Common washerwoman thinks she has not had a proper Breakfast without Tea and hot buttered Bread …'.[6]

The new products demanded new industrial production arrangements, but the old ones could still be made by the potter and his family, often combining pottery with farming. The factory system became established in Staffordshire but not in Ticknall. A comparison between Josiah Wedgwood and Joseph Tetley of Heath End illustrates the differences between families which started from a similar base. Both came from potting families and learned the trade in the family, though Wedgwood was formally apprenticed to his brother.[7] When he came of age he inherited £20 from his father, far less than Joseph Tetley inherited from Henry. Wedgwood started at the Churchyard Works, Burslem, which a contemporary illustration shows was a timber-framed jettied thatched house with two hovels beside it. An open-fronted working area was built against the gable end.[8] It is comparable in size and scale to Ley Farm at Heath End (site 20), a timber box-frame house built by Joseph Tetley's father with a brick and tile extension; the house is still recognisable from Henry Tetley's 1684 inventory which was worth £270 0s 6d. There were workshops to the side of the house and a kiln behind it, making typical Ticknall pottery as well as mottled wares. Churchyard Works made similar products, 'of a common description, consisting chiefly of black and mottled ware, baking dishes, pitchers, milk-pans, porringers, and such like. Butter pots were made in large numbers'.[9] Both families had other property. So far, so similar.

However, Henry Tetley, like many Ticknall potters, was heavily involved in agriculture and Joseph continued farming on a small scale. The Wedgwoods were not involved in farming. Joseph Tetley stayed at Heath End and worked on his own. He had enough capital to buy Marriott's pottery and cottage in Ticknall for £40 in 1711, which he used as security to raise another £40, but he did not succeed financially. When he died in 1729 his inventory only totalled £19 15s. His son (also Joseph) continued the pottery but sold the cottage to pay off the debts. The Tetleys' decline, typical of Ticknall potting families, contrasts sharply with the rise of the Wedgwoods; they showed no entrepreneurial skills or drive to develop their products. There was no investment to develop the pottery beyond the basic workshop/drying shed and kiln. Wedgwood went into partnership with Whieldon after his apprenticeship, and learned new methods and ideas. He moved from this partnership to a pottery similar to the Churchyard Works, the Ivy Works at Burslem, in around 1760. It consisted of 'two kilns, a few tile-covered sheds and rooms, and the adjoining ivy-covered cottage'.[10] Small as it was, it was larger than most Ticknall potteries, only a few of which had two kilns; but it was still the type of works like Ley Farm, designed for small-scale operation. As his business expanded, Wedgwood rented a second works, the Brickhouse or Bell Works,[11] and the pattern of specialisation among the pottery workers became common here as it never did in Ticknall. Eventually he recognised that both the scale and methods of production for his new wares demanded an innovative approach. He bought the Etruria estate and developed a factory system for the production of his pottery and housing for his workers in 1765–6.[12] He was able to finance it partly through the profits of his Burslem works, but mainly because he had married an heiress, Sarah Wedgwood, a distant relative who brought him about £20,000 in 1764.[13] Nobody in Ticknall married an heiress; there was no capital injected for growth.

Wedgwood provided technical, social, business and artistic leadership for the Stoke-on-Trent area. He had contacts with political leaders that were useful when lobbying for the canal or the turnpikes. He had business and social contacts at the highest levels through his supply of pottery to royalty both at home and abroad. Ticknall had no dominant figure with such vision, energy and organisational skills.

The factory system mechanised many processes. There were economies of scale which made it worth while, for example, to use steam power for clay pressing or water power for grinding flints. There is no evidence of mechanisation in the Ticknall potteries other than the use of the lathe, which can be operated by hand. It was too expensive to install, and the scale of production was too small. By the time it became available the Ticknall potteries were in decline and there was neither the incentive nor the capital to introduce it.

Part of the problem seems to have been the attitudes of the Ticknall potters. Fathers trained their children; the little evidence for formal apprenticeships has been discussed above. The failure to apprentice children meant that there was no training on new ideas or techniques, and they did not move to other potteries as journeymen to become familiar with new products. Sons probably made the same things in the same ways as their fathers and grandfathers had done. It is clear that the crucial generation was that which entered the trade in the late seventeenth and early eighteenth centuries. Their parents had done well from potting; they expected to, but found that their living standards gradually declined in the face of competition from Staffordshire. If their children became potters, they struggled to make ends meet. Many families moved out of potting in this generation. The peak numbers of potters in Ticknall were found in the 1720s, when the trade was already doomed (Figure 84). By the 1780s that was clear even to the potters themselves, and the failure of Melbourne (site 25) and site 24 to thrive in their attempts to make creamwares confirmed their fate. It is noticeable that the potters who were buying property did so mainly in the late seventeenth and early eighteenth century, as the Houghs did in 1694, supporting the suggestion that this was a period of prosperity.

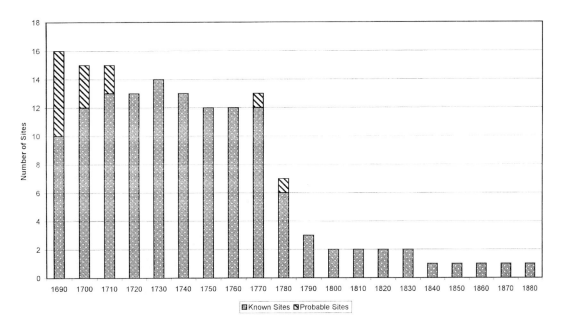

Figure 84 The decline of the Ticknall potteries 1690–1886

Most of the Ticknall potters retained links with farming, and they seem to have seen themselves primarily as farmers rather than manufacturers. When there was money to invest, the inventories show that it went into farmland and stock rather than into the pottery. As the Stoke-on-Trent potters accumulated capital they moved away from agriculture and concentrated on potting. Ticknall's potters clung on to their farms, however small. As we have shown in Chapters 3 and 4, a number of potters, such as John Smallwood or Richard Gardener, leased their own homes and workshops but also bought property to rent out or to farm themselves. Some, such as the Hanburys, rented it to other family members. The Blores, who eventually became dependent on the parish, had bought their own pottery in 1719. The Drapers had inherited property and they also bought two messuages and land they were renting in Ticknall. The property they bought in 1691 cost £95 and it remained in the family until 1824. The wealthiest potter was Thomas Hanson, worth £449 14s 2d when he died in 1724. Although he rented his pot site, he owned freehold properties in Hartshorne and Ashby de la Zouch. His younger son Joseph acquired a property in Atherstone in payment of a £140 debt, and this seems to have enabled him to move out of potting altogether in favour of farming, clearly seen as a more desirable investment than the pottery.

Thomas Hanson's estate shows how little money there was for capital investment in Ticknall, and perhaps explains why there was no move to factory development here. Advertisements in the *Staffordshire Advertiser* sought the kind of capital that was never available in Ticknall. In 1800 a Lane End pottery advertised for a partner to put in at least £400, and Richard Johnson sought a partner with at least £500 in 1804.[14]

Joseph Tetley was the only local potter who rented a pottery to someone else, but the practice was common in Staffordshire.[15] The difference may be that the Staffordshire potters saw themselves as manufacturers not farmers and invested accordingly; they also bought cottages to let. A significant number of Staffordshire potters who eventually had large factory premises built up their fortunes this way. They insured their property too. A study of the Sun Fire and Royal Exchange insurance records from the establishment of their offices in 1710 and 1713 up to 1795 shows that nobody in Ticknall insured any property. Either they could not afford it or did not consider their property worth insuring. Thomas Astbury and William Tittensor, both potters in Hanley, insured their property between 1714 and 1731.[16] In Derbyshire in 1793–4 a Tideswell cotton spinner insured with the Sun; in Staffordshire there were eight gentlemen, a farmer, five tradesmen, a potter, a victualler, two maltsters and two millers insuring property, as well as Wedgwood who insured property he owned in Liverpool.[17] Local people clearly knew about insurance as there were four instances of domestic and one of industrial insurances. Richard Shepherd, gentleman, of Swarkestone insured with the Sun in 1718, as did Thomas Bainbridge Esq. of Derby. In 1780 William Haines of Melbourne insured with the Royal Exchange and John Burton of Bretby Hall Park did likewise in 1785.[18] The screw mill in Hartshorne was insured in 1793.[19] Plenty of potteries were insured — in London alone between 1713 and 1786 there were thirteen. Staffordshire potteries were insured in 1782 and 1784, with two in 1787. In 1713–14 there were five pottery and glass sellers insuring across the country. This had grown to nineteen by 1777–95, but none was in either Staffordshire or Derbyshire.[20] Examples of the Staffordshire potters investing in property to build capital include John Harrison of Stoke-on-Trent, who insured two houses in Red Lion Square in Newcastle-under-Lyme for £100 each which he rented to Mrs Hyatt, a grocer, and W. Wood, also a grocer. There were warehouses and a stable in the yard (£70), a house in the yard (£30) and a warehouse and brewhouse (£50). William Tittensor of Hanley insured a house in Lane End for £200 that he rented to Richard Johnson, another adjoining it was rented to John Tollfree (£100), two other houses (£50 each), a thatched stable to Johnson's house (£50), a thatched house (£20) and three further houses, together insured for £30. Charles Bagnall of Shelton, Stoke-on-Trent, insured his own house for £700 and his furniture for £300 in 1786.[21] These potters are a world away from Ticknall's modest expectations.

The most significant reasons for Ticknall's decline can be summarised as competition from Staffordshire in terms of products, inventions and the entrepreneurial spirit; the mindset of the local potters who, still regarding themselves as farmers, never modernised their industry or rationalised production; and the lack of any significant investment or development of capital. In the light of its shortcomings, it is surprising that the industry hung on for as long as it did; but our evidence clearly shows that it had been a significant industry with a well-developed distribution system for several centuries. From 1790 a new pottery industry had started in Swadlincote, Church Gresley and Woodville, and it is possible that some of the Ticknall potters found employment there. If its potteries had developed on an industrial scale it might have become Ticknall-on-Trent, its neigbouring villages subsumed into grimy suburbs, and suffering all the problems of industrial decline. Instead it has become a desirable commuter village in an attractive rural setting.

# References

1 Brears, P. C. D. (1971), pp40–1
2 Item 4690 DLSL
3 Smiles, S. (1897)
4 ibid.
5 Hampson, R. (2000), pp5, 6, 7, 40, 41, 42, 58, 69, 82, 83
6 Ayscough, G. (ed.), C. Deering, *Nottingham Vetus and Nova* (1751), p72, quoted in Marshall, D. (1956), p172
7 Smiles, S. (1897), p21
8 Thomas, J. (1971), facing p84
9 Smiles, S. (1897), p21
10 ibid., p42
11 ibid., pp43–4
12 ibid., pp85–7
13 ibid., p66
14 Hampson, R. (2000), pp67, 71
15 ibid. has examples
16 Sun Fire, both in drawer 17817/31, l. 1793 GL
17 Sun Fire Register MS 11937 vol. 1 (1793–4) GL
18 Sun Fire policy no. 8/411 (1718); Sun Fire policy no. 9/108 (1718–9); Royal Exchange MS 7253/5, policy no. 78006 (1780); Royal Exchange MS 7253/11, policy no. 94829 (1785); all GL
19 Royal Exchange Register, policy no. 136108 (1793) GL
20 All information from Sun and Royal Exchange fire insurance registers GL
21 Sun Fire Register MS 11963/257, policy no. 38498 (1778); Sun Fire Register MS 11937 vol. 1, policy no. 622497 (1794); Royal Exchange Register MS 7253/12, policy no. 98226 (1786); all GL

# Appendix 1:
# Ticknall Pottery in Leicestershire, 1537–1760

Leicestershire is the only county for which we have studied all the inventories; because they are bound in year volumes, it was a relatively straightforward task. As they have all been used, it may seem that there is an over-emphasis on Ticknall ware in the county, but we felt it was better to produce a thorough study where one was possible. Much as we would have liked to do a survey of all the inventories within a radius of, say, 30 miles to produce a more balanced picture, it would have been prohibitive in terms of time and access.

The maps group the early years and the last years together, with dates for each reference to Ticknall ware. As more references appear, the county has been mapped by decade and the sequence shows the changes in the market patterns both over time and geographically.

The main market towns are numbered on each map as follows.

1. Leicester
2. Loughborough
3. Hinckley
4. Ashby de la Zouch
5. Melton Mowbray
6. Market Harborough
7. Lutterworth
8. Market Bosworth

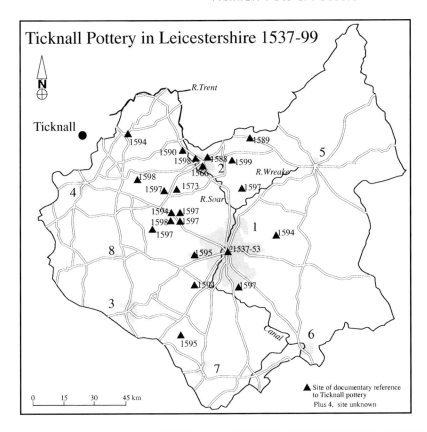

Ticknall Pottery in Leicestershire 1537-99

N

Ticknall

R.Trent

1594

1590
1598
1588
1599
1566
2
1589
R.Wreake
1598
1597
1573
1597
R.Soar
4
1594
1597
1598
1597
1597
1
1594
?1537-53
8
1595
1594
1597
3
6
Canal
1595
7

0    15    30    45 km

▲ Site of documentary reference
   to Ticknall pottery
Plus 4, site unknown

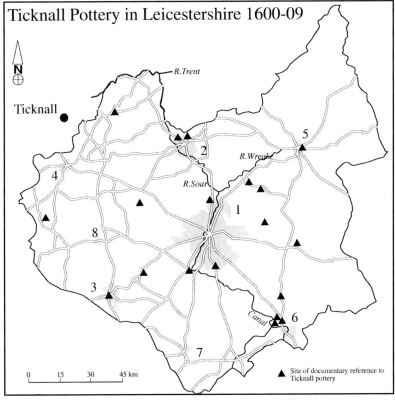

Ticknall Pottery in Leicestershire 1600-09

N

Ticknall

R.Trent

2
5
R.Wreake
4
R.Soar
1
8
3
Canal
6
7

0    15    30    45 km

▲ Site of documentary reference to
   Ticknall pottery

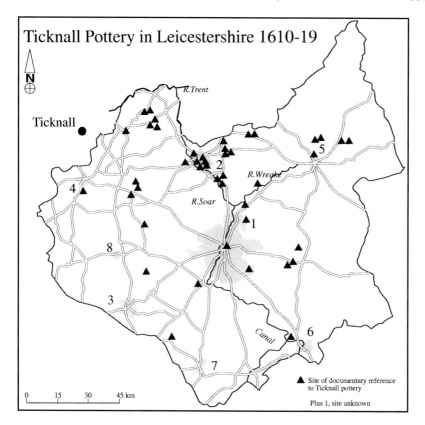

Ticknall Pottery in Leicestershire 1610-19

N

Ticknall ●

R.Trent

R.Wreake

R.Soar

Canal

▲ Site of documentary reference
to Ticknall pottery

Plus 1, site unknown

0    15    30    45 km

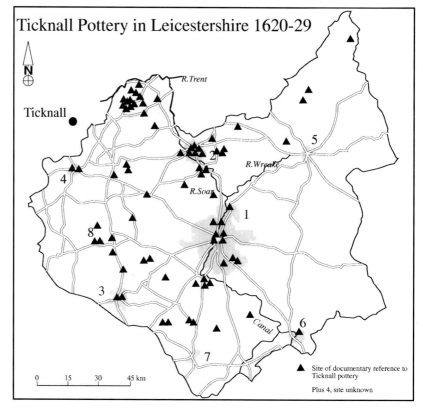

Ticknall Pottery in Leicestershire 1620-29

N

Ticknall ●

R.Trent

R.Wreake

R.Soar

Canal

▲ Site of documentary reference to
Ticknall pottery

Plus 4, site unknown

0    15    30    45 km

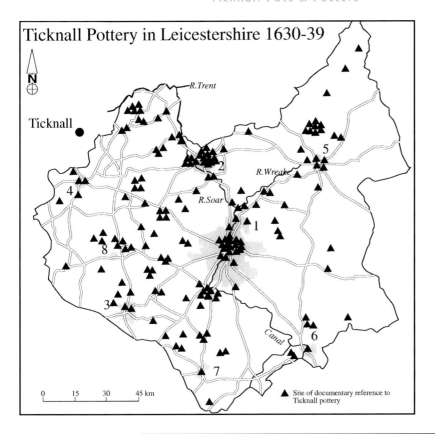

Ticknall Pottery in Leicestershire 1630-39

0  15  30  45 km

▲ Site of documentary reference to
Ticknall pottery

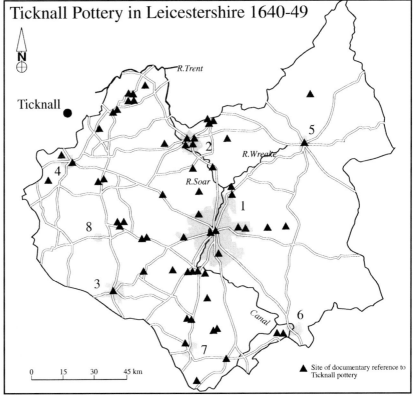

Ticknall Pottery in Leicestershire 1640-49

0  15  30  45 km

▲ Site of documentary reference to
Ticknall pottery

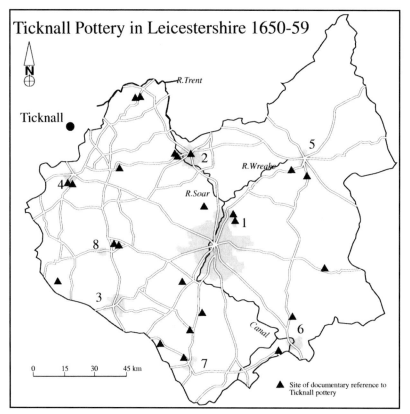

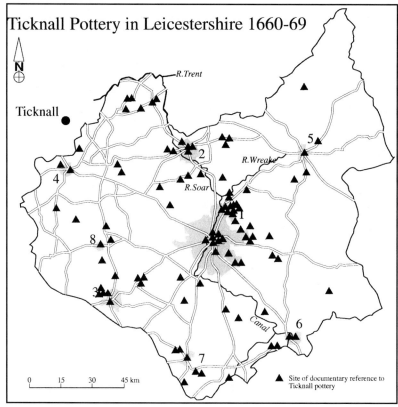

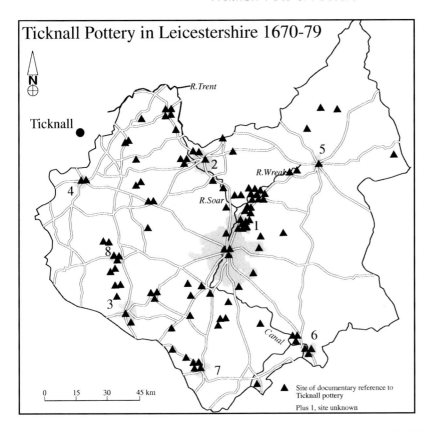

Ticknall Pottery in Leicestershire 1670-79

N

Ticknall ●

*R.Trent*

5

*R.Wreak*

2

*R.Soar*

4

1

8

3

6

7

0    15    30    45 km

▲ Site of documentary reference to
Ticknall pottery

Plus 1, site unknown

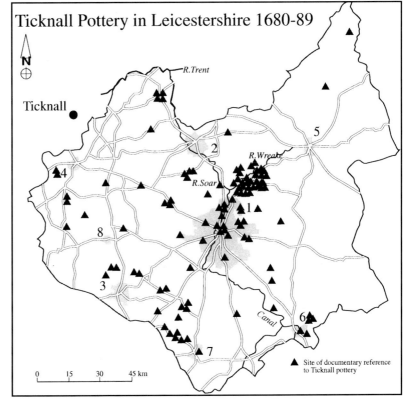

Ticknall Pottery in Leicestershire 1680-89

N

Ticknall ●

*R.Trent*

2

*R.Wreak*

5

*R.Soar*

4

1

8

3

6

7

0    15    30    45 km

▲ Site of documentary reference
to Ticknall pottery

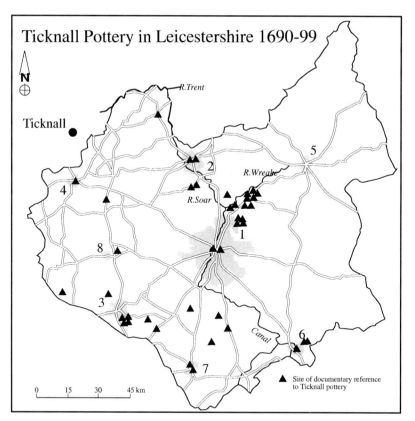

Ticknall Pottery in Leicestershire 1690-99

N

Ticknall ●

R.Trent

R.Wreake

R.Soar

Canal

▲ Site of documentary reference
to Ticknall pottery

0    15    30    45 km

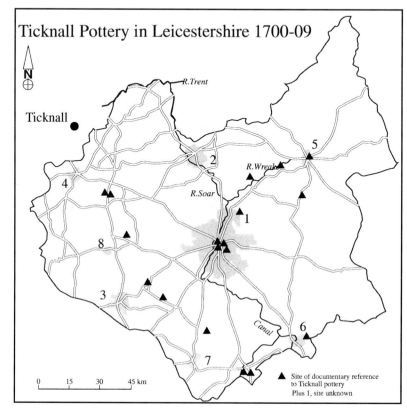

Ticknall Pottery in Leicestershire 1700-09

N

Ticknall ●

R.Trent

R.Wreake

R.Soar

Canal

0    15    30    45 km

▲ Site of documentary reference
to Ticknall pottery
Plus 1, site unknown

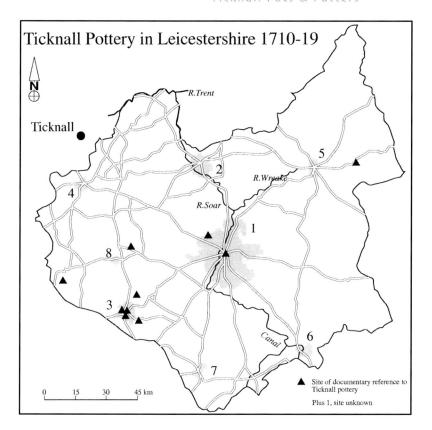

Ticknall Pottery in Leicestershire 1710-19

N

Ticknall ●

R.Trent

5

2

R.Wreake

4

R.Soar

1

8

3

Canal

6

7

0    15    30    45 km

▲ Site of documentary reference to
Ticknall pottery

Plus 1, site unknown

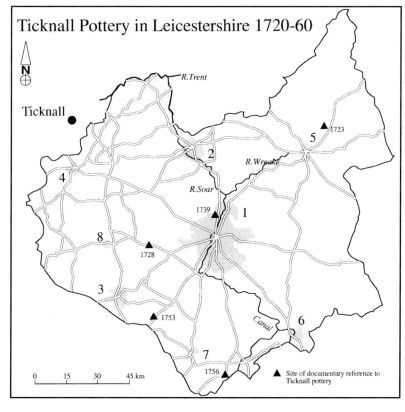

Ticknall Pottery in Leicestershire 1720-60

N

Ticknall ●

R.Trent

1723
5

2

R.Wreake

4

R.Soar

1739
1

8

1728

3

1753

Canal

6

7

1756

0    15    30    45 km

▲ Site of documentary reference to
Ticknall pottery

# Appendix 2:
# Drawings of Selected Pots from Ticknall Pot Sites

All drawings reproduced at a quarter size.

Cistercian Ware (Black): Nos. 2, 3, 4, 5, 7, 10, 11, 13, 14, 15, 16, 20, 23, 25, 30, 31, 36, 37, 38, 44, 46, 47, 56.

Cistercian Ware (Yellow): Nos. 24, 32, 33.

Black Ware: Nos. 1, 12, 17, 18, 19, 21, 22, 26, 27, 28, 29, 34, 35, 39, 40, 43, 45, 48, 49, 50, 51, 52, 53, 54, 55.

Yellow Ware: Nos. 6, 8, 9, 41, 42, 57.

## Site 1

## Site 7

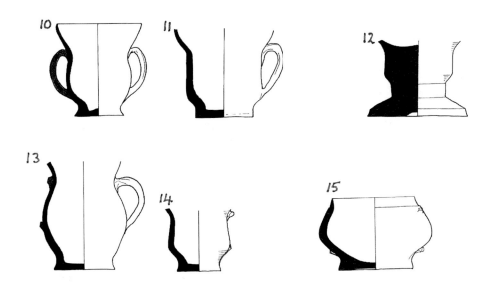

## Site 6

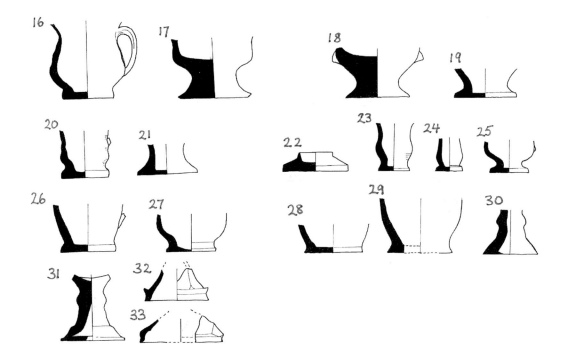

**Site 11**

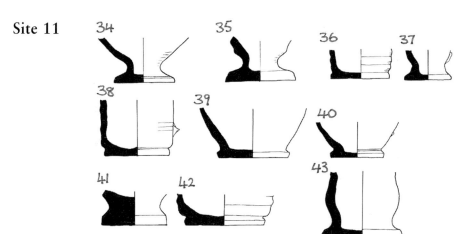

**Site 17**

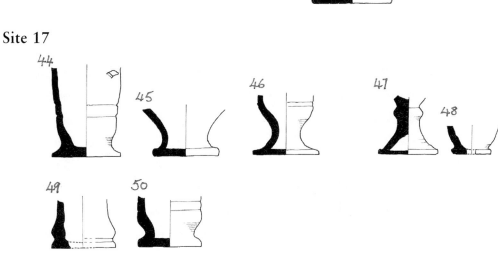

**Site 24**

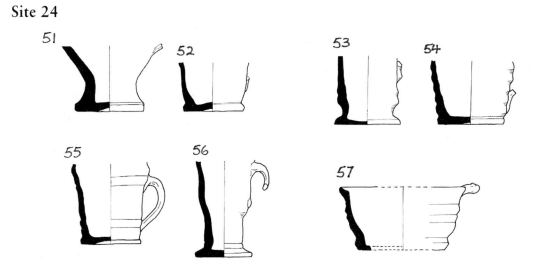

# Appendix 3:
## List of Potters' Wills and Inventories

| Name | place | will | inventory | value | probate |
|------|-------|------|-----------|-------|---------|
| Richard Hanburye | Ticknall | * | * | £10-18-00 | 7 June 1587 |
| Henry Hanburie | Scaddows T | * | * | £11-16-10 | 17 February 1597/8 |
| Homfrey Makepeace, alias Taylor | Scaddowe yard T | * | | £106-05-04 | 28 June 1611 |
| Richard Gardener | Ticknall | * | * | £188-07-10 | 18 July 1614 |
| John Beighton | Ticknall | * | * | £64-18-10 | 6 February 1620/1 |
| Henry Blest | Ticknall | * | * | £15-18-00 | 31 May 1621 |
| John Coggreave | Ticknall | | * | £13-15-06 | 5 August 1626 |
| Richard Holland | Ticknall | * | * | £42-14-08 | 21 March 1628/9 |
| Robert Fisher | Ticknall | | * | £27-10-04 | 3 January 1639 |
| William Holland | Ticknall | * | * | £23-15-00 | 9 June 1663 |
| John Standlye | Ticknall | * | * | £333-18-00 | 11 December 1667 |
| William Hanberye | Scaddows T | | * | £15-15-11 | 3 March 1672 |
| Timothy Beighton | Ticknall | * | * | £50-12-04 | 13 October 1674 |
| George Hough | Ticknall | * | * | £56-00-00 | 19 September 1679 |
| Thomas Tetley | Ticknall | * | * | £82-08-10 | 10 June 1681 |
| Henry Tetley | Inner Southwood A | * | | £270-00-06 | 23 September 1684# |
| Samuel Potter | Ticknall | * | * | £48-01-00 | 24 April 1688 |
| John Cox | Ticknall | * | | £9-12-09 | 4 October 1695 |
| Joseph Morley | Ticknall | * | * | £11-11-02 | 14 November 1701 |
| John Marriott | Ticknall | * | * | £17-14-04 | 28 April 1709 |
| Joseph Standley | Ticknall | | * | £22-09-02 | 29 April 1709 |
| James Hough | Ticknall | Admon. only | | | 2 October 1712 |
| Edward Long | Ticknall | | * | £38-03-06 | 14 June 1718 |
| Joseph Beighton | Ticknall | * | * | £15-11-08 | 29 March 1720 |
| John Draper | Heath End S | | | | 14 March 1721# |
| William Pemberton | Ticknall | * | * | £19-13-03 | 13 April 1724 |
| Joseph Potter | Ticknall | * | * | £38-08-10 | 29 May 1724 |
| Thomas Henson | Ticknall | * | * | £449-14-02 | 28 September 1725 |
| Thomas Henson | Ticknall | * | * | £233-19-00 | 14 November 1729 |

| Name | place | will | inventory | value | probate |
|------|-------|------|-----------|-------|---------|
| Joseph Tetley | Inner Southwood A | | * | £20-05-00 | 11 November 1730# |
| Richard Cox | Ticknall | | * | £19-06-08 | 14 November 1732 |
| John Smallwood | Whitehollow R | | | | |
| | | * | * | £17-00-00 | 4 October 1733 |
| Thomas Jones | Heath End A | * | | | 9 October 1734# |
| Robert Draper | Heath End S | | | | 8 July 1742# |
| Anthony Hood | Broadstone R | * | * | £18-05-00 | 24 April 1744 |
| William Hide | Heath End A | | | | 28 July 1756# |
| Joseph Hanson ** | Ticknall | * | | | 1 December 1758 |
| John Knifton | Ticknall | * | * | £17-18-11 | 21 April 1766 |
| Isaac Hill | Ticknall | Admon. only | | | 23 December 1771 |
| Joseph Bosworth ** | Heath End S | * | | | 23 August 1773# |
| John Cox | Calke | * | | under £20 | 23 November 1793 |
| Joseph Hide | Ticknall | * | | | 30 April 1811 |
| Thomas Hill | Ticknall | * | | | 16 April 1816 |
| Samuel Hill | Ticknall | * | | | 15 October 1816 |
| Martha Hill | Ticknall | * | | under £100 | 20 November 1832 |
| Joseph Hyde | Ticknall | * | | under £200 | 8 October 1833 |
| Ann Hide | Ticknall | * | | under £100 | 20 April 1847 |

**Key:**
* indicates a document exists
** indicates that the testator was not described as a pot maker in his will or inventory

**Place column:**
A = Ashby de la Zouch parish
R = Repton parish
S = Staunton Harold in Breedon parish
T = Ticknall parish

All probate documents are to be found at LJRO except for those marked # which are at ROLLR

# Bibliography

## Books

Adams, M., Cox, B., Usher, H. and Woodward, S., *Ticknall Reflections* (1989)

Bagshaw, S., *History, Gazetteer and Directory of Derbyshire* (1846)

Barker, D., *Slipware* (1993)

Barker, T. and Gerhold, D., *The Rise and Rise of Road Transport 1700–1990* (1993)

Beresford, J. (ed.), *The Diary of a Country Parson 1758–1802 by James Woodforde* (1935)

Bestall, J. and Fowkes, D., *Chesterfield Wills and Inventories*, vols 1 and 2 (1997 and 2001)

Brears, P. C. D., *The English Country Pottery, Its History and Techniques* (1971)

Bruyn Andrews, C. (ed.), *The Torrington Diaries. The Tours of the Hon. John Byng between the Years 1781 and 1794*, vol. 2 (1935)

Bulmer, T., *History, Topography and Directory of Derbyshire* (1895)

Chaffers, W., *Marks and Monograms on Pottery and Porcelain* (1903)

Cockroft, J., *Nantwich Wills. Transcripts of Wills and Inventories 1603–1688* (1999)

Colvin, H., *Calke Abbey, Derbyshire: A Hidden House Revealed* (1985)

Cox, J. C., *Notes on the Churches of Derbyshire*, vol. 3 (1875–9)

Cunnington, C. W. and Cunnington, P., *Handbook of English Costume in the Sixteenth Century* (1954)

Cunnington, P., *Costume in Pictures* (1964)

Davies, Revd D. P., *A New Historical and Descriptive View of Derbyshire* (1811)

Defoe, D., *A Tour Through the Whole Island of Great Britain*, vols. 2 and 3 (1983)

Edelen, G. (ed.), *The Description of England, The Classic Contemporary Account of Tudor Social Life by William Harrison 1587* (1994)

Edwards, D. G. (ed.), *Derbyshire Hearth Tax Assessments 1662–70* (1982)

Farey, J., *General View of the Agriculture and Minerals of Derbyshire*, vol. 3 (1817)

Fraser, W., *Field Names in South Derbyshire* (1947)

Fussell, G. E., *The English Dairy Farmer 1500–1900* (1966)

Garratt, H. J. H. (ed.), *Derbyshire Feet of Fines 1323–1546* (1985)

Gibson, H., *A Case of Fine China* (1993)

Gillen, M., *The Founders of Australia* (1988)

Glover, S., *History, Gazetteer and Directory of the County of Derby* (1829)

Hampson, R., *Pottery References in the Staffordshire Advertiser 1795–1865* (2000)

Harding, A., *England in the Thirteenth Century* (1993)

Havinden, M., *Household and Farm Inventories of Oxfordshire, 1550–1590* (1965)

HMC, *Report on the Manuscripts of Lord Middleton* (1911)

Holme, R., *Academy of Armory*, Book 3 (1688)

Honey, W. B., *English Pottery and Porcelain*, 2nd edn (1945)

Hughes, B. and Hughes, T., *The Collectors' Encyclopaedia of English Ceramics* (1968)

Jeayes, C., *Derbyshire Charters* (1906)

Jewitt, L., *Ceramic Art of Great Britain*, vol. 2 (1878)

Johnson, R., *History of Alfreton* (1968)

Johnston, J. A., *Probate Inventories of Lincoln Citizens 1661–1714* (1991)

Kelly, E. R., *Kelly's Directory of Derbyshire, Leicestershire, Rutland and Nottinghamshire* (1888)

Kelly and Co., *Kelly's Directory of Derbyshire* (1891)

Kiernan, D., *The Derbyshire Lead Industry in the Sixteenth Century* (1989)

Kinder P., MSS *History of Derbyshire* (1663) with Notes and Observations by J. J. Briggs FRSL (1870)

Kirkham, N., *Derbyshire Lead Mining Through the Centuries* (1968)

Kirkland, T., *A Commentary on the Apoplectic* (c.1774)

Kitching, C. (ed.), *Squire of Calke Abbey: The Journals of Sir George Crewe 1815–1834* (1995)

Leics. FHS, *Leicestershire Strays 4* (1985)

Lysons, W., *Magna Britannia* (1817)

Mammatt, E., *A Collection of Geological Facts of the Ashby Coalfield* (1834)

Manpower Services Commission, *A Survey of the Park and Gardens at Calke Abbey. Vol. 1: Park and Garden Development.* Archival research by P. Heath (1988)

Marshall, D., *English People in the Eighteenth Century* (1956)

Miller, T., *Our Old Town* (1857)

Mingay, G. E. (ed.), *Arthur Young and His Times* (1975)

Nesfield Cookson, Mrs, *The Costume Book* (1934)

PRO, *Calendar of Fine Rolls* (1451), vol. 18 (1911–62)

Passmore, R. and Robson, J. S. (eds), *A Companion to Medical Studies*, vol. 3 parts 1 and 2 (1974)

Percival, T., *Observations and Experiments on the Poison of Lead* (1774)

Phillips, C. B. and Smith, J. H., *Stockport Probate Records 1620–1650* (1992)

Pigot, J., *Pigot and Co's New Commercial Directory for Cheshire, Derbyshire and Lancashire* (1828)

Pigot, J., *Pigot's Directory of Derbyshire* (1857)

Pilkington, J., *A View of the Present State of Derbyshire*, vol. 2 (1789)

Pitt, W., *General View of the Agriculture of the County of Leicester* (1809)

Plot, R., *The Natural History of Staffordshire* (1686)

Plumb, J. H. and Weldon, H., *Royal Heritage: The Story of Britain's Royal Builders and Collectors* (1977)

Rackham, B. and Read, H., *English Pottery* (1924)

Rees, A., *The Cyclopaedia; or Universal Dictionary of Arts, Sciences, and Literature*, vol. 21(1802–20)

Reeves, D., *Furniture: An Explanatory History* (1947)

Rice, D. G., *Derby Porcelain: The Golden Years 1750–1770* (1983)

Richardson, J., *The Local Historian's Encyclopedia*, 2nd edn (1986)

Roberts, E. and Parker, K. (eds), *Southampton Probate Inventories 1447–1575*, vol. 1 (1992)

Scott, W., *The Story of Ashby de la Zouch* (1907)

Smiles, S., *Josiah Wedgwood F. R. S. His Personal History* (1897)

Spufford, M., *The Great Reclothing of Rural England: Petty Chapmen and their Wares in the Seventeenth Century* (1984)

Steer, F. W., *Farm and Cottage Inventories of Mid-Essex 1635–1749* (1969)

Strong, R., *Gloriana* (1987)

Thirsk, J. and Cooper, J. P. (eds), *Seventeenth Century Economic Documents* (1972)

Thomas, J., *The Rise of the Staffordshire Potteries* (1971)

Towner, D., *Creamware* (1978)

Usher, H., *Ticknall Pottery and the Calke Collection* (1989)

Usher, H., *The Ticknall Limeyards* (1995)

Venn, J. and Venn, J. A. (eds), *Alumni Cantabrigiensis* part 1 vol. 2 (1922)

*Victoria History of the Counties of England, Derbyshire* vol. 2 (1970)

*Victoria History of the Counties of England, Staffordshire* reprints: all Greenslade, M. W. (ed.), *History of Stoke-upon-Trent; History of Tunstall; History of Burslem* (all 1963)

Walford, C., *Fairs Past and Present, A Chapter in the History of Commerce* (1883)

Weatherill, L., *The Pottery Trade and North Staffordshire 1660–1760* (1971)

Wedgwood, H. A., *People of the Potteries* (1970)

White, F., *History, Gazetteer and Directory of the County of Derby* (1857)

Wilcox, R. T., *The Mode in Costume. A History of Men's and Women's Clothes and Accessories*, 2nd edn (1958)

Wolley, W., *History of the County of Derby 1066–1712* (1712)

## Unpublished Theses and Dissertations, Nottingham University

Brown, S., *Pot hawkers in north west Leicestershire in the eighteenth and nineteenth centuries* (1999, MA)

Griffin, C. P., *The Economic and Social Development of the Leicestershire and South Derbyshire Coalfield 1550–1914* (1969, PhD)

White, A. J., *Post-Medieval Pottery in Lincolnshire 1450–1850* (1989, PhD)

### Newspapers

*Derby Mercury* DLSL

*Leicester Journal* ROLLR

# Articles

Alvey, R. C., 'The Pottery' in Todd, M., 'Excavations on the Medieval Defences of Newark, 1972' in *Transactions of the Thoroton Society*, vol. 78 (1974)

Barrett, F., 'Description of the Finds', part 2 of a paper entitled 'Furnace Farm Pottery' and presented to a conference at the Victoria and Albert Museum, 14 January 1961, published in the proceedings

Brittan, F., 'The Pickleherring Potteries: an inventory', *Journal of the Society for Post-Medieval Archaeology*, 24, 1990

Brown, R. B., 'The Furnace Site at Melbourne' in *Northern Ceramic Society Journal*, vol. 3 (1978–9)

Brown, R. B., 'Potteries of Derbyshire', *Journal of the Northern Ceramic Society*, vol. 11 (1994)

Coppack, G., 'Medieval and post-medieval pottery' in Hall, R. A. and Coppack, G., 'Excavations at Full Street, Derby, 1972', *DAJ*, 92 (1975)

Cox, J. C., 'Derbyshire in 1327–8: being a Subsidy Roll', *DAJ* vol. 30 (1908)

Daneill, J., 'A Lost Leicestershire Industry' in *Leicestershire Archaeological Society Transactions*, 38 (1962–3)

Draper, J., 'Inventory of Ann Shergold, ceramic dealer in Blandford, Dorset', *Post-Medieval Archaeology*, 16 (1982)

Everitt, A., 'Country carriers in the nineteenth century' in *Journal of Transport History*, 10 (1976)

Gooder, E. A., 'Clayworking in the Nuneaton Area Part 2', microfiche in Mayes, P. and Scott, K., *Pottery Kilns at Chilvers Coton, Nuneaton*, Society for Medieval Archaeology Monograph Series, 10 (1984)

Hart, W. H., 'A List of the "Alehouses, Innes, and Tavernes" in Derbyshire, in the Year 1577', *DAJ* vol. 1 (1879)

Hyde, J., 'Tickenhall Pottery' in *Derbyshire Life*, May 1974, vol. 39, no. 5

Irving, A. L., 'The Cistercian Ware Products of Ticknall, South Derbyshire', to be published by the Medieval Pottery Research Group in 2005

Jewitt, L., 'On a Tile-Kiln and some Paving and Other Tiles Recently Discovered at Repton, Derbyshire', *The Reliquary*, January 1868

Kirkham, N., 'Early Lead Smelting in Derbyshire', *Trans. Newcomen Society*, vol. XLI (1968–9)

Kirkham, N., 'Great Hucklow Mines', *Collected Works*, vol. 2 (1978)

Lockett, T., 'The Mystery of Melbourne', *International Journal of Ceramics and Glass*, vol. 1 (1985)

Marshall, G., Palmer, M. and Neverson, P., 'The History and Archaeology of the Calke Abbey Lime-yards', *Industrial Archaeology Review*, vol. XIV part 2 (1992)

Mountford, A. R. and Celoria, F., 'Some examples of sources in the history of 17th Century Ceramics', *Journal of Ceramic History*, 1 (1968)

Pearce, J. and Vince, A., 'Surrey Whitewares' in *A Dated Type-Series of London Medieval Pottery*, part 4 (1988)

Pears, Revd S. R., 'On the Discovery of a Tile Kiln at Repton, Derbyshire', *The Reliquary*, January 1868

Sinar, J., 'Calke and Ticknall', *Derbyshire Miscellany* vol. 8 part 5 (1979)

Thorpe, A., 'Excavation of the Site', part 1 of a paper entitled 'Furnace Farm Pottery' and presented to a conference at the Victoria and Albert Museum, 14 January 1961, published in the proceedings

Towner, D., 'The Melbourne Pottery', paper read at the Victoria and Albert Museum, 17 January 1970

Weatherill, L., 'The growth of the pottery industry in England, 1660–1815 Some new evidence and estimates', *Post-Medieval Archaeology* 17 (1983)

White, A. J., 'A Stamford Potseller's Stock in 1720', *Post-Medieval Archaeology*, 13 (1979)

Wilson, J., 'An Account of the Disease called Mill-Reek by the miners at Leadhills, in a Letter from Mr James Wilson, Surgeon at Durisdeer, to Alexander Munro, P.A.', Article 22 in *Essays and Observations, Physical and Literary, Read before the Philosophical Society in Edinburgh*, vol. 1, 2nd edn (1771)

Woodland, R., 'The Pottery' in Mellor, J. E. and Pearce, T., *The Austin Friars, Leicester*, CBA Research Report 35 (1981)

## Maps

David and Charles reprints of the first edition of the 1-inch Ordnance Survey of England
   and Wales, sheets 26, 27, 28, 29, 33, 34, 35, 36, 41, 42, 43, 44, 51, 52

Harley, J. B., Fowkes, D. V. and Harvey, J. C. (eds), *Burdett's Map of Derbyshire 1791* (1975)

Ordnance Survey 25-inch 1882 (2nd edition) sheets: LVII – 7, 8, 11, 12, 15, 16; LVIII – 5,
   9, 10, 12, 13, 14; LX – 4; LXI – 1, 2

Ordnance Survey 6-inch 1924 sheet LVIII SW

Ordnance Survey 6-inch geological map 1904 sheet Derbyshire LXI NW

Ordnance Survey 6-inch geological map 1953 sheet 155

Yates, W., *The County of Stafford Map* (1798, reprinted Staffordshire Record Office)

# Index